ITER

Publications of

ITER INC.

&

CENTRE FOR REFORMATION AND RENAISSANCE STUDIES

Victoria University in the

University of Toronto

THE OTHER VOICE IN
EARLY MODERN EUROPE:
THE TORONTO SERIES, 2

Series Editors

Margaret L. King and Albert Rabil, Jr.

Love in the Mirror

GIOVAN BATTISTA ANDREINI

~

Edited and translated by

JON R. SNYDER

Iter Inc.
Centre for Reformation and Renaissance Studies
Toronto
2009

Iter: Gateway to the Middle Ages and Renaissance
Tel: 416/978–7074   Fax: 416/971–1399

Email: iter@utoronto.ca   Web: www.itergateway.org

CRRS Publications, Centre for Reformation and Renaissance Studies
Victoria University in the University of Toronto
Toronto, Ontario M5S 1K7 Canada
Tel: 416/585–4465   Fax: 416/585–4430
Email: crrs.publications@utoronto.ca   Web: www.crrs.ca

Library and Archives Canada Cataloguing in Publication
Andreini, Giovan Battista, 1576-1654
Love in the mirror / by Giovan Battista Andreini ; edited and translated by Jon R. Snyder.

(The other voice in early modern Europe : Toronto series ; 2)
Co-published by: Centre for Reformation and Renaissance Studies.
Translation of: Amor nello specchio, with original Italian text on facing pages.
A play.
Includes bibliographical references and index.
Also available in electronic format.
ISBN 978–0–7727–2051–1
I. Snyder, Jon R., 1954– II. Victoria University (Toronto, Ont.). Centre for Reformation
and Renaissance Studies III. Iter Inc IV. Title. V. Series: Other voice in early modern
Europe. Toronto series ; 2

PQ4562.A7A8313 2010
852'.5   C2009–906949–0

Cover illustration: Rome, Galleria Nazionale d'Arte Antica in Palazzo Barberini, attr
Guido Reni [now attr Elisabetta Sirani], *Portrait of Beatrice Cenci*, inv. 1944
Credit: Archivio Fotografico, Soprintendenza Speciale per il Patrimonio Artistico ed
Etnoantropologico e per il Polo Museale della Città di Roma

Cover design: Maureen Morin, Information Technology Services, University of Toronto
Libraries
Typesetting and production: Iter Inc.

Contents

Acknowledgments

I wish to thank series co-editor Albert Rabil, Jr., for his unwavering support of this project. With consummate professionalism and scholarly acumen, he has shepherded the manuscript through the editorial and publication process from start to finish. My thanks also go to Margaret L. King, series co-editor and scholar of the Andreini family, for her interest and support.

I am grateful to the dedicated staff of the Biblioteca Nazionale Universitaria di Torino for their assistance, and to the Academic Senate of the University of California, Santa Barbara, for research and publication funds.

John Bernard organized a panel on early modern Italian comedy at the 2006 Renaissance Society of America conference in San Francisco that gave me the impetus to complete this book. Nancy Canepa (Dartmouth College) and Francesco Erspamer (Harvard University) kindly invited me to present abbreviated versions of the introduction to their respective colleagues and students. Edward Tuttle answered with his usual blend of erudition and grace my many queries about Andreini's use of the Italian language. Julia Hairston, Erika Milburn, and Luca Marcozzi helped me to identify some of Andreini's most elusive poetic sources. The anonymous reader for The Other Voice in Early Modern Europe series offered many invaluable suggestions for improving the translation and introduction. I am truly indebted to Robert Henke, *il miglior fabbro*, who freely gave of his time in reading and commenting on an early draft of the introduction. My greatest debt, however, is to Salvatore Maira and Anna Michela Borracci, the co-editors of the 1997 edition of *Amor nello specchio*, who have so generously shared with me their expertise and materials concerning this remarkable play.

Although these friends and colleagues saved me from many mistakes, any shortcomings of this book are wholly my own.

Jon R. Snyder
Santa Barbara, California

The Other Voice: Amor nello specchio

There are two principal reasons for including *Amor nello specchio* (Love in the Mirror, 1622), by Giovan Battista Andreini (1576–1654), in the Other Voice series.

The first has to do with the highly unusual theme of this Baroque work, set in Florence early in the seventeenth century. For *Love in the Mirror* represents the triumph of women over the early modern patriarchal system that defined and regulated sexuality and gender roles. The play features a passionate, consensual love affair between its two female protagonists, Florinda and Lidia. Andreini knew the Italian theatrical tradition as few others could have, but in *Love in the Mirror* chose to break openly with the great sex comedies of the sixteenth century. In these works women may fall in love with women, but because of disguise and deceit the erotic bond between these earlier female characters is always seen as a comic error to be corrected by the end of the play. Instead, in Andreini's experimental comedy, Florinda and Lidia choose to love one another freely and openly, "breast to breast and mouth to mouth," with full awareness of their actions. Neither has a father or other male relative to command her; they fear no one and nothing; both are financially and intellectually independent; unwanted suitors are spurned, scorned, jailed, and even beaten by them; and the most powerful male figure in the play (the Wizard) cannot help to bring them back into line, even though he commands the art of natural magic. The conventions of the comic genre, whose roots may ultimately derive from the fertility rituals of ancient Greece, require that the two women be married off at the end of the play, for order must be restored to society, usually through marriage, so as to guarantee its rebirth in a new generation. Andreini, however, supplies an ingenious—if wholly Baroque—means of preserving Florinda's love for Lidia, even within the confines of her marriage to Lidia's brother. The love story between Florinda and Lidia is, in short, a milestone for the European stage, although destined to languish in oblivion for centuries after its initial publication.

The second reason for inclusion of *Love in the Mirror* in this series is biographical. Andreini was the eldest child of Isabella Canali

Andreini (1562–1604), the greatest actress of her age, and one of the leading European women of letters of the late sixteenth century. She married the actor Francesco Andreini (1548–1624) of the Compagnia dei Gelosi, one of the premier *commedia dell'arte* troupes, in 1575: Isabella was only fourteen years old when Giovan Battista was born, and her career as an actress and writer lay almost entirely in front of her. Although her son was eventually sent to study in Bologna, a profound and lasting bond formed between a young mother and son extremely close in age. By the 1580s, Isabella was a diva whose legendary performances as a chaste young lover (*innamorata*) made her a celebrity throughout Italy and France, in an age in which relatively few women appeared on stage in Europe.[1] Her range was remarkable, and she could cross over gender boundaries with ease: she was not only a supreme improviser as a lovestruck maiden but was also known to play male roles. Isabella could appear on stage, in other words, not only as the transvestite of Italian learned comedy (*commedia erudita*) or *commedia dell'arte*, in which a female character dressed like a young man before returning to her subordinate place in the patriarchal order, but also in the role of the main male character.[2] She seems to have transmitted some of her interest in publicly crossing gender boundaries to her son, who was later to write the transgressive *Love in the Mirror*, with its story of same-sex love and desire, in order to showcase two actresses. Compared with his theatrical contemporaries, Andreini was remarkably attuned to the range of women's experience and was himself deeply devoted to the cult of the Magdalen, to whom he dedicated several sacred works.

Both parents hoped, after investing in his education, that their son would practice a more socially respectable profession such as law. Giovan Battista chose the theater instead and was acting with

---

1. Women performed more freely in Italy than anywhere else in Europe, but they did perform in Spain, despite periodic but only temporary injunctions against actresses there, and sometimes in France as well. For Italy, see M. A. Katritzky, "Reading the Actress in Commedia Imagery," *Women Players in England, 1500–1660: Beyond the All-Male Stage*, ed. Pamela A. Brown and Peter Parolin (Burlington, VT: Ashgate, 2005), 109–43. See, for Spain, Part 2 ("Actrices") of *Genealogía, origen y noticias de los comediantes de España*, ed. N. D. Shergold and J. E. Varey (London: Tamesis Books, 1985), 365–570.

2. For instance, Isabella is believed to have played the title role in the pastoral *L'Aminta* by Torquato Tasso. Aminta is a male shepherd who falls in love with a nymph, Silvia, who cannot return his love because she has devoted herself to the goddess Diana. See Valeria Finucci, "Isabella Andreini," *Routledge Encyclopedia of Italian Literature*, 2 vols. (New York: Routledge, 2006), 1: 39.

his parents' troupe by the time he was eighteen. As the *innamorato* named Lelio he would, presumably, have appeared regularly on stage with his mother, since she played a similar role, while Francesco Andreini usually played the role of Capitano Spavento—a brilliant refashioning of the traditional braggart warrior role (*miles gloriosus*). We may suppose that Giovan Battista learned his actor's craft from his parents but especially from his mother, whose principal stage role was closest to his own: he would in fact continue to play Lelio for decades after her death. Isabella was a gifted poet as well as the first published professional woman playwright in Italy, and, here again, her son followed her lead, publishing volumes of verse, both sacred and profane, as well as plays ranging from comedies to tragicomedies to tragedies. In this choice of a writing as well as an acting career, he took after his mother more than his father, although the latter also published several works (but not full-length plays of his own). Outside of England, no contemporary actor-writer in Europe even came close to matching Giovan Battista's literary output in the first few decades of the seventeenth century. Unlike many children of famous artists, Andreini was, in developing his own voice and creative direction, seemingly uninhibited by his mother's renown in Italy and abroad. Instead, she was a primary source of inspiration throughout his long life on the stages of Europe. His writings for the theater are highly original and stand on their own merits, but they may legitimately be viewed as the commemoration and transmission of the legacy of Isabella Andreini. Small wonder that, as an old man approaching death, when Giovan Battista wrote a letter recounting his life and that of his family, he signed it simply "Lelio, figlio d'Isabella"—Isabella's son Lelio.[3]

Text and Context

The Baroque, born in Italy, was the first global aesthetic. Spreading quickly across a large swath of the planet, from Rome to Goa and Manila, from Madrid to Mexico City and Lima, it not only internationalized Italian culture as never before but introduced a fundamentally new way of seeing, representing, and narrating. How did the Baroque differ from what came before it? The answer is to be found chiefly in its deliberate break with the tenets of ancient and Renaissance

3. Maurizio Rebaudengo, *Giovan Battista Andreini tra poetica e drammaturgia* (Turin: Rosenberg & Sellier, 1994), 25.

art, in particular with the principle of mimesis, i.e., the imitation of nature or the real. If, prior to the late sixteenth century, artists and writers thought of their work in terms of a stable series of categories and norms such as verisimilitude, credibility, harmony, proportion, symmetry, balance, measure, unity, decorum and the like, it was because these were thought to derive ultimately from the order of nature itself. This proximity to the origin (the true, the real) granted artworks their authenticity and legitimacy. Baroque artists and writers instead called into question the necessity and even the possibility of mimesis, seeking to free art from the tyranny of rules by distorting—and even breaking—the mirror of nature. Once the imperative of imitation was weakened or done away with in art, as the Piedmontese Jesuit Emanuele Tesauro (1592–1675) noted approvingly in his famous treatise on Baroque metaphor, *Il cannocchiale aristotelico* (The Aristotelian Spyglass), "everything is licit."[4] The freely creative faculty of the human imagination, or what the Italians called "ingegno," was to take the place of the canons of classical beauty. This same word was translated as "wit" in England from the late sixteenth century on, becoming the first term in the history of Western aesthetics without either a Greek or Latin etymology. For the Baroque, beauty was to be made anew, not discovered in what already exists: representation did not repeat the real but rather altered it irrevocably. The result of this revolt was cultural tumult, a free-for-all of new techniques of representation that transgressed against long-established aesthetic codes by disorienting and overwhelming the senses of the spectator, reader, or listener. And no artist or writer, in Italy or elsewhere, embraced the artistic freedoms of the Baroque more wholeheartedly than did Giovan Battista Andreini in *Love in the Mirror*.

These freedoms came, however, at a price. The Baroque aesthetic was a key component of what José Antonio Maravall calls the "lyrical engineering of the human world" in early modernity.[5] The scientific and geographical discoveries of the age had irreversibly transformed Western knowledge: the microscope and the telescope were the emblems of the Baroque discovery of infinity, whether in a drop of water or in deep space. The epistemological foundations and certainties of the past were shaken to their very core by these dis-

---

4. Emanuele Tesauro, *Il cannocchiale aristotelico* (Savigliano: Editrice Artistica Piemontese, 2000 [1670]), 735.

5. José Antonio Maravall, *Culture of the Baroque: Analysis of a Historical Structure*, trans. Terry Cochrane (Minneapolis: University of Minnesota Press, 1986 [1975]), 263.

coveries. The widespread sense of cultural decentering and dispersion that accompanied this paradigm shift in knowledge was not met, however, without resistance from those who had the most at stake in preserving the status quo. One of the principal ways in which the profoundly conservative social and political system of hereditary privilege, which we now call the Old Regime, reacted to the new epistemological instability was through patronage of the arts. In what amounted to the first European mass societies with huge urban centers, the role of communication was understood by those in power to be central, and art was seen as the most persuasive means with which to reach the masses and integrate them into the Old Regime hierarchy of values. The Baroque artistic product, charged with intellectual and emotional force, was intended not only to sway but to transport the spectator, overcoming any possible resistance to its message. The patronage programs of seventeenth-century popes and princes, sometimes remaking entire cities in the process, have been widely studied in recent years. This "lyrical engineering," with its search for new modes of deployment of power through aesthetic innovation and experimentation, accounts in no small part for the remarkable intensity and variety of Baroque artwork. Although Andreini was a complex and multifaceted intellectual, we cannot think of his writings for the theater without recalling the paradoxical situation of the Seicento, in which a radically transgressive aesthetic was often—although not always—in the service of those who held tightly to the reins of power.

For much of Andreini's life, Italy experienced a period of relative peace known as the Pax Italica.[6] The Italian Wars (1494–1559), which had devastated the peninsula, were brought to an end with the signing of the Treaty of Cateau-Cambrésis in 1559. This did not mark a return, however, to the old medieval and Renaissance system of fiercely independent city-states. The treaty instead confirmed Spain, whose world empire was still expanding, as the dominant power in Italy. From the Ionian Sea to the Alps, dynastic absolutism was the order of the day. The Spanish crown directly controlled Milan, Naples, Sicily, and Sardinia, with garrisons along the west coast of

---

6. See the dedication by the printer Pandolfo Malatesta to Andreini's *Lo schiavetto*: "From those years, when beautiful Italy began to enjoy a tranquil peace, almost as a restorative to the hardship of such continuous wars, the most valiant persons began to rediscover the ancient forgotten practice of performing comedies." As cited in Anne MacNeil, *Music and Women of the Commedia dell'Arte in the Late Sixteenth Century* (New York: Oxford University Press, 2003), 165.

central Italy. Spain also kept on a tight leash the rulers of Tuscany, Genoa, and most other regional states north of Rome: as its gateway to northern Europe, Genoa played a particularly crucial role in Spanish military and economic affairs. Relations with the papacy were complex but the Pontifical States and the Spanish Empire were allies.[7] That left the Republic of Venice, which was losing its grip from the eastern Mediterranean to the Ottoman Empire, and the Duchy of Savoy in Piedmont as the only fully independent Italian states of the Old Regime. If in the 1570s Italy still seemed to figure prominently in the calculations of the European powers (the Holy League fought at Lepanto in 1571 with, among others, Genoese, Venetian, Tuscan, and Piedmontese warships), by the turn of the century the situation had changed, as the peninsula became increasingly peripheral to the central events of continental and global politics. Even after the Pax Italica finally collapsed, and despite the ups and downs of the great empires of Spain, France, and England, the system of the Italian states changed relatively little in the course of Andreini's long lifetime: this was the political world that he knew and that figured largely in the writing of *Love in the Mirror*.

Andreini was born in Florence, the capital of the Grand Duchy of Tuscany, but spent most of his working life in the Po River valley, which was—politically speaking—a patchwork of dynastic regimes large and small, with the exception of "La Serenissima" (as the venerable Venetian Republic was called). To travel from Venice to Ferrara, and thence to Mantua and Milan—a distance of a few hundred kilometers across the Po's rich alluvial plains—meant to traverse the respective territories of at least four states, each with its own distinct political and cultural coordinates. The members of the Gonzaga dynasty in Mantua, who had managed to cling to power against considerable odds, were Andreini's chief patrons in this period, and it is not surprising that he purchased a home in the nearby countryside in 1616. He also had, however, powerful supporters in Spanish Milan: the Count Pedro Fuentes, governor of Milan, was perhaps the godfather of one of the Andreinis' children, and there the itinerant actor-author published several of his most important devout works.[8] In autonomous Venice, on the other hand, with its deep-

---

7. On the role of Spain in Italy in this period, see Thomas J. Dandelet and John A. Marino, eds., *Spain in Italy: Politics, Society and Religion 1500–1700* (Leiden and Boston: Brill, 2007).

8. Fabrizio Fiaschini, *L'"incessabil agitazione": Giovan Battista Andreini tra professione teatrale, cultura letteraria e religione* (Pisa: Giardini, 2007), 67.

rooted theatrical culture and important printing trade, he published or republished many of his comedies, whose colorful dialogues risked violating the rules of Counter-Reformation decorum or, far worse, earning the opprobrium of zealous local authorities. His most avant-garde plays—including *Love in the Mirror*—may or may not have ever been performed in Italy, but Andreini waited to publish them until his company was ensconced in far-off Paris, with patrons from among the highest-ranking French nobility.[9] As a professional actor and man of letters, Andreini had to negotiate constantly the visible and invisible boundaries—territorial, economic, political, and linguistic, as well as cultural—that fractured or splintered the peninsula.

When armed conflict finally returned to northern Italy, as the War of the Mantuan Succession (1628–31), Andreini suffered serious losses: his property was sacked by the marauding armies, and his first wife died (perhaps of the bubonic plague that followed the Spanish army into Italy) the following summer. Financially speaking, his fortunes seem never to have recovered from this catastrophe, which occurred in a period of overall economic and demographic decline. Central-north Italy was the most densely populated area in Europe in the sixteenth and seventeenth centuries.[10] However, plague, famine, and disease repeatedly decimated the population between 1575 and 1630, especially in the towns and cities, which were the mainstay of Andreini's itinerant acting company. The decline in economic prosperity in central-north Italy, where traditional industries such as silk and wool had fallen on hard times, forced the *capocomico* and his troupe farther and farther afield in search of patrons and public alike (Vienna, Prague, Florence, Lucca, Paris).[11] The precarious economics of the profession and the transitory nature of theatrical fame and fashion, as well as fierce competition from other Arte companies, meant that Andreini, even at the peak of his powers, faced a daily struggle to keep his theatrical enterprise afloat. The dedicatory

9. The only known performance of *Love in the Mirror* appears to have taken place in Paris in 1622.

10. Paolo Malanima, "A Declining Economy: Central and Northern Italy," *Spain in Italy*, ed. Dandelet and Marino, 386. For a different viewpoint, see Giovanni Muto, "Dopo 'l'estate di San Martino' dell'economia italiana," *Italia 1650: Comparazioni et bilanci*, ed. Giuseppe Galasso and Aurelio Musi (Naples: CUEN, 2002), 71–86.

11. Malanima, "A Declining Economy," 388–89. Robert Henke, *Performance and Literature in the Commedia dell'Arte* (New York: Cambridge University Press, 2002), 215, adds: "In Italy, the commedia dell'arte did wane after the 1630s because the northern courts that had patronized [the companies] declined in power and prestige."

preface to *Love in the Mirror*, with its fawning and hyperbolic praise of Andreini's patron, François de Bassompierre, will give even readers wholly unfamiliar with Italian Baroque culture a sense of the asymmetrical social and economic relations that marked the age of absolutism and defined the limits of Andreini's sphere of action. Those who were at the margins of the world of the great and powerful had, with few exceptions, to conform to the latter's demands or face the consequences: as Elizabeth S. Cohen has remarked, in early modern Italy "subordination was the norm for nearly everyone."[12] The players' independence—in crossing borders between states and in marketing their "products" wherever they went—nevertheless did not place them outside of this norm. Thus, despite its revolutionary gestures, in the end Andreini's sex-comedy restores the established order of things, as the Governor's wishes are carried out and the characters obediently return to their "proper" places in society.

The Counter-Reformation authorities' intolerance of the theater did have an impact on both the composition and production of comedies in Italy. In Milan, the devout Charles Borromeo (1538–84) censored comedy and even called for an end to Carnival itself, sifting through the scenarios of the Compagnia dei Gelosi in 1583 in search of scandalous dialogues and situations to suppress before they could appear on stage. Comedies, as he saw them, made a dangerous display of every kind of vice, from adultery to prostitution, and actors were mere nomads and vagabonds to be expelled from the city.[13] Actors were barred from burial in consecrated ground, and in the Papal States actresses were banned from the public stage.[14] Andreini was intimately familiar with the ecclesiastical critique of comedy, and sought to forestall it (wherever possible) in writing his plays. *Love in the Mirror* contains none of the bawds, ruffians, or parasites of earlier Renaissance comedies. There are no adulterers, thieves, frauds, corrupt priests, or crooked public servants. No patriarch (the *senex* of the

12. Elizabeth S. Cohen, "Evolving the History of Women in Early Modern Italy: Subordination and Agency," *Spain in Italy*, ed. Dandelet and Marino, 329.

13. For Borromeo's attitude toward comedy, see his "Lettera al Cardinale Gabriello Paleotti, Arcivescovo di Bologna (luglio 1578)," in Ferdinando Taviani, *La commedia dell'arte e la società barocca: la fascinazione del teatro* (Rome: Bulzoni, 1991 [1969]), 23–24. Taviani, 315–526, has also republished the Jesuit Giovan Domenico Ottonelli's (1584–1670) important critique of the Baroque theater in Italy.

14. Richard Andrews, *Scripts and Scenarios: The Performance of Comedy in Renaissance Italy* (Cambridge: Cambridge University Press, 1993), 224.

Plautine tradition) is tricked or humiliated by the younger generation. Although biblical figures and episodes are briefly mentioned, no religious sentiment is expressed, in order to avoid any possible controversy. Finally, all the characters are reconciled at the end of the play.[15] However, the difference between theory and practice was great indeed in the case of clerical antitheatricalism in early modern Italy. Borromeo's proscription was not in fact followed by many other members of the clergy, who saw in the theater a didactic and propaganda tool of great efficacy for the faith: Andreini's sacred plays, such as his three versions of the Mary Magdalen story, bear witness to this. Besides, many members of the Italian aristocracy—upon which the church depended for political and financial support—had no intention of depriving themselves of either the pleasures of the theater or of the possibilities it afforded them to display their own status and enhance their prestige through patronage.

Above all, however, it was the new phenomenon of the professional theater that ultimately proved unstoppable. Because of Shakespeare's canonical status, many English-language readers are likely already familiar with the story of the explosive growth of theatrical culture in London between the late sixteenth and early seventeenth centuries. In Italy the first permanent theaters were built at court in Mantua and Ferrara in the mid-Cinquecento, followed soon afterward by smaller professional theaters in Venice, Florence, and Naples.[16] (Although built for an academy rather than for the commercial stage, the oldest surviving early modern theater in Europe, Andrea Palladio's Teatro Olimpico in the city of Vicenza, was begun in 1575 and completed in 1585, long before ground was broken for the Globe Theatre in London.) Venice, with its vast wealth, quickly became the new theatrical center of Italy: in the seventeenth century, in fact, its network of theaters was larger and more important than that of any other European city.[17]

---

15. Compare this to Malvolio's last line in the final act of *Twelfth Night* (V.i): "I'll be revenged on the whole pack of you!" This is hardly consonant with the principles of comic closure.

16. Siro Ferrone, *Attori mercanti corsari: la commedia dell'arte in Europa tra Cinque e Seicento* (Turin: Einaudi, 1993), 56. The Teatro Baldracca in Florence, for instance, was a second-floor space of the Dogana outfitted into a theater. See Annamaria Evangelista, "Le compagnie dei comici dell'arte nel teatrino di Baldracca a Firenze: notizie dagli epistolari (1576–1653)," *Quaderni di Teatro* 24 (1984): 50–72.

17. Siro Ferrone, "Il teatro," in *Storia della letteratura italiana*, ed. Enrico Malato (Rome: Salerno, 1997), 5:1086.

After the expulsion of the Jesuits in 1606, the Venetian nobility threw its entrepreneurial energy and financial resources into the building and management of theaters. Audiences, in which different social strata intermingled, embraced enthusiastically this new professionalized mode of spectacle, especially opera. As Venetian commerce contracted in the eastern Mediterranean, the city's theatrical industry attracted increasing amounts of investment capital: the theaters were money-making enterprises, with performances put on for a paying public, and more and more extravagant productions were needed in order to keep the box-office receipts flowing in.[18] The Compagnia dei Fedeli worked frequently in the city, and Andreini's unconventional comedies, some of which were published (if not performed) in Venice, could well have been written with the needs of this new class of impresarios in mind. His plays not only reached beyond the Arte tradition in terms of theme and plot, but, as in the case of *Love in the Mirror*, sometimes may have been staged with elaborate crowd-pleasing special effects (mirrors, flames, and monsters are mentioned in the stage directions) requiring the newest theatrical-industrial technology. These "new comedies," as Andreini called them,[19] could not be easily played on the small stages that the Arte actors used in most northern Italian cities: they instead called for a performance space with the kind of technically advanced equipment found only where the new theatrical system flourished. Even if *Love in the Mirror* was never seen in public on the peninsula in Andreini's lifetime, the play needs to be read in the context of the far-reaching process of professionalization and technological innovation of the early modern theater that was then underway.

Although the Fedeli continued for many years to mount Arte performances as part of their repertory, the *commedia dell'arte* was the target of frequent censorship by the Venetian authorities, to say

18. Ellen Rosand, *Opera in Seventeenth-Century Venice: The Creation of a Genre* (Berkeley: University of California Press, 1991), 15, notes that in Venice "commercial success was of primary concern, and that could be achieved only by creating works with broad audience appeal."

19. The purpose of the "new comedy" was to be, he argued, free of the frank immorality so often found in the learned comedies of the Renaissance, which would allow it to flourish in the Counter-Reformation climate. For, as Andreini remarked in the prologue to *Lelio bandito*, "Although in comedies we often see lascivious acts and profane actions, they are not put there in order to teach us [how to perform] them, but in order to show us the way in which we may avoid them." See G. B. Andreini, *Lelio bandito: tragicommedia boschereccia* (Venice: G. B. Combi, 1624), 12.

nothing of those in less tolerant cities across Italy. Comedy is, generally speaking, a conservative genre, but the bold irreverence of the Arte players could be perceived, in some places, as subverting not only official "high" culture but public order. As a number of scholars have shown, however, one of the main reasons for the authorities' concern was the prominence of actresses in the companies. Municipal officials and clergymen railed against them, accusing actresses of every conceivable public and private impropriety, but it was too late: in most of post-Renaissance Italy, professional acting companies that included women were an established fact of life. Indeed, even before Andreini's birth in 1576, women were not only the leading attractions of their companies, but may have functioned as troupe leaders as well.[20] Life in the professional theater might have been a choice that relatively few women outside of the lowest ranks of society made willingly, given the marginal social status of all but a handful of famous actresses in Italy, but within that profession it was possible for women to play a prominent role. If performance on stage was like writing on water, namely, a transient and ever-changing event that left no permanent trace behind, the very fact of public performance—particularly in the case of actresses—nevertheless in itself marked a signal moment in the slow transition toward modernity in Italy.

Andreini was *capocomico* (lead actor and director) of the Fedeli as well as the resident playwright, but Virginia Ramponi and the rest of the troupe had a great deal of input into the writing of his comedies. We know that Andreini often worked, in fact, by composing in performance, drawing on the company's extensive experience in Arte improvisation. As Anne MacNeil observes of the comedy *Lo schiavetto* (The Little Slave), "while Andreini's name appears on the title page, the contents of the play are in fact a collaborative effort, representing the ideas and talents of all the members of his troupe."[21] If the Fedeli's actresses had to speak on stage through conventions set by male playwrights and reworked by Andreini, there is nevertheless good reason to think that their voices came through onto the printed pages of *Love in the Mirror*, in which they figure as its indisputable protagonists. Andreini himself was, as Lelio, to play only a secondary role on stage.[22] In the play the chief female characters walk boldly—

---

20. Henke, *Performance and Literature in the Commedia dell'Arte*, 85.

21. MacNeil, *Music and Women*, 165.

22. Piermario Vescovo, "Virginia Ramponi e Virginia Rotari nello specchio di Giovan Battista Andreini," *Donne e teatro*, ed. Daria Perocco (Venice: Ca' Foscari/Comitato per le

and sometimes unaccompanied—into the streets of the city, although they are not prostitutes or bawds. They control their own wealth, and can choose or refuse suitors as they please. "Domestic" scenes are often played in public spaces, including the ritual beatings that the women administer to the men, and power relations between the sexes are reversed until the final scenes of the last act. On stage, at least, the protagonists are not constrained by prescribed gender roles nor are they contained within the walls of houses, legal codes, or social practices.[23] *Love in the Mirror* is a fairy tale rather than a mirror of the early modern condition, but its text allows aspects of these other voices to emerge today, like long-lost relics, from the swirling, shifting sands of time.

Life and Works

Giovan Battista Andreini was born in Florence on February 9, 1576, the eldest child in a professional theatrical family. His was no ordinary childhood, for this was no ordinary family. His father, Francesco Andreini, was at that time the most important member of the renowned comic troupe La Compagnia dei Gelosi, specializing in the *commedia dell'arte* role of Capitano Spavento.[24] Of the many captains to appear in the Arte tradition, Francesco Andreini's was unusually poetic: although rooted in the stock character of the braggart warrior of ancient comedy, Capitano Spavento was an elegant dreamer who struggled at times to distinguish between fantasy and reality, rather than a vainglorious or ridiculous blowhard. His fame as an actor eventually earned the elder Andreini the role of *capocomico* in the company, a role he retained for several decades. Isabella Canali Andreini, Giovan Battista's mother, was soon to become not only an acclaimed poet and woman of letters but the first great diva of the European stage. Following her eldest son's birth, she developed and performed extensively

---

pari opportunità, 2004), 45.

23. Cohen, "Evolving the History of Women in Early Modern Italy: Subordination and Agency," 327; and Jane Tylus, "Women at the Windows: Commedia dell'Arte and Theatrical Practice in Early Modern Italy," *Theater Journal* 49 (1997): 323–42.

24. Although a "maschera" or stock role with roots in medieval Liguria, Capitano Spavento was made famous by Francesco Andreini's performances. For English-speaking readers unfamiliar with Arte terminology, traditions, and performance practices, see Andrews, *Scripts and Scenarios*, 169–203, and Henke, *Performance and Literature in the Commedia dell'Arte*, 1–49.

the role of the *prima donna innamorata*, or young woman in love: after her death this stock character came to be called "Isabella," the first to be named in honor of an Arte actress. The only woman to belong to the learned Accademia degli Intenti in Pavia, she was able, with her excellent humanist training and knowledge of languages, to play with the Compagnia dei Gelosi not only Arte roles but those of many other theatrical genres as well, from pastoral to tragicomedy.[25] Her pastoral, *Mirtilla* (Mirtilla, 1588), was the first play to be published in Europe by a professional woman of the theater, and her collection of Petrarchan verse, entitled *Rime* (Verse, first ed. 1601), confirmed her reputation as one of the leading women poets of her generation and a legend in her own time. After she died suddenly of complications from a pregnancy (which would have been her eighth child[26]) at age forty-two, her grief-stricken husband disbanded the company, and her eldest son devoted several works to her memory. In his 1606 poem of mourning for his beloved mother, *Il pianto d'Apollo* (Apollo's Tears), Giovan Battista movingly imagines the climactic moment of his reunion in heaven with her: "when one day I may be / Welcomed up above, leaving behind this prison; / There, o mother, gazing at your beautiful face / (...) I will step forward."[27]

By 1595, Giovan Battista was appearing with his parents' company using the stage name "Lelio," which was to be his trademark for the next six decades. In the Arte plays, Lelio was principally a *primo innamorato*, or young man in love, whose seemingly spontaneous flights of ornate speech and complex verbal conceits required mental agility and linguistic creativity (the usual technique for comic actors was to stitch together, often on the fly, previously memorized fragments of speeches). Thus, in countless performances with his mother and father in many different venues, Andreini began his career as an itinerant actor. Early modern companies of players lived largely on the road and were rarely in residence in any

---

25. See MacNeil, *Music and Women*, 77–126; and Eric Nicholson, "Romance as Role Model: Early Female Performances of *Orlando furioso* and *Gerusalemme liberata*," *Renaissance Transactions: Ariosto and Tasso*, ed. Valeria Finucci (Durham, NC: Duke University Press, 1999), 246–69.

26. Giovan Battista's siblings included Domenico (a captain in the service of the Duke of Mantua), Pietro Paolo (a friar), and four sisters, Lavinia, Osanna, Claridiana, and Caterina (of which at least the first three were nuns).

27. *Il pianto d'Apollo: Rime funebri in morte d'Isabella Andreini Comica Gelosa, & Accademica Intenta* (Milan: Girolamo Bordoni and Pietro Martire Locarni, 1606), 29, as cited in Rebaudengo, *Giovan Battista Andreini tra poetica e drammaturgia*, 26.

one place for more than a few months at a time. In 1601 he married Virginia Ramponi, a beautiful actress-singer from Milan, who soon took the stage name "Florinda" (and bore him several children). Not long afterward Andreini founded his own troupe, La Compagnia dei Fedeli, of which he was the director and leading man. Although reorganized numerous times, the Fedeli were to endure for about half a century, and to play for the great and powerful in many of the capital cities of Europe.

From the first, Andreini pursued an ambitious project to transform the social and cultural status of the actor. If his parents had managed to earn the acclaim and admiration of leading literati in Italy and France, their profession was nevertheless generally considered disreputable: in the eyes of many, including religious authorities, actors were little more than common vagrants and the theater a scandalous threat to public decency. Throughout his long lifetime of performing and writing, Andreini consciously sought to create a new figure in Italian culture, namely the actor-intellectual who served as an interface between the world of official culture and the world of the stage (especially the comic stage). Andreini's tireless work as an actor, a poet, and a cultural operator aimed to integrate comedy and comedians into the very fiber of contemporary literary and artistic life and to show that the former was inseparable from the latter. The Baroque aesthetic privileged the shock of the new, and the experimentalism of his brand of comedy, he contended, was essential—rather than marginal—to that aesthetic.[28]

In 1604, Andreini's new troupe took up residence for a time at the Gonzaga court in Mantua. The Fedeli, who worked throughout northern Italy, took part in spring 1608 in the festivities in Mantua for the marriage of Prince Francesco Gonzaga to Margarida of Savoy (daughter of Duke Charles Emmanuel I). There, Virginia Ramponi Andreini successfully sang the title role in Monteverdi's new court opera *Arianna* (Ariadne). Contemporary accounts relate that the ladies of the Gonzaga court were moved to tears by Virginia's inaugural performance of the great "Lament," and she became a celebrated diva in her own right. Music generally played a role in the Fedeli's *commedia dell'arte* productions, as well as in Andreini's own comedies, which he likely began to introduce into the company's repertory in these same years. He was familiar not only with the intricate Renaissance court spectacle of the *opera regia*, but with the new art of opera that

---

28. I am indebted here to Fiaschini, *L'"incessabil agitazione,"* 12–13.

had emerged in Italy around the turn of the century, and understood the challenge that its innovations posed to the traditional theatrical genres. For example, Andreini's musical comedy entitled *La Ferinda* (Ferinda, 1623) is clearly modeled on the first early modern operas by Monteverdi and Peri, and *Love in the Mirror* (1622), like many other dramatic works of his, includes a number of songs. He understood that the system of genres inherited from antiquity and the Renaissance had lost its relevance for the Baroque theater, in which generic boundaries no longer could be defended, and multiform, multimedia works had taken hold.[29] Indeed, in his dazzling *La centaura* (The Centaur, 1622), the first act is a comedy, the second is a pastoral and the third is a tragedy. As one of the characters in the play aptly sings in the prologue: "Out of an indelible and fatal desire / I've brought new things into the world; / Everything in [this] work is both concordant and discordant, / All is calm, and all is stormy; / And it's the first to appear artfully / On paper as comedy, pastoral and tragedy."[30]

During the Fedeli's first decade, Andreini published a steady stream of texts, ranging from defenses of the comic art to collections of verse, from religious drama to tragedy and, of course, comedy. His varied output, balanced between many different genres, sought to define new points of intersection between theatrical and literary culture. Andreini made his living, however, as an actor and director. His mastery of stagecraft and lighting, like his firsthand knowledge of trends in theatrical representation, was put in the service of the crowd-pleasing Baroque aesthetic of wonder (*meraviglia*), whose chief contemporary exponent, the celebrated poet G. B. Marino, argued that artists should seduce the public through daringly inventive conceits intended to astound and delight with their extreme artifice.[31] As a sign of the company's growing stature, the Fedeli played in Paris in 1613–14, following a royal invitation, at the Hôtel de Bourgogne and at the court in Paris and Fontainebleau. After returning to Mantua, Andreini purchased a residence nearby in 1616 (Ca' di Mandraghi),

---

29. Giovanni Battista Guarini (1538–1612), who first developed the tragicomedy in the late sixteenth century, influencing greatly European literature, theater, and music of the Seicento, had ardently defended the notion of the hybrid genre in the Italian critical debates of his time. See Bernard Weinberg, *A History of Literary Criticism in the Italian Renaissance*, 2 vols. (Chicago: University of Chicago Press, 1961), 2: 679–84.

30. G. B. Andreini, *La centaura* (Genoa: Il Melangolo, 2004), 52.

31. On Marino's poetics and aesthetics, see my *L'estetica del Barocco* (Bologna: Il Mulino, 2005), 34–36.

which was long to remain a touchstone in his life. Shakespeare and Cervantes died in 1616, but Andreini, who was forty years old, was instead about to enter the prime of his theatrical career. With the rapid development of the professional theater in early modern Europe—in an age of increasing prestige for products that exploited art's capacity for illusion, nothing could compete with the theater—he now had a unique opportunity, as a playwright, to reach beyond the Italian comic tradition, of which he was an acknowledged master, in order to explore the very limits of the art form.

The Fedeli traveled steadily throughout northern Italy in the following years, which were marked by dissension in the ranks of the company, with members coming and going. During this time Andreini published occasional verse, a religious drama (with music by, among others, Monteverdi), and more comedies, sometimes using pseudonyms. On January 31, 1620, he signed an act of emancipation from his aged father, providing public proof of his financial success. Around this same time, he likely began a liaison with the actress Virginia Rotari, a member of the company specializing in servants' roles, who was one day to play the role of Lidia in *Love in the Mirror* (and, eventually, to become his second wife). In autumn 1620, the Fedeli once more departed for Paris: Andreini's fame was such that the company remained there until the end of the 1622 Carnival season, with King Louis XIII regularly attending the performances at court. It was during this long sojourn in the French capital that Andreini published, in Italian, five of his finest plays, including *Love in the Mirror* and *The Centaur*.[32] Most of these works are built around a concept that pushes traditional representational practices of the theater to the breaking point. (Some or most of these may have been composed years earlier, and may have already been part of the repertory of the Fedeli.) Doubles and doubling devices or themes are common in them, and the only rule is a relentless deconstruction of all notions of the real and the authentic. In *Li duo Lelii simili* (Lelio and Lelio, the Identical Twins), there are identically named identical twins who appear and speak together on stage in the final act, in defiance of the laws of verisimilitude. In *Love in the Mirror*, the same-sex desires of the leading female character are resolved through marriage to an hermaphrodite, whose body combines the traits of male and female. In *The Centaur*, there are—among other

---

32. See my "Publish (f)or Paris? G. B. Andreini in France," *Renaissance Drama* 36–37 (2010): 351–75; and Siro Ferrone, *Arlecchino: vita e avventure di Tristano Martinelli attore* (Bari: Laterza, 2006), 209–20.

doublings—mythological hybrid beings, half-human and half-animal. In *Le due commedie in commedia* (The Two Plays Within the Play), published in 1623 in Venice, there are two competing plays within a play, performed by two different "troupes." Andreini's works for the stage reverse the traditional Western notion of the relationship between art and life: they suggest that reality itself is representation and that the theater is a metaphor, rather than a mirror, of the real.[33]

Andreini and members of his company had at least two further sojourns in Paris between 1622 and 1625, although the Hôtel de Bourgogne was forbidden to Italian troupes after 1622. He continued to publish verse (both occasional and devout), learned apologies for comedy, and works for the stage. He took the Fedeli to the court of the Holy Roman Emperor Ferdinand II in 1627–28, with stays in Prague and Vienna. After the disaster of the War of the Mantuan Succession, followed by the death of his wife Virginia Ramponi in 1631, Andreini traveled with the remnants of his company throughout northern and central Italy until 1642, struggling with legal and financial problems while continuing to write and publish. His final two comedies appeared in these years, in which he devoted himself increasingly to religious compositions and to verse. He returned to Paris between 1643 and 1647, apparently without the Fedeli, and acted with other Italian troupes. He sought, and failed to obtain, the patronage of such prominent figures as Cardinal Mazarin and the Gonzaga-Nevers Duke of Mantua, Charles II. We know that he was in Rome by 1651, where he played Pantalone for another company at Carnival, leaving behind manuscript copies of his retelling of the Don Giovanni legend, *Il nuovo risarcito 'Convitato di Pietra'* (The New "Guest of Stone," first published in 2003).[34] Although the Fedeli were formally disbanded in 1652, Andreini continued to work in the theater, and in that same year completed his final play, the devout *La Maddalena lasciva e penitente* (Mary Magdalen, Sinner and Penitent), which he staged in Milan with his second wife, Virginia Rotari, in the role of Martha.[35] He died on June 7, 1654 in Reggio Emilia, leaving extensive debts to his heirs.

---

33. "Il gioco e i suoi 'generi': conversazione con Luca Ronconi," ed. Aldo Viganò, in *La centaura*, 215.

34. Silvia Carandini and Luciano Mariti, *Don Giovanni o l'estrema avventura del teatro: 'Il nuovo risarcito Convitato di Pietra' di Giovan Battista Andreini* (Rome: Bulzoni, 2003), 395–707.

35. Giovan Battista Andreini, *La Maddalena lasciva e penitente*, ed. Rossella Palmieri (Bari: Palomar, 2006).

A *Reading of* Love in the Mirror

Love in the Mirror is a play about magic of many different kinds. Some of these may sound familiar enough to modern readers: the magic of mirrors, of sexuality, of love, of illusion. Yet, in this play, these and other kinds of magic possess meanings specific to Andreini's Baroque vision of existence. The title itself tells of two of them. The magic of love in the play is not to be confused with what we today think of as "romantic" love: it is instead to be attributed to a powerful divinity, Eros or Cupid. His is a superhuman force, external to the human mind and heart, which no human can influence or, for that matter, explain. The love god is capricious and arbitrary, yet all are subject to his will, and he takes his revenge on those who defy his edicts, as Florinda learns. Because of the love god, things happen to the characters without warning and without any evident logic, like a *coup de foudre* or the sudden reappearance of a long-lost and never-mentioned twin. When we think today of the magic of the mirror, on the other hand, we are likely to consider it as an optical device, chiefly for viewing what cannot otherwise be seen by the unaided eye. Although it has this function in *Love in the Mirror*, the mirror is, more to the point for Andreini, a metaphor: or rather, it is a metaphor for metaphor, the uncontrollable proliferation of signs, images, and figures—leading to doubling upon doubling, ad infinitum—that defines the Baroque aesthetic as one of radical ungrounding. Furthermore, following the classic comic tradition, the play is concerned with the magic of sexuality (the remote origins of Western comedy may perhaps lie in ancient fertility rites), but once again this is not to be understood in a modern sense. Here, sexual magic is about the truly inexplicable—in 1622—reproductive mysteries of the organism, from pregnancy and childbirth to the failure of nature to differentiate adequately between its creations when twins are conceived, to the doubling of sexual organs in the body of the hermaphrodite. Finally, the magic of illusion is represented in the play, at the level of the plot, by the wizard Arfasat. He is a master of natural or sympathetic magic, capable of discovering buried treasure or controlling the weather; even more astonishingly, however, he can produce a seemingly identical double of the body of a sleeping person, summoning a spectacle out of thin air. Yet, for all this, in *Love in the Mirror* the magic of the *magus* stands above all as a metaphor for the very function of the theater itself in Baroque culture. Magic is, like the theater, the supreme instrument of illusion,

and Arfasat is but a figure for the playwright, who can conjure a spectacle—and the world that it evokes—out of thin air too, using a pen instead of a magic wand.[36]

Like one of the many monstrous beings mentioned in it, *Love in the Mirror* is a hybrid text combining other forms of theater, a skillful assemblage of elements taken from the Western comic tradition. The stage set displays a piazza or street, with three houses fronting onto it: Lidia's, Florinda's, and Orimberto's. The sixteenth-century Italian *commedia erudita* or learned comedy (so called because it imitated the classic Roman stage) adopted this device from the ancient comedies of Plautus and Terence, and Andreini maintains it in his own "new comedy." The action takes place primarily in front of the three houses, but there are scenes (such as II.6 or IV.2) in which characters are seen at a window. Therefore, unlike the rudimentary stage of the *commedia dell'arte*, which could be quickly set up or struck by the itinerant troupe, Andreini's comedy seems to have required the construction of a fixed scene, as was the norm for learned comedy.

The 1999 film adaptation of the play beautifully displays several versions of this set.[37] There are a number of other, less immediately visible, differences between the play and its immediate predecessors in the early modern comic genre. The Arte players generally used scenarios instead of full-length scripts like *Love in the Mirror*, leaving room for them to improvise, whereas the play's five-act structure clearly refers to the scripted model of learned comedy originally derived from the Plautine tradition. No masked actors appear on stage, although several roles or "maschere"—Lelio, Lidia, Florinda—come directly from the Arte plays for which the Compagnia dei Fedeli was renowned. Nor is there the slightest hint of a transclass love affair in *Love in the*

---

36. The first known performance of Shakespeare's *The Tempest* was only a little over a decade before the publication of *Love in the Mirror*. Andreini is certainly not Shakespeare, and there is no evidence that he knew the latter's work. Both were, however, professional men of the theater, keenly attuned to the tastes of the public and well-versed in the new Baroque aesthetic. Given Shakespeare's familiarity with a variety of Italian literary sources, from Petrarch to the *commedia dell'arte*, it is not surprising that these two prolific dramatists shared some important themes. Corneille's *L'Illusion comique* (The Comic Illusion) was to return to this same notion just a few years later, in 1639.

37. This is clear from the performance instructions that Andreini included at the end of the play, where he notes: "If there should be more streets, as is the case in some theaters, there should be even more actors dressed as Death." Luca Ronconi instead used facing Renaissance palaces, and the street in between them, for his 2002 open-air production of *Love in the Mirror* in the historic center of Ferrara.

Mirror, although this was a mainstay of both learned comedy and Arte scenarios (e.g., Pantaloon pursuing a housemaid). The servants speak the language of the body, while their masters and mistresses speak the language of love, and no erotic charge passes between these two social classes. Although there is no *beffa* or *burla*, the elaborate and sometimes cruel practical joke or hoax so often at the heart of the learned comedy, there are trace elements of comic violence taken from the resources of the Arte. When the women beat the men with stiff parchment sticks, for instance, Andreini understands this as slapstick comic relief in the Arte tradition (the only real injury is to the men's pride), although, as we have seen, it also has a very serious thematic function.

Furthermore, the playwright makes almost no attempt to (re)-construct the characters' identities or their backgrounds. We know virtually nothing of Florinda except for the passions that she displays on stage; she has no family, no past, and she mentions only one friend once. This makes her more like an Arte character than a protagonist of learned comedy. What we do come to know is her sexual odyssey, the complex and at times tormented exploration of sexuality that takes place on and off stage: her lovers—Lidia and Eugenio—represent different facets of her journey, rather than autonomous personalities in their own right. It bears repeating that one must abandon any expectation of realism or naturalism in reading Andreini's work for the theater. The rapid passages in Florinda's personality, from misanthrope to lesbian to wife, are not psychologically plausible. But, then again, neither are they meant to be. According to the Spanish moralist Baltasar Gracián (1601–58), one of the greatest of all Baroque prose writers, Homer's invention, in the *Odyssey*, of the wanderings of Ulysses was a universal symbol of human life as a tempest-tossed crossing of a world swarming with strange, hybrid beings.[38] This fits perfectly with what happens to Florinda in *Love in the Mirror*, for her stormy voyage of discovery in search of sexual "truth" finally leads her into the embrace of just such a being, namely, the hermaphrodite Eugenio, with unexpected consequences for them both.

Following the dedication, which firmly establishes the centrality of the twin themes of love and the mirror, act 1 begins with a dialogue between Guerindo, who is in love with Florinda, and Coradella, his servant. Their very first words refer to armed conflict: describing his beloved's aversion to him, Guerindo speaks of enemy

---

38. See my *L'estetica del Barocco*, 9.

warriors and "war to the death," as symbolized by the eternal enmity between fern and reed. The audience quickly comes to understand, as the opening dialogue unfolds, that this is to be a war of the sexes, in which the two sides will engage in hand-to-hand combat. Like Andreini's patron Bassompierre, at once gallant lover and skilled soldier, *Love in the Mirror* is born not only under the sign of Cupid, god of love, but also under that of Mars, god of war. We should not be surprised at the mythological references throughout the play: the international literary culture of classicism recirculated and recycled an encyclopedic repertory of mythologies, ancient and early modern, texts, epigrams and commonplaces, providing an inexhaustible supply of thematic material to writers such as Andreini.[39] The tension between the two opposing poles of love and war informs the play from beginning to end, always threatening to collapse them into a single entity in which, in a typically Baroque poetic conceit pilfered from antiquity, love and war amount to the same thing. If the work starts by raising martial and amorous themes, it concludes with the conversion of the failed suitors to a life under arms, as well as Florinda's marriage to a soldier.

The female protagonists of Andreini's comedy are unarmed, but ready for battle. Florinda and Lidia both belong to the bourgeoisie that was nourished by the urban culture of Italy in the Middle Ages and the Renaissance. Although not great noblewomen, they are members of polite society, or what Stefano Guazzo called, in his famous 1574 treatise on conduct, "the civil conversation."[40] Unusual for the seicento, the women, never married, are independent in every sense of the term: financially (they have houses, servants and no apparent lack of funds), intellectually, and legally (they are without close male relations). The only father figure to appear in the play, Sufronio, is—ironically— unable to command his wayward son, Silvio, rather than dominate a daughter. Florinda is clearly somewhat older than Lidia, although the text of the play does not give their ages, but both are beautiful, quick-witted, eloquent, and virginal. They are much cleverer than the men around them, and have their way with the men in argument after argument. Because of their complete freedom from social and familial

---

39. See my "*Mare magnum*: the Arts in the Early Modern Age," *The Oxford Short History of Italy, Vol. 4: Early Modern Italy 1550–1796*, ed. John. A. Marino (Oxford and New York: Oxford University Press, 2002), 158.

40. Stefano Guazzo, *La civil conversazione*, ed. Amedeo Quondam, 2 vols. (Modena: Mucchi, 1993).

controls, these women would have appeared as figures of impossibility to the seventeenth-century public, lending the play the aura of a fairy tale for adults, at a time in which the very first such literary fairy tales in the Western tradition were beginning to be composed in Italy.[41]

We first meet Florinda in act 1, scene 3, in which she engages in a duel of wits with her suitor, Guerindo. His manservant Coradella refers to her as "this furious female" ("questa femmina arrabbiata"), but Florinda in fact coolly counters every argument that Guerindo puts forward in favor of her surrender to him. The two exchange a series of commonplaces drawn from the long-running Renaissance debate over the equality of women, to which women themselves, such as Moderata Fonte, had begun to contribute only fairly recently. When Guerindo tries to argue for the biblical basis of women's inferiority to men, his lady love easily demolishes his logic, sending him packing. Florinda's other suitor, Lelio, fares no better. After a brief and fruitless clash with the object of his desire in act 1, he returns to her house in the opening scene of act 2. Here he attempts to convince Florinda to fall in love with him, citing mythological, natural, and historical examples of famous lovers, from Venus to Cleopatra. His beloved, however, responds that her only lover is honor itself, of which Lelio is the "enemy," because sexual congress with a man would deprive her of her physical and emotional integrity. He could do her a favor, she adds, by transforming himself into Adonis, while changing her into Diana, goddess of the hunt. Instead of Florinda being dismembered through the loss of her virginity, Lelio would thus be gored to death—penetrated, in a phallic reversal, by the tusk of a wild boar sent by the goddess.

In fact, Florinda's love is reserved for only one person: herself. In two lengthy monologues (I.3 and II.1) designed to let Virginia Ramponi play the *prima donna* in spectacular fashion, she worships her own image in a mirror. Florinda's narcissistic self-regard adds to the many meanings of the title, *Love in the Mirror*. Mesmerized by her reflection, "the portrait of the one I adore," she embraces the glass and declares herself to be "always pleasured by it." There are, in fact, overt suggestions of onanism in these two speeches. If Florinda is at first amazed "that I myself should sigh with love for myself," she soon sings of the mirror as "a flame in which I, burning like a phoenix, am born

---

41. The first to write collections of literary fairy tales is Giambattista Basile, *Lo cunto de li cunti*, ed. Michele Rak (Milan: Garzanti, 1998 [1634–36]). The English title of this work is usually given as *The Pentameron*, but see Giambattista Basile, *The Tale of Tales, or Entertainment for Little Ones*, trans. Nancy Canepa (Detroit: Wayne State University Press, 2007).

and die": this metaphorical phoenix-like cycle of death and rebirth is that of repeated sexual rapture, climax, and release.[42] She lists the numerous advantages of loving only herself in the mirror, which include protection from pregnancy and preservation of her freedom, instead of taking a lover who will violate her body, subordinating her sexually and socially. The autoerotic charge of these monologues, in which Florinda appears absolutely sure of the object of her own desire, prepares the way for the important scene (II.6) in which Lidia's face accidentally appears as a reflection in Florinda's mirror while the latter is gazing at herself in it. Wearing a man's hat, as was the fashion of the day in Florence, while looking out of her window, Lidia is mistaken by Florinda in the looking glass for a very beautiful and melancholy young man. The sudden juxtaposition in the mirror of this tearful face with her own triggers an extraordinary change of heart in Florinda, thus adding yet another layer of meaning to the title of the play. As in the Renaissance tradition of transvestite sex comedy, in which women fall for women in male disguise because they make the most attractive men, Florinda feels a sudden, mad longing for this unknown "man," declaring: "Oh if men were really like this, I wouldn't be such a fierce enemy of theirs." But of course men are not really "like this," because Lidia is most decidedly not a man. Overcome by passion, from that moment Florinda abandons her principled self-love and sets off on a frenzied search for her newly beloved. Act 2 closes on a comic note, with Florinda in despair at her failure to find the enigmatic source of the new image in her mirror.

When act 3 opens, Florinda discovers Lidia's true identity at last (III.1), exclaiming "Why, this is a gentlewoman!" So that there can be no room for error, Lidia simply replies: "I am a woman." This scene contains the first of two key turning points in the plot of the play. Florinda, when she learns that Lidia is pining for the love of Silvio, whom she has unjustly had jailed in a fit of anger, decides to "cure" this lovesick young woman by disabusing her of any romantic notions. "Leave Love," Florinda tells her bluntly. There ensues a debate between the two women about the nature and worth of love, in which the Baroque taste for far-fetched metaphors is ably put on display, along with many commonplaces from this well-worn discourse: when Florinda declares, for instance, that "Love is a pestilent worm that

42. For more on the music in Andreini's plays, see John S. Powell, *Music and Theatre in France, 1600–1680* (New York: Oxford University Press, 1998), 167–70, and MacNeil, *Music and Women*, 163–84.

gnaws at the heart," Lidia immediately responds, "If Love is a worm, it's a silkworm, whose small but honored mouth spins silk for us." Lidia defends love so skillfully, in the face of Florinda's frontal assault on it, that the latter—able to outwit any man, but not another woman—is eventually overcome with emotion and swoons into her new friend's arms. The women's debate on love then takes an unexpected turn. Florinda awakens to find herself still in Lidia's embrace. Transported by the erotic power of Lidia's words in praise of love, they fall in love … with one another. After sealing their bond with kisses and embraces, they swear to "despise all men and love only each other."[43] The clear inference in the text of the play—and (too) much has been made in recent years of the fact that Andreini's wife and lover would have been playing these roles on stage in 1622—is that the two women consensually choose tribadism or lesbianism, although this is never said directly by them.

The rest of the third act is devoted to the suitors' nocturnal attempts to possess the women (Florinda and Lidia) by magic, with the help of the wizard Arfasat. All three suitors gratefully accept the wizard's unsolicited offer of help in conquering the women, but fail miserably at the tasks to which he sets them. Thanks to Arfasat's enchantment, the beloved, deeply asleep, appears to her suitor, through the phenomenon of bilocation (in which a person seems to be in two distinct places at the same time). In each case, however, the overexcited suitor fails to follow the wizard's instructions carefully enough, with disastrous results.[44] Monsters and evil spirits materialize and wreak havoc with panicking suitors and servants alike, as flames shoot out of the stage, providing an occasion for the spectacular theatrical special effects that the Baroque public favored. Only the courtier Orimberto is beaten and physically humiliated by the spirits, but the others are all equally terrified out of their wits, and by the next day have renounced love in favor of military service far away from Florence.

---

43. Harriette Andreadis, *Sappho in Early Modern England : Female Same-Sex Literary Erotics, 1550–1714* (Chicago: University of Chicago Press, 2001), offers a very useful account of early modern lesbianism, although in another part of Europe.

44. If the wizard's magic had worked, Florinda would have been taken by both Lelio and Guerindo, rivals for her hand: their use of his magic was destined to fail, in other words, from the outset. See Piermario Vescovo, "Narciso, Psiche e Marte 'mestruato': una lettura di *Amor nello specchio* di Giovan Battista Andreini," *Lettere italiane* 56, no. 1 (2004): 73.

For a modern-day audience, the long unfolding and undoing of the suitors' schemes in act 3 may seem not organically related to the love affair between Florinda and Lidia. If we consider, however, that the men intend to rape the sleeping women, in order to impregnate them (recalling at least one important variant of the Sleeping Beauty fairy tale) and force them into marriage, the relationship between these central episodes becomes clearer. Act 3, scene 1, in which the two women fall in love with one another, shows the irresistible power of Cupid to create a consensual erotic and emotional bond, disregarding prescribed gender roles. The rest of the same act instead displays the failure of human beings—even with the aid of natural magic, which taps the unlimited but occult power of nature—to undo the divine magic of the great god of love. The suitors are human, all too human: although the wizard knows how to harness the power of nature and to put it at their service for the purpose of sexual conquest, the men prove innately incapable of overthrowing Cupid's reign, and are severely punished for their revolt against his rule. Thus—to return to the conflation of love and war with which the play began—we witness the rout of those who would use male violence as a weapon in the war of the sexes. In a neat reversal, the men who planned to violate the defenseless, sleeping women, who do not love them, are themselves subjected to a night of terror.

In act 4, another unexpected plot twist occurs. Day returns, and Florinda and Lidia, having spent the night together, take leave of one another. Continuing the intertwined themes of Mars and Venus, Florinda recounts how she "ravaged her [Lidia] with an army of kisses" (IV.3). When Bernetta mocks them for their inability to have genital intercourse, Florinda dismisses such criticism: she and her lover are united, in body and soul, by their great disdain of the opposite sex. What they do not know is that Lidia's near-identical and long-lost twin brother, the soldier Eugenio, has suddenly come to town. In the soliloquy signaling his arrival in Florence (IV.4), he too reprises the play's original theme of the conflict between Mars and Venus. The young soldier weighs the respective virtues of arms and letters, attributing masculine traits to arms and feminine traits to letters, suggesting to the audience that there are conflicting forces at work in him. This soliloquy doubtless was intended to be played for comic effect, inasmuch as the same actress plays both Lidia and Eugenio, thus giving the soldier an unmistakably androgynous appearance. Not surprisingly, given the newcomer's ambiguous physique and voice,

a comedy of errors ensues, spilling over into act 5: first Orimberto (IV.5), then Bernetta (V.4), and finally Florinda (V.5) in fact mistake Eugenio for his cross-dressed sister.

In the play's final act, Florinda seduces Eugenio, believing him to be her lover Lidia in disguise. There are many precedents in Italian literature for this (offstage) scene of seduction due to misrecognition. This is perhaps the first time on stage, however, that the seductress consciously seeks to conquer another woman, while knowing her to be a woman, albeit one dressed as a man. Eugenio of course does not know what to make of Florinda's entirely unexpected proposal that he come to bed with her, although he cannot believe his good fortune: "only a knave could refuse her offer. My lady, I'm the woman named Lidia, the man called Eugenio; I'm Cupid, dressed or undressed; I'll be anything you like, but let's go to bed" (V.5). These remarks by the excited young soldier signal the second major turning point in the plot of the play. Recounting their first sexual encounter to a crowded stage two scenes later (V.7), Florinda reveals that when she was about to make love with Eugenio, he said to her: "Know, then, madam, that I am not a woman like you, but am (if you've ever heard the term before) an hermaphrodite, that is to say, I am more man than woman." Andreini, by introducing here the hybrid figure of the hermaphrodite, offers a typically Baroque solution to the puzzle of the third and final phase of Florinda's sexual odyssey in the play.

There are a number of hints, scattered throughout the play, that anticipate the appearance of the hermaphrodite in act 5. The dedication to the great nobleman and libertine Bassompierre, "the most faithful follower" of both "Mars and Venus," might well have reminded readers that the French were obsessed with this theme: the hermaphrodite was often seen in early modern France as not only highly sexualized, but as a direct threat to hierarchy and civil order.[45] Hermes/Mercury, who is mentioned in act 1, scene 1, was often identified with hermaphroditism, as was the alchemical magic of the wizard Arfasat (III.2), in early modern culture. The phoenix (I.3), because it was self-

---

45. Kathleen Long, *Hermaphrodites in Renaissance Europe* (Burlington, VT: Ashgate, 2006), 2. Long points out that Henri III (King of France from 1574–89) was denounced as an hermaphrodite both in political pamphlets and in Thomas Artus's novel, *L'Isle des Hermaphrodites, nouvellement descouverte* (The Island of Hermaphrodites, Newly Discovered), which was first published around 1605. See also the anonymous political tract *L'Hermaphrodite de ce temps* (1612–15) for further use of this same theme.

engendering, was sometimes connected to this same theme.[46] In Greek mythology, Hermaphroditus was the son of Hermes and Aphrodite, combining elements of the male and the female in a single body.[47] The hermaphrodite body is androgynous, belonging fully to neither sex. Its gender too can be ambiguous: the hermaphrodite is neither man nor woman, although usually inclined toward one or the other of these two, as Eugenio is inclined toward the male gender. In her retrospective narration of her sexual encounter with Eugenio, Florinda attributes to her new lover first one gender and then another, switching back and forth with comic effect until finally deciding that he is "all man" (V.7).[48] As Kathleen Long has shown, "discourse cannot encompass the hermaphroditic body" because that body violates the system of binary oppositions upon which gender depends.[49] It is not identical with itself, in other words, and therefore cannot be embodied in language (as a "s/he"). If the play's first turning point involves the mirror, in which Florinda and her lover are brought together, the second one centers instead on the hermaphrodite Eugenio, who once more brings together Florinda and Lidia, but with a difference. The mirror is both Narcissus and Echo, we are told earlier in the play (I.3 and II.1), or, in other words, both male and female, and so is the hermaphrodite. Thus the mirror and Eugenio's body "mirror" one another, in a dizzying play of reflections, or *mise-en-abîme*, of the very sort favored by Andreini's artistic temperament.

Like the mirror, Eugenio is a "whole," a union of male and female; everyone else in the play is partial, incomplete, and in search of a way to overcome this condition. If so much of the play is about male *versus* female, Eugenio breaks that pattern by presenting himself to Florinda as male *and* female. Unlike the traditional early modern view of the hermaphrodite, however, there is nothing monstrous about him. On the contrary, the other characters remark upon his

---

46. On the phoenix as a multivalent emblem in early modern culture, see José Julio García Arranz, *Ornitología emblemática: las aves en la literatura simbólica ilustrada en Europa durante los siglos XVI y XVII* (Cáceres: Universidad de Extremadura, 1996), 333–61.

47. Orimberto's misrecognition of Eugenio (IV.5) echoes the myth of Hermaphroditus: in ancient art, the youth is sometimes shown being assaulted by a satyr, who mistakes him for a female.

48. See Nicolas Boileau, *Satires, Épîtres, Art poétique*, ed. Jean-Pierre Collinet (Paris: Gallimard, 1985 [1660–68]), 12, II.1–3, for an analogous reflection on the gender of the hermaphrodite in the Romance languages: "Du langage français bizarre hermaphrodite, / De quel genre te faire, équivoque maudite / Ou maudit?"

49. Long, *Hermaphrodites in Renaissance Europe*, 56.

beauty (V.7), and of course Florinda falls in love with him. This hermaphroditic unity of being, however, is not stable, but oscillates between the poles that it binds together, like an electrical charge. The hermaphroditic body is, as Louis Marin notes, "neither the true sex nor the false" and thus cannot be the final resolution of difference or the binding synthesis of the sexes.[50]

This explains the play's profound ambiguity concerning Eugenio's sexuality. Andreini, in a gesture that we may find everywhere in his work, elides and collapses categories: if Eugenio is "all man" at one moment, he is something else again at another, successive moment, namely a *semivir* (or "half-man"). There is no progression toward the "perfection," as early modern culture held it to be, of maleness. Nor does her sudden marriage to Eugenio mean that Florinda has developed emotionally into a mature woman ready to embrace her traditional role as wife and mother. On the contrary, after her tryst with Eugenio, which effectively transforms her into his wife, Florinda nonetheless declares to his twin sister Lidia that "now—more than ever—you're mine" (V.7).

What could be meant by this? Florinda has presented herself before as being entirely sure of her sexual preferences, i.e., autoeroticism (acts 1 and 2) and lesbianism (acts 3 and 4). Each time, she states with great enthusiasm that this is what she wants; each time, however, something happens to change her mind. In act 5, she announces that she is convinced of Eugenio's manhood, but only after some extraordinary linguistic wriggling. There is nothing in the text of the play to suggest that this claim too might not be subject to further revision. Indeed, in the scene following Florinda's blow-by-blow description of her seduction of Eugenio, we learn from her servant Bernetta that Eugenio has been left bleeding heavily—from the nose—after having had sex with her mistress. In his present state, with his head held over a basin, he cannot return to the stage: thus there is no scene of recognition (*anagnorisis*) between brother and sister in the play, which would show the audience that these are in fact distinct individuals. Until her encounter with the young soldier, Florinda was a virgin—she's told the audience so several times (see, for instance, II.1)—but afterward, it is the androgynous Eugenio who seems to have been deflowered, if not emasculated.[51] Andreini finds

---

50. Louis Marin, "Neither the True Sex nor the False," *Cross-Readings*, trans. Jane Marie Todd (Atlantic Highlands, NJ: Humanities Press, 1998 [1992]), 228–34.

51. See Vescovo, "Narciso, Psyche e Marte 'mestruato,'" 70–71, who suggests instead that

in the ambiguous figure of the hermaphrodite a fittingly Baroque solution to the problem of comic closure, which traditionally requires the restoration of patriarchy through marriage. Florinda abandons her vow of virginity, but not, as we have seen, her vow of love for Lidia (first taken in III.1). With her hermaphrodite husband, who both is and is not his sister Lidia, she will be able to explore all sides of her sexuality without outside interference from the system of social controls. By marrying Eugenio, Florinda chooses a partner who has both, as Bernetta says, "as much in his trousers as I have under this skirt" and, as the soldier adds, "something more besides." Because it represents both sexes in one, Eugenio's androgynous body offers this unique comic heroine the chance to create a space of freedom for herself—the freedom to love as she pleases and to look at herself in whatever mirror she chooses—within the confines of early modern society.

Afterlife of the Play

Most, although not all, of Andreini's literary and dramatic output was published in his lifetime. Today we know of fewer than twenty full-length non-religious plays, along with a rather larger number of volumes containing verse, criticism, or sacred works.[52] This corpus was largely forgotten after his death, even before Baroque poetics and aesthetics went out of fashion in Europe.[53] Both the Enlightenment and Romanticism bluntly rejected the principles of Baroque art and culture. In fact, the very term "Baroque" was first used in the eighteenth century as a derogatory reference to the style of the preceding century: Andreini instead thought of himself simply as "modern." Giammaria Mazzuchelli, one of the most important eighteenth-century Italian literary historians, does mention a handful of Andreini's works in his classic *Gli scrittori d'Italia* (Italian Writers).[54] After 1674, however,

---

early modern medical theory would have required a periodic release of blood from a male after having had it "stirred" in this way by sexual intercourse.

52. For a complete list of Andreini's works, see Carandini and Mariti, *Don Giovanni*, 50–57.

53. On the end of the Baroque, see Vernon Hyde Minor, *The Death of the Baroque and the Rhetoric of Good Taste* (Cambridge: Cambridge University Press, 2006). Only the comedy *La campanazza* was given posthumous publication in the seventeenth century (Milan: Pandolfo Malatesta, 1674).

54. Giammaria Mazzuchelli, *Gli scrittori d'Italia; cioè, notizie storiche, e critiche intorno alle vite, e agli scritti dei letterati italiani* (Brescia: Giambatista Bossini, 1753), 1: 710–11.

no text by Andreini was to be reprinted until the nineteenth century; only in 1982 did the first comedy reappear in print.[55] Even today there are just a handful of modern editions of his work for the stage, most notably *Love in the Mirror* and *The Centaur*. This long neglect may be attributed to many factors, ranging from the difficulty of the works themselves to the process of canon-formation in modern Italy, which banished Baroque literature as the product of a "decadent" culture under foreign domination. Given the nineteenth-century novelist Alessandro Manzoni's scathing critique of seventeenth-century Italy in his classic novel *I promessi sposi* (The Betrothed), the subsequent refusal of both liberals and fascists to recognize any value in this phase of the peninsula's past, and the influential neo-idealist philosopher Benedetto Croce's blanket condemnation of Baroque art as "il brutto" ("the ugly"), it is no wonder that Andreini, along with many other artists and writers of the Seicento, languished in oblivion for so long.[56]

Andreini's reputation has revived in Italy in recent decades, as interest in seventeenth-century art and culture has grown exponentially there and throughout the West. Both of the above-mentioned comedies have been staged in Italy by the renowned director Luca Ronconi, who has shown a particular affinity for Andreini's brand of daring Baroque experimentalism. In staging these works, Ronconi made some (necessary) cuts to Andreini's performance texts, but on the whole remained very faithful to the playwright's words and intentions. The director noted, in an interview concerning his 2004 production in Genoa of *The Centaur*, that Andreini printed relatively simple stage directions with the text of this work, as if to suggest that stage machinery was far less important than the audience's imaginative involvement in the events taking place on stage, despite the playwright's defiance of all psychological naturalism or realism.[57] There are, however, stage directions for specific special effects included in the original edition of *Love in the Mirror,* and Ronconi's two productions of it (1987 and 2002) did not try to do away with them. A major motion picture entitled *Amor nello specchio* (Love in the Mirror), freely adapting the play for the screen, was released in 1999, although not in the United

---

55. *Lo schiavetto* (1612) was anthologized in *Commedie dei comici dell'arte,* ed. Laura Falavolti (Turin: UTET, 1982), 57–213; *Le due commedie in commedia* (1623) can be found in *Commedie dell'arte,* ed. Siro Ferrone, 2 vols. (Milan: Mursia, 1985–86), 2: 17–105.

56. See the remarks by Giuseppe Galasso, "Il Seicento a mezzo del cammino," *Italia 1650,* ed. Galasso and Musi , 8.

57. "Il gioco e i suoi 'generi': conversazione con Luca Ronconi," 215.

States.[58] Starring Anna Galiena and Peter Stormare, this period film was mostly shot on location in and around Sabbioneta, the unspoiled sixteenth-century ideal city in the Po valley, south of Mantua (which also served as a location for Bertolucci's *The Spider's Stratagem*). The director, Salvatore Maira, who coedited the 1997 critical edition of the play, had previously made two full-length feature films examining the lives of women in contemporary Italy.[59]

His striking cinematic adaptation of *Love in the Mirror* interweaves the story of the Fedeli's rehearsals for the first performance of the play in 1622 with the development of the love triangle between Andreini and the two Virginias. Although only a few scenes from the original play are included in the film, Maira tries to capture the creative process that led Andreini to write and stage *Love in the Mirror*, in an attempt to provide a plausible psychological framework for the play's plot and characters (who at one point even argue onstage with the author, à la Pirandello, about their lack of psychological depth). In a surprising twist, Maira turns the tables on Andreini by having the love story at the center of the play—i.e., the affair between Florinda and Lidia—subsequently inspire the two actresses to abandon the playwright and become lovers in real life. In this, of course, the film takes its cue from the Baroque aesthetic itself, in which life and art, truth and fiction, reality and illusion, original and copy, are indistinguishable from one another.

Maira also takes a postmodern step into anachronism by including the character of Athanasius Kircher (1602–80), a Jesuit priest whose claim to have invented the "magic lantern," the first practical apparatus for projecting pictures onto a screen through the use of mirrors and lamps, dates to many years after Andreini's death.[60] In the film are included a number of complex special effects based on Baroque catoptric devices, which do in fact beautifully capture the magic of Florinda's first encounter with Lidia in the mirror: both women

---

58. *Amor nello specchio*, Italy, 1999, 104 minutes, with Anna Galiena, Peter Stormare, and Simona Cavallari. Story, screenplay, and direction by Salvatore Maira. A Factory and G. M. F. production, in collaboration with RAI Radiotelevisione Italiana.

59. *Riflessi in un cielo scuro* (1991) and *Donne in un giorno di festa* (1993).

60. Athanasius Kircher, *Ars magna lucis et umbrae n X. libros digesta. Quibus admirandae lucis & umbrae in mundo, atque adeò universa natura, vires effectusque uti nova, ita varia novorum recondiitiorumque specimum exhibitione, ad varios mortalium usus, panduntur* (Amsterdam: J. Jansson, 1671). On Kircher and his work, see Paula Findlen, ed., *Athanasius Kircher : the Last Man Who Knew Everything* (New York: Routledge, 2004).

are transformed into moving images. At the end of the film, after a final performance of the play *Love in the Mirror* in the magnificent theater of Sabbioneta, the company's players yield their place on stage to Kircher and his magic lantern, which enthralls the public with the projection of monstrous and bizarre beings onto a screen.[61] By including the magic lantern and other early modern optical devices in the film, Maira makes the point (which he confirms in the final sequence) that Andreini's inexhaustible and restless experimentalism seems, both technically and intellectually, to anticipate the cinema.[62] A film about *Love in the Mirror* has, in this sense, to be a metafilm, a Baroque folding of layer upon layer of representation and illusion. Before the final credits roll, a caption reminds viewers that Molière saw Andreini perform in Paris in the mid-1640s, thus confirming a fragile link between one of the greatest early modern European comic playwrights, whose canonical status is unquestioned today, and his almost forgotten Italian predecessor.

Remarks on the Translation

Inevitably there are many difficult decisions to be made by any translator of Baroque literature, no matter what the target language may be. In the 1600s, witty conceits and far-fetched metaphors were in vogue in many parts of Europe. Theatergoers in the English-speaking world can readily comprehend the obstacles faced by translators trying to bring Shakespeare over into another tongue, whether it be Portuguese, Hindi, or Japanese. For if a good deal of Shakespearean dialogue is challenging for the modern ear, some of it is quite obscure—even for fluent speakers of English—without an annotated text at hand. In the rapid-fire exchanges of wit in *Twelfth Night*, for instance, the puns and jokes hover at times on the edge of incomprehensibility. Finding equivalent expressions for elaborate rhetorical figures in another language, without doing violence to the underly-

61. On the relationship between the magic lantern and magic itself, see Koen Vermeir, "The Magic of the Magic Lantern (1660–1700): On Analogical Demonstration and the Visualization of the Invisible," *British Journal of the History of Science* 38, no. 2 (2005): 129.

62. For a description of the projection devices available to Andreini during his own lifetime, see Laurent Mannoni, Donata Pesenti Campagnoni, and David Robinson, *Light and Movement: Incunabula of the Motion Picture 1420–1896/Luce e movimento: incunaboli dell'immagine animata 1420–1896/Lumière et mouvement: incunables de l'image animée 1420–1896* (Gemona, Italy: Le Giornate del Cinema Muto, 1995), 62–63.

ing meaning of the original version, is no simple matter, and this was certainly the case in translating *Love in the Mirror* into English. On the other hand, the translator of early modern drama has the luxury of being able to unravel its dense verbal and figural textures, back-filling and expanding through modulation and paraphrase what has become linguistically or semantically alien to us. Every translation is a priori an interpretation, of course, but in this case the loss of poetic force through the act of translation may prove at least to be a gain in coherence for today's reader.

I have sought to translate the play, as nearly as possible, into our contemporary idiom. It was my aim to produce a version that could be transformed, without insurmountable linguistic barriers, into a performance text, or, in other words, into a script for today's players. I avoided archaisms whenever I could, while leaving intact the tissue of often obscure classical references woven throughout Andreini's text. Although it might have seemed logical to a nineteenth-century translator to imitate the syntactical and lexical choices of Shakespeare, Jonson, and other Anglo-Saxon contemporaries of Andreini, I have tried to keep as far as possible from any echo of Elizabethan/Jacobean speech patterns,[63] while respecting forms of address then in use. Nor have I transposed the northern Italian dialect spoken on rare occasion in the play into an English-language equivalent such as Cockney or Brooklynese: for this would limit overmuch the possibilities of the performance text. However, mindful of the Italian proverb "traduttore traditore" ("the translator is a traitor"), I have tried to translate faithfully the original text, making no attempt to eliminate any of its elements for the sake of a smoother end result in contemporary English. The only exception is the list of demons in III.10, which I thought untranslatable, since they seem to be an invention of Andreini's bor-

---

63. The one exception is Granello's pun (I.6) on the genitive case in Latin, for which I owe a particular debt to Shakespeare's *Merry Wives of Windsor*, IV.1:

EVANS. What is your genitive case plural, William?

WILLIAM. Genitive case?

EVANS. Ay.

WILLIAM. Genitive: horum, harum, horum.

QUICKLY. Vengeance of Jenny's case; fie on her! Never name her, child, if she be a whore.

EVANS. For shame, oman.

QUICKLY. You do ill to teach the child such words. He teaches him to hick and to hack, which they'll do fast enough of themselves; and to call "horum;" fie upon you!

dering on nonsense and serving chiefly for the purposes of rhyme and meter: the facing Italian text contains these names, for those who wish to know them. If this present version is to be employed for a modern staging, directors and dramaturgs will want to adapt it. In translating *Love in the Mirror*, in short, I have taken seriously the question of performance, but without trying to determine the direction in which future readings or stagings may go.

One difficulty that presents itself immediately to the translator, as well as to the reader, of *Love in the Mirror* is that of honorific titles and forms of address. The Baroque was a culture in which distinction mattered a great deal and could even—as in anything concerning honor—be an issue of life and death. Andreini employs a welter of titles and forms of address in ways that are difficult to convey to a modern reader, accustomed as she may be to a more casual system of social interaction. In the play some are interchangeable, while others may be used variously to signal deference, respect, or (at times) contempt. Andreini leaves the social rank of some of the play's most important characters deliberately unclear: Lelio, Guerindo, Florinda, and Lidia seem to belong to the uppermost stratum of the urban bourgeoisie, as would be appropriate for the *innamorati* roles of the *commedia dell'arte* whose names they share.[64] I have generally translated the title "Madonna" literally, i.e., "Madam" or "My lady," and have kept the same translation for "Signora." I have, however, also used "Mistress" frequently. Given that "Mister" did not come into usage in English until well after this period, in translating "Signore" I have opted for "Master" instead. This form of address was the forerunner of "Mister," and was by the early 1600s used as a respectful form of address for men of this same social stratum among speakers of English. Occasionally I have used "Sir" in the body of the play, but only where it does not suggest that the addressee was a noble. The one exception is in V.4, in which Bernetta mocks Eugenio, whom she believes to be a woman trying to pass as a man.

The noble to whom the play is dedicated, the Marquis de Bassompierre, is addressed by the playwright as "Eccellenza Vostra Signoria Illustrissima," "Signore Illustrissimo," and "Vostra Signoria Illustrissima," all of which I have translated as "Your Most Illustrious Lordship." A version of this same title is accorded to the Judge and

---

64. The actors in the Compagnia dei Fedeli generally played the same stock roles in different plays in the repertory and would have been known to the public as "Lelio" (G. B. Andreini), "Florinda" (Virginia Ramponi), "Lidia" (Virginia Rotari), and so on.

the Governor, the highest-ranking characters in the play, socially speaking, although both would have been far below Bassompierre's own exalted status. Andreini also addresses Bassompierre in the dedication as "Signore," however, which in this case means "(Your) Lordship." There is, however, an important caveat to be made here. The similar-sounding title "Vostra Signoria" is employed on many occasions by the characters in the play. A servant may use it to indicate respect (I.4, III.8, V.5, V.9), as may characters of equal social rank (I.5: the exchange between Lidia and Sufronio; III.1: between Lidia and Florinda, IV.6, V.6–V.7); or it may sometimes be employed in a facetious fashion (I.3, II.6, III.3). I have translated this term throughout as "Your Lordship/Ladyship" or "Your Excellency." None of the characters has anything like the rank of Andreini's Parisian patron, and so the use of these terms in their conversations needs to be seen in the context of the play, rather than in relation to Andreini's delicate negotiations with the uppermost crust of the French nobility. The ambiguities in his use of Italian would, in short, make a mockery of any machine translation.

Because there is meant to be much music in the play, I have freely translated the songs and incantations into rhymed verses, following Andreini's rhyme schemes as closely as possible. In each case I have provided a literal translation in a note, since there is considerable variance between the rhymed and unrhymed versions. The vocative case occurs frequently in Andreini's Italian, moreover, as it does in Shakespeare's English.[65] I have tried to distinguish carefully between 'O' (vocative) and 'Oh' (emotional interjection), although the seventeenth-century Italian text often does not provide any orthographic difference between them.

Finally, the title of the work, *Amor nello specchio* or *Love in the Mirror*, contains a crucial play on words. "Amor(e)" refers to two things at once: one of these is love, but the other is the mythological god known as Eros or Cupid. The mirror is the means through which love may be ignited in the play (for instance, between Florinda and Lidia), but it is also the chosen residence of the love god himself: we learn from Florinda (I.3) that this personification of love is, literally, *in the mirror*. In the play, the powers of the Greco-Roman deity of love are often discussed and his attributes described in detail (see, for instance,

---

65. See, again, the *Merry Wives of Windsor*, IV.1:
EVANS. "What is the focative case, William?"
WILLIAM. "O-vocativo, O."

I.3 and III.1). Sometimes, however, the characters speak of love, which, even if the word is capitalized in the text, is not to be understood as a reference to the god himself. The dedication emphasizes the double meaning of "Amor(e)," shifting back and forth between the passion and its personification, which cannot be easily separated from one another, and this undecidability remains throughout the rest of the work. I have therefore based the translation of "Amor(e)" on the context in which the term appears each time. Although there are instances in which both meanings may be plausible, this is, of course, just what Andreini—with his ardent Baroque wit—intended.

This edition of *Love in the Mirror* is based on the 1622 first edition and the 1997 critical edition established by Salvatore Maira and Anna Michela Borracci. It is dedicated to my daughter, Isabella, whose love of the theater since early childhood has inspired me in my work.

Amor nello specchio
Commedia di Giovan Battista Andreini fiorentino

All'Illustrissimo Signore Basampiere dedicata.
In Parigi.
Apresso Nicolas della Vigna, stampatore nella strada Cloopi\<n>
allo Scudo di Francia, vicino al Piccolo Navarro.
M. DC XXII.

Illustrissimo Signore,

Allo specchio di gentilezza cavallieresca, allo specchio d'intrepido valor guerriero, allo specchio di vertù pellegrina, oggi s'apresenta questo AMOR NELLO SPECCHIO, commedia amorosissima.

Né poteva io, né sapeva dedicarla a cavaliero che più se li convenisse che a Vostra Signoria Illustrissima, intendendomi che questo AMOR NELLO SPECCHIO sia quello nel quale ella stessa mirandosi, così n'ha invaghito Amore, che non solo si compiacque di star nel suo volto, ma di soggiornar lieto colà dentro, dove la bella imagene sua alcuna volta si trasfonde rimirandosi.

E ben certo ella è tale, che non solo ha dato occasione ad infiniti pittori di colorarla in mille tele, ma ad Amore d'inciderla in mille e mille cuori.

Narciso si specchiò nel fonte e s'invaghì follemente di sé stesso. Eccellenza Vostra Signoria Illustrissima, specchiandosi nel fonte della gloria, saggiamente conobbe come amando sé medesimo far si debba per divenir immortalmente glorioso.

Gli Egizi, per le fonti limpide rimirando, cercavano colà dentro il sole. Eccellenza Vostra Signoria Illustrissima, riguardando nello specchio tersissimo de' grandi antenati suoi (aquila d'immensa gloria) vede e s'abbaglia a quel sole d'eroiche azzioni che non tramonterà giamai, se non al tramontar del mondo.

Lo specchio, ricevuti in sé i vivi raggi del sole, gravido di quella accesa luce, la prole de' lampi dilatando d'ogni intorno, abbaglia.

Eccellenza Vostra Signoria Illustrissima, specchio d'immensa chiarità di grandezza, gravido del diluvio di que' tanti splendori che derivano dal sole della illustrissima prosapia sua, d'ogni intorno i lampi della sua gloria dilata e spande.

Love in the Mirror

A Comedy by Giovan Battista Andreini of Florence

Dedicated to His Excellency Lord Bassompierre.
Published in Paris
By Nicolas de La Vigne, printer in the Rue Clopin
At the (sign of the) *Coat of Arms of France*, near the College of Navarre.[i]
1622.

Your Excellency,

To you—the mirror of chivalric courtesy, the mirror of intrepid warrior valor, and the mirror of remarkable virtue—I present today my LOVE IN THE MIRROR, a comedy wholly about Love.

I could not, and would not know how to, dedicate my play to a gentleman more worthy than Your Most Illustrious Lordship.[ii] I understand this LOVE IN THE MIRROR to be that same mirror in which you, gazing at yourself, have made Cupid so infatuated that not only is he pleased to become one with your face but to dwell happily there: sometimes, when you look at yourself, his handsome image is infused with yours.

And certainly this is so. For this same image has not only given an infinite number of painters the occasion to paint it on a thousand canvases, but has given Cupid himself the occasion to engrave it in thousands and thousands of hearts.

Narcissus saw his image reflected in a spring and fell wildly in love with himself.[iii] Your Most Illustrious Lordship, seeing himself mirrored in the spring of glory and loving what he saw there, wisely knew what to do to become immortally glorious.

The Egyptians, when gazing into pure spring waters, used to seek the sun in them. Your Most Illustrious Lordship, when gazing into the pellucidly clear mirror of his great ancestors, like an eagle of immense glory sees himself in—and yet is dazzled by—the sun of their heroic deeds, which will never set before the end of the world itself.

Having received into itself the sun's living rays, and pregnant with that glowing light, the mirror dazzles as it sends forth in every direction the offspring of lightning bolts.

Your Most Illustrious Lordship is a mirror of greatness, graced with immense clarity, which is swollen with the flood graced of splen-

Lo specchio, parimente dal sole percosso, se dietro lui l'arida esca si oppone, tosto in quella sfavilla il fuoco.

Eccellenza Vostra Signoria Illustrissima, specchio lucidissimo di fama trasparente, percosso dal sole de' gesti magnanimi suoi, accende fiamme inestinguibili d'amore.

Propriamente adunque questo *Amor nello Specchio* a Vostra Signoria Illustrissima si conveniva; e tale esser doveva per aver nome di commedia, la quale dai più savi ritrovata fu, quasi specchio nel quale ciascuno rimirando potesse le macchie de' cattivi costumi levarsi.

Platone commandava che l'uomo adirato si guardasse nello specchio, onde veggendosi dall'esser suo fatto diverso s'astenesse dall'ira.

E qui forse giustamente dir si potrebbe che lo specchio che 'ntendeva questo gran filosofo altro non fosse che lo specchio della commedia, detta speculum vitae humanae.

E ben certamente più si converrebbe a Talia lo specchio della prudenza che la maschera in mano; se non per altro per far noto almeno con quanta prudenza m'abbia questa commedia dello specchio a Vostra Signoria Illustrissima dedicata.

Ricevala adunque benigno, che a guisa di quegli ordigni composti di varii specchi fra' quali ponendosi il capo bellezze varie e infinite si discoprono, così spero anch'io che fra gli specchi varii qui dentro artificiosamente posti dal grande ingegnero Amore, non potrà se non virtuosamente dar vario diletto a' seguaci di lui; tra i quali più cari è 'l gentilissimo e amorosissimo Signor Baron Basampiere.

E qui per non accendere una lite inestinguibile fra Marte e Amore, ciascuno pretendendo che 'l seguace suo più fido Vostra Signoria Illustrissima sia, finisco e le m'inchino, celebrator inestancabile e perpetuo di quelle molte grazie che dalla sua mano liberalissima mi sono state compartite in due volte che m'è occorso (scenico peregrino) venir alla Francia, per servigi reali. Iddio la feliciti.

Di Parigi il dì 18 marzo 1622.
Di Vostra Signoria Illustrissima divotissimo servitore
Giovan Battista Andreini.

dors coming from the sun of his most illustrious lineage: everywhere the lightning-flashes of his glory continue to spread and expand.

The mirror, likewise struck by the sun, will quickly start a blaze if dry tinder is set before it.

Your Most Illustrious Lordship, who is the brightest mirror of transparent fame, struck by the sun of his own magnanimous gestures, lights inextinguishable flames of love.

Hence this *Love in the Mirror* was most suited to Your Most Illustrious Lordship. It had to be thus in order to be called a comedy, which the wisest men have found to be a near-mirror in which all might see the blemishes of bad habits removed.[iv]

Plato called for the angry man to look in a mirror, for in seeing himself so noticeably altered from his usual state, he would abstain from anger.[v]

And here perhaps it would be right to say that the mirror to which this great philosopher referred was none other than the mirror of comedy, called a *speculum vitae humanae*.[vi]

Indeed it would be more fitting for Thalia to hold in her hand the mirror of prudence rather than a mask,[vii] if for no other reason than at least to point out how prudently I have dedicated this comedy about mirrors to Your Most Illustrious Lordship.

Therefore receive it favorably, for like those devices made of different mirrors in which, if one places one's head in them, various infinite beauties may be discovered, thus I too hope that the several mirrors artfully placed herein by the great engineer Cupid cannot but virtuously give delight to his followers.[viii] Among the dearest of all to him is His Lordship, Baron Bassompierre, renowned as a great noble and a great lover.

In order not to start an endless quarrel between Mars and Venus,[ix] both of whom would claim Your Most Illustrious Lordship as his or her most faithful follower, I come here to the end of my discourse and bow before you, celebrating tirelessly and perpetually those many graces that your most liberal hand has granted to me on the two occasions in which I (a wandering actor) came to France by royal invitation. May God bless you.

Paris, 18 March 1622.
Your Most Illustrious Lordship's most devoted servant,
Giovan Battista Andreini.

Interlocutori

Florinda
Bernetta serva

Guerindo
Coradella servo

Sufronio
Silvio figlio
Testuggine servo

Orimberto uomo di Palazzo

Lidia sola

Lelio
Granello servo

Mago
Griffo
Orco
7 spiriti in forma di marinari

Spirito mostruoso
Menippo
Cruone
7 spiriti da facchini
4 vesti\<ti\> da Morte

Latanzio governatore
Notaro
4 labardieri

Eugenio fratello simile di Lidia

Melina serva
Peruccio servo
Giudice

Dramatis personae[x]

Florinda
Bernetta (her servant)

Guerindo
Coradella (his servant)

Sufronio
Silvio (his son)
Testuggine (his servant)

Orimberto (courtier)

Lidia (alone)

Lelio
Granello (his servant)

Wizard [Arfasat]
Griffon
Ogre
7 spirits in the form of sailors

Monstrous spirit [Death]
Menippus
Cruon
7 spirits in the form of porters
4 [spirits] dressed as Death

Latanzio (the Governor)
Notary
4 halberdiers

Eugenio (Lidia's twin brother)

Melina (servant)
Peruccio (servant)
Judge

ATTO PRIMO

Scena Prima
[Guerindo, Coradella]

GUERINDO Non credo che tanto sia nemica della serpe l'ombra dell'alloro e del frassino, quanto assai più m'è contraria Florinda; e credo per simboleggiar questo si potrebbe far come facevano gli antichi combattenti, che alor che mostravano in alto sollevato, quasi in istendardo, la filitide e la canna, dimostravano di non voler se non guerra mortale.

CORADELLA Io che son Coradella tutto cuore, m'avvalorate tanto all'essempio di questa filitide che bramo di saper qual cosa sia.

GUERINDO La filitide è quell'erba trivialmente detta felice; quella, che dicono queste donnicciuole, che fa tante cose maravigliose raccogliendosi il seme di quella in tempo di notte; ma tutte scioccherie. Or quando l'agricoltore intendente vede un campo ripieno di questa filitide, e che non può col fuoco incenerire il tronco e disperder le radici, alora al vomere del suo aratro lega una canna e ara il luogo; e così avviene, che per la gran nemicizia che la canna ha con la felice, e la filitide con la canna, che 'l campo si netti e purghi da quella infezzione, e 'l contadino vi semina poi il frumento e ne fa le desiderate raccolte.

CORADELLA Oh che bella cosa! Volete ch'io vi dica che voi potreste servir per ceratano, tante belle cose sapete, e guadagnereste vedete.

GUERINDO Ignorante. Questo è 'l guiderdone che riportano i virtuosi parlando con gente sciocca; ma lasciamo il parlar di cose tali, or che siam giunti alla casa di questa ingrata Florinda. Ohimè, talor ch'io la miro, cagionano questi marmi in me effetti contrari di quello che facessero le colonne di Mercurio, poiché se l'une infondevano parole, e queste mi fanno rimaner muto.

CORADELLA Signor Guerindo, non abbiate paura di cosa alcuna, che alora che vi mancherà il cuore, e Coradella ve l'infonderà. O di casa?

ACT I

Scene One
[Guerindo, Coradella]

GUERINDO The shade of the laurel and the ash tree may be the enemy of the snake, but Florinda is set against me more harshly still, I think.[xi] To symbolize this, one could do as the warriors of old when they raised high the hart's tongue and the reed, almost like a standard, to show that they wanted only to wage war to the death.

CORADELLA I'm Coradella, whose name means "all heart," and you give such prominence to the example of the hart's tongue that I'm dying to know what it might be.

GUERINDO The hart's tongue is a plant commonly known as a fern.[xii] Silly women say that it possesses marvelous powers when its seeds are gathered by night; but this is mere foolishness. When a farm foreman sees a field full of hart's tongue, knowing that fire cannot burn the trunk and destroy the roots, he ties a reed to the ploughshare and plows the entire field. Because of the great enmity that the reed has for the fern, and that the hart's tongue has for the reed, the field can be cleared and purged of that infestation, and peasants can then plant and harvest wheat.[xiii]

CORADELLA What an amazing thing! Let me tell you something: you know so many of these amazing things that you could work as a charlatan and make money at it. You'll see.

GUERINDO Ignoramus! This is the reward the virtuous get for talking with morons. Let's drop the subject, for we've come to the house of the ungrateful Florinda. Alas, every time I see it, these stones have an effect on me that is the opposite of Mercury's column, which, for the ancients, inspired the use of words; these stones instead leave me speechless.[xiv]

CORADELLA Master Guerindo, don't be afraid of anything: if your heart fails you, Coradella will inspire it for you. Hey, anybody home?

Scena Seconda
[Bernetta, Guerindo, Coradella]

BERNETTA O signor Guerindo mio, siete voi; poveruccio, quanto mi dispiace che quella crudelaccia della mia padrona vi sprezzi. Uh, vedete là che viso pizzuto, che occhi incassati, che boccuccia livida avete fatto! O Florinda ciorcinataccia, son pur tanto, tanto compassionevole alla carne umana io, uhimè.

CORADELLA Sorella, n'ho un pezzo che patisce, mi ti ricomando.

BERNETTA Se patisce puzza; se puzza è fracida, s'è fracida abbruciela.

CORADELLA Più tosto biscottianla, però prestami il tuo forno ch'è di bocca larga ed è sempre caldo.

BERNETTA Fratello, è un pezzo che non cuoce, e però è più tosto freddo e agghiacciato.

CORADELLA C'è remedio: impiccerò due fascine di spino, e ficcandole colà dentro si scalderà.

GUERINDO O cara Bernetta, tu se' tutta contenta, ma io misero?

BERNETTA Vedete signor Guerindo quanto Florinda è nemica dell'uomo e io amica; e quando vedo patire uno di questi poverucci amanti, ohimè, non mi fate dire, tutta mi rodo, tutta mi struggo come cera al foco, sì alla fé, sì certo; uh, non me lo fate più replicare! Si vede bene che le morose non vi stanno a torno; guardate qua questo collarino com'è storto, bisogna tirar questi pizzi.

CORADELLA Cara sorella, tira su un po' i miei pizzi ancora; ma ve', è collaro da uomo alla veneziana, c'ha un pizzo solo tondo per parte.

Scene Two
[Bernetta, Guerindo, Coradella]

BERNETTA So it's you, my good Master Guerindo; poor thing, how sorry I am that that wickedly cruel mistress of mine should hold you in disdain. Tsk, you see there what a drawn face, what sunken eyes, and what a wan little mouth you've got? Wretched Florinda! I'm instead so very, very compassionate for the flesh of others, oh dear.

CORADELLA Sister, I've got a piece of flesh that's suffering: I put myself in your hands.

BERNETTA If it suffers, it stinks; if it stinks, it's rotten; if it's rotten, burn it.

CORADELLA I'd rather bake it, so lend me your oven, which has a wide mouth and is always warm.

BERNETTA Brother, it hasn't cooked anything in a while, so it's rather cold and frozen over.

CORADELLA That can be fixed: first I'll light two bundles of thorns on fire, and then things will warm up if I shove them in there.

GUERINDO O my dear Bernetta, you're all happy, but what about poor me?

BERNETTA You see how Florinda is the enemy of men, while I'm instead their friend; and when I see one of these poor darling lovers suffering—oh dear, don't make me say it—I pine away, and I melt completely like wax near a flame, yes I swear it, I really do; now don't make me go saying it again! It's obvious that you two don't have girlfriends around: just look how crooked this little collar is; you need to pull on these tips.

CORADELLA Dear sister, do give mine another tug; but mind you, I've a man's collar in the Venetian style, and each part has only one round tip.[xv]

BERNETTA Ho inteso che tante volte gli hai bagnati nelle pignatte di salda cattiva, che sono ormai vicini all'andar in nulla al toccar loro. Oh furfantello, to', acconcio ancor il tuo, to' che ti fo bello.

CORADELLA Oh, così a maneggiarsi una volta per uno, e dove più all'uomo piace.

GUERINDO O cara Bernetta gentile.

BERNETTA Ora sto bene in questo mezo; vorrei esser tutta intorno intorno cinta dagli uomini.

CORADELLA Sì, ma che tu non tirassi coregge.

BERNETTA Oh nasa lì! Che parole! Oh, furfantello!

Scena Terza
[Florinda, Guerindo, Coradella, Bernetta]

FLORINDA In casa sfacciata, in casa temeraria.

BERNETTA Oh poverina me, conciava loro i collari.

FLORINDA Che collari; via furfantella sciagurata.

CORADELLA È vero signora, guardava se la salda era dura o tenera.

FLORINDA Che duro, che tenero ancor tu. Vedete, ancor è su la porta. Entra in casa dico, disonesta.

BERNETTA Voleva domandarle, se con la salta le piace il ravanello.

FLORINDA Sì, sì.

BERNETTA Così m'immaginava, perché noi altre donne siam tutte d'un appetito col ravanello. Me n'entro.

BERNETTA I take it you've soaked them so many times in pots of bad starch that now, at the least little touch, they risk falling apart altogether. Come here, you little rogue, I'll straighten yours out too and make you look nice.

CORADELLA Oh, to get handled just once like that, and where men like it the most.

GUERINDO O my dear sweet Bernetta!

BERNETTA Now I'm just fine here, in between the two of them; I'd like to be surrounded on all sides by men.

CORADELLA Sure, but only as long as you don't fart.

BERNETTA Get a whiff of that! How dare you use such words with me, you little rogue!

Scene Three
[Florinda, Guerindo, Coradella, Bernetta]

FLORINDA Get in the house, you reckless, shameless woman!

BERNETTA Poor little me, I was just straightening their collars.

FLORINDA What collars? Get going, you wicked wench!

CORADELLA It's true, my lady; she was just looking to see if the starch was stiff or limp.

FLORINDA Don't you go talking to me about "stiff or limp." Look, the door is still open. I'm telling you to get in the house, you indecent woman.

BERNETTA I just want to know if you like a radish with your salad.

FLORINDA Yes, yes.

BERNETTA Just as I thought: because we women all hunger after radishes. I'm going in now.

CORADELLA Credo pur che colei del ravanello faccia un sol boccone, tanto n'è golosa.

FLORINDA Signor Guerindo, abborrisco tanto questo sesso maledetto dell'uomo che per non vederlo, che per non udirlo, mi conterei d'esser nata e cieca e sorda; di grazia, non mi comparite giamai alla presenza.

CORADELLA Signor Guerindo arrivederci; che diavolo ha questa femmina arrabbiata? Pos' tu crepare.

GUERINDO Ah signora Florinda, dunque così fieramente come nemica degli uomini lacerate nel sesso virile il povero Guerindo? Or non sapete, adunque, che quelle cose ch'hanno bisogno d'aiuto presupongono debolezza; tale fu la donna, che per la nascita sua dell'uomo ebbe di necessità, adunque è più nobile, e però Guerindo merita d'esser amato.

FLORINDA V'ingannate signore; il mancamento fu nell'uomo, e però vi si aggiunse la donna per farlo più perfetto.

GUERINDO Signora Florinda, per vita sua dia bando allo sdegno.

FLORINDA Udite signore, poiché mal mio grado mi convien parlar con voi: chi tenete per materia più nobile, questo fango o questa carne?

GUERINDO Questa carne, senza alcun dubbio.

FLORINDA Cedete adunque, poiché la donna è fatta di carne e l'uomo di loto, e quanto voi fate più nobile la carne di questa terra, tanto anch'io fo più nobile la donna dell'uomo; sì che come men degno di me, e a me soggetto, v'impongo ch'andiate a far i fatti vostri.

GUERINDO Piano signora; questa sola ragione, e mi parto. Quelle cose che prima furono create, non son più nobili di quelle create doppo, onde si veggono le progeniture valer tanto?

FLORINDA Sì signore.

CORADELLA I bet she's so greedy that she eats a radish in just one gulp.

FLORINDA Guerindo, I so detest the accursed male sex that, in order not to see it and not to hear it, I'd be happy to have been born blind and deaf; so I'll thank you not to appear before me again.

CORADELLA Farewell Master Guerindo. What the devil has gotten into this furious female? The hell with her.

GUERINDO Florinda, do you thus—as the enemy of men—so fiercely wound your poor Guerindo in his very maleness? You don't know, then, that things in need of help presuppose weakness; such was woman, who was born from man and was necessarily helped by him. Thus man is more noble, and thus Guerindo deserves to be loved.

FLORINDA You deceive yourself, sir; the original lack was in man, and woman was added in order to make him more perfect.

GUERINDO Florinda, for pity's sake give up this disdain of yours.

FLORINDA Listen to me, my good sir, for I must speak with you in spite of myself: which do you consider a more noble material, mud or the flesh?

GUERINDO The flesh, without a doubt.

FLORINDA Yield then, for woman is made of flesh and man is made of lotus.[xvi] And as much as you may make the flesh more noble than the soil, I may make woman more noble than man. Thus, since you are less worthy than me and subject to me, I command you to go away and leave me alone.

GUERINDO Not so fast, my good lady. Let me say but this, and I will leave you. Are not those things that were created first more noble than those that were created afterward, for which reason the firstborn are valued so highly?

FLORINDA Yes indeed.

GUERINDO Oh, siete convinta! L'uomo non fu creato prima della donna?

FLORINDA Sì signore.

GUERINDO Dunque è più nobile; dunque mi siete soggetta, né voglio partire.

FLORINDA Oh, oh, c'è risposta, e bella, e la risposta vi sarà commiato. Non dite che le cose create prima sono più degne di quelle che sono create dopo?

GUERINDO Signora sì.

FLORINDA Gli animali non furono creati prima dell'uomo?

GUERINDO È vero.

FLORINDA Dunque l'asino è più nobile della signoria vostra. Uh, dalli dalli!

GUERINDO Addio signora, vo al molino.

[*Exeunt Guerindo & Coradella*]

FLORINDA Amor possente, che tu ignudo fra l'acque animoso nuotatore le tue faci accendendo, ardano del tuo fuoco inestinguibile i numi cerulei e gli squamosi pesci, non è maraviglia.

Amor, che tu, di faretra armato, le foreste scorrendo, ogni belva fugando, piagando risani e cacciando depredi, è poco al tuo valore.

Amor, che tu, su le bellissime ali leggerissimo alzandoti all'aria, al cielo innamori gli uccelli e gli dei, poco o nulla io lo stimo.

Ma che tutto raccolto in te stesso, in maestà sovrana sedendo, abbi eletto per tuo seggio, per tua reggia, questo picciolo specchio, io mi confondo.

E pur è vero; né già traveggio appassionata, ma saggia discorrendo dico che mi fai credere, in questo vetro mirando, che quant'hai di buono, Amore, tutto qui dentro in bel compendio s'accolga.

GUERINDO Ah, then you are convinced! Was not man created before woman?

FLORINDA Yes indeed.

GUERINDO Therefore he's more noble: therefore you're subject to me, and I've no desire to leave.

FLORINDA Oh, there's an answer for that, and a good one too, which will serve to give you your leave. Did you not say that things created first are more worthy than those created afterward?

GUERINDO Yes indeed.

FLORINDA Were not animals created before men?

GUERINDO That is true.

FLORINDA Then a donkey is more noble than you are, sir. So take that!

GUERINDO Farewell, madam, I'm going to the mill.

[*Exit Guerindo & Coradella*]

FLORINDA O powerful Cupid, you who boldly swim naked through the waters while lighting your torches, no wonder the azure gods and the scaly fish both burn with your inextinguishable flame.[xvii]

O Cupid, you who race through the forests armed with your quiver, putting to flight the wild beasts, who heal by wounding and plunder by hunting, this is but little compared with your true worth.

O Cupid, you who rise lightly through the air on beautiful wings, and in the heavens make birds and gods fall in love, I esteem little or not at all these powers of yours.

But it bewilders me that, all intent upon yourself and enthroned in sovereign majesty, you have chosen this little mirror for your seat, indeed for your palace.

And yet it's true: though I don't yet dote with passion, speaking prudently I say you make me believe, by looking in this glass, that whatever good there is in you, god of Love, may be found wholly

O fanciullo amoroso, o ingegnero glorioso, a te già non mancavano i modi ne' quali essercitar si potesse la tua immensa gloria, s'oggi ancor di picciolo vetro fatto signore, maravigliose cose a trattar non prendevi. Che ami la terra il cielo, l'amante ami l'amata, e 'l tutto senta amore, io ben l'accerto; ma ch'io medesma, me medesma amando sospiri, desiando languisca, idolatrando adori, ben questi gli ultimi sforzi della tua forza sono.

> S'ama dunque Florinda, e sì di core
> ch'entro uno specchio inamorata more;
> ch'entro bel vetro ha tutto posto il core.

Ben assai più di te gloriosa è la mia sorte, o innamorato Narciso, poiché s'alla limpida fonte specchiandoti t'invaghisti, onde te stesso amasti, t'amasti perché bello, t'insuperbisti perché vago in te stesso credevi d'essere face di mille cuori, strale di mille petti; ma io sola di me medesma vaga, per apprezzar me stessa, ciascuno disprezzo.

Però se stelle lucidissime quest'occhi io chiamo, stelle son di Diana, e non di Venere; onde ben si vede che per mantener loro sempre luminose e vaghe, drudo carnal non cerco, che 'n pianto trasformandole, piovose Pleiadi nomar le faccia; che saggia ben m'avvidi, che sì come la stella di Venere in un momento duo nomi acquista, così ancor in un medesmo istante queste gioie d'Amore nell'acquistar son alba, nel tramontar son sera. Se d'oro il crine già non cur'io, che disanellato e vagabondo ad arte, quanto più disciolto tanto maggiormente allacci, e ventilante abbagli, ma che raccolto umile ad altrui si celi, a me sola si scopra, a me sola diletti.

O vetro non vetro, ma sfera dove si raggira Amore.

O vetro non vetro, ma gemma più viva del sole.

O vetro non vetro, ma strale che dolcemente per gli occhi m'impiaghi.

O vetro non vetro, ma fiamma dov'ardendo fenice, e nasco, e moro.

O vetro non vetro, ma cielo dove quest'occhi sono le stelle, anzi la luna, e 'l sole.

Partiti Florinda, e degli amanti a scorno così parla:

> Non perch'io viva amante
> entr'un lucido vetro
> e di vetro il mio bene,
> ch'il vetro Amor fa divenir diamante;
> però dolci le pene
> narrando i' vo festante;

gathered herein.

O amorous youth, o glorious wit, surely you weren't lacking in ways to exercise your immense glory, even if today, though lord of this little glass, you hadn't chosen to deal in marvelous things. I well ascertain that heaven loves earth, the lover his beloved; and that everything feels love. But that I myself should sigh with love for myself; that I should languish in desire; that I should adore in idolatry: these are indeed your supreme show of strength.

> So much herself Florinda thus does love,
> That, dying in the mirror for desire thereof,
> Her heart's all in this glass, like hand in glove.[xviii]

My fate is much more glorious than yours, o enamored Narcissus, for if at the clear spring you were attracted to yourself, gazing at your own reflection, and thus you came to love yourself, you loved yourself because of your beauty, and you grew proud because, desiring yourself, you thought that you were the light of a thousand hearts and the arrow in a thousand breasts. I instead desire only myself and, to esteem myself, I despise all others.[xix]

But if I call these eyes shining stars, they are Diana's stars and not Venus's.[xx] Thus, in order to keep them always bright and desiring, I don't seek a carnal lover, who would, transforming them through tears, rename them rainy Pleiades.[xxi] Wisely I realize that, as Venus's star acquires two names at the same time, thus in one single instant these jewels of Cupid's are dawn in their coming and evening in their waning. I'm heedless of my golden locks, artfully unadorned and vagabond, which, the looser they are, the more they ensnare me. If winnowing them in the wind dazzles the eye, that humble harvest should hide itself from others, revealing itself only to me, and to me alone give pleasure.

O glass that is not glass, but a sphere wherein Cupid revolves.

O glass that is not glass, but a gem more vivid than the sun.

O glass that is not glass, but an arrow that sweetly wounds me in the eyes.

O glass that is not glass, but a flame in which I, burning like a phoenix, am born and die.

O glass that is not glass, but a heaven in which these eyes are stars, or rather moon and sun.

Go, Florinda, and mock your lovers thus:

> Not though as lover I live
> In a brightly shining glass,

e grido ognor felice
arde in un vetro chi è d'Amor fenice.

Scena Quarta
[Sufronio, Testuggine]

SUFRONIO E la signora Lidia m'invia questa lettera? Quant'è? Che vuole? Dillo tosto.

TESTUGGINE È poco, non lo so, ho finito.

SUFRONIO Da Roma in fino al cul, buon di buon anno. Quest'è un modo di parlare.

TESTUGGINE E quest'è un modo di rispondere. Vorrà forse dir che Vostra Signoria è 'l suo cuore e 'l suo amore, e vorrà far l'amor con voi.

SUFRONIO Eh, fratello! Amor si dipinge così giovine seguitato da pargoletti, per insegnar che non vuol compagnia di vecchi.

TESTUGGINE Veramente i vecchi stanno mal principi assoluti, perché non mai tengono diritto lo scettro della giustizia.

SUFRONIO Testuggine mio, noi altri vecchi siamo come il pappagallo, non possiamo parlare né far carezze senza il becco torto.

TESTUGGINE Certo che i vecchi sono come gli oriuoli di villa, discordati; poiché non mai il raggio tocca il segno, non mai l'ore battono a tempo, e non mai i contrapesi sono giusti, poiché uno va in su e l'altro in giù.

SUFRONIO Orsù, leggiam questa lettera.

And of glass my love is made,
Does Cupid diamonds for glass give;
　　　But this pain's such a sweet trade
With joy I tell him I'll forgive,
And cry aloud, in bliss at last:
I am Love's phoenix, who burns in a glass.[xxii]

Scene Four
[Sufronio, Testuggine]

SUFRONIO Lidia sends me this letter? How much is [in] it? What does she want? Tell me quickly.

TESTUGGINE I don't know… not much. I've finished now.

SUFRONIO All the way from Rome right up the ass: have a nice day, have a great year. That's one way to talk.

TESTUGGINE And this is one way to answer. Perhaps she means to say that Your Excellency is her heart and her love, and that she wants to make love with you.

SUFRONIO My good fellow! Cupid paints himself as a youngster followed around by cherubs in order to teach us that he doesn't want the company of old men.

TESTUGGINE In truth old men are poor absolute princes, because they can't hold upright the scepter of justice.

SUFRONIO My dear Testuggine, we old men are like parrots: we can't speak or caress without a bent beak.

TESTUGGINE Old men are indeed like the clocks on country estates, which don't keep time: they never strike the hours on time, because the hands can't get up to the top of the dial, and the counterweights are always off, since as one goes up the other goes down.

SUFRONIO Very well, let's read this letter.

TESTUGGINE Sì, sì; che questo ragionamento non fa per voi, perché non si può star troppo sul duro con la persona vostra.

SUFRONIO D'ogni travaglio è la vecchiezza piena. Ecco 'n verso, ed ecco aperto questo foglio. Leggiamo: "Molto Magnifico Signor mio Osservandissimo, scrivo col sangue."

TESTUGGINE Lasciate un poco vedere. Oh, che sangue nero com'inchiostro!

SUFRONIO È un modo di scriver figurato questo, non è che scriva col sangue.

TESTUGGINE È perché ogni fin di mese le donne così scrivono.

SUFRONIO "Scrivo col sangue, e come questo è sparso per questo foglio, e 'l vostro si spargerà per lo terreno."

TESTUGGINE Signor Sufronio, v'ha ella tolto per un porco da scannarvi per le strade.

SUFRONIO Io non l'intendo. "Chè ben dovere che chi dà morte altrui debb'esser morto."

TESTUGGINE Avete ammazzato alcuno voi?

SUFRONIO Ho paura che tu burli, a dirtela. "Il sangue di Sufronio pagherà il debito."

TESTUGGINE Udite, se siete voi.

SUFRONIO "Ammazzar chi vuol bene sta molto male, e 'l carnefice ne darà la riccompensa. Troppo amor, troppo odio, condurrà la casa Zizolieri in dispersione."

TESTUGGINE Come le vostre zizole vanno in bordello state fresco.

TESTUGGINE Yes, yes, this line of argument doesn't suit you, because no one can be too hard with you.

SUFRONIO Old age is full of travails of every kind. Here's the back of it, and now let's unfold this sheet of paper. Let's read: "My most magnificent and excellent lord, I am writing to you with my blood."

TESTUGGINE Let me have a look at that. Oh heavens, blood as black as ink!

SUFRONIO She employs figures of speech; she's not writing with her own blood.

TESTUGGINE It's because at the end of every month women write that way.

SUFRONIO "I am writing to you with my blood, and just as it is spilt across this sheet of paper, your own blood will be spilt on the ground."

TESTUGGINE Master Sufronio, she has taken you for a pig to be slaughtered in the streets.

SUFRONIO I don't understand. "It is right that anyone who deals death to another should die himself."

TESTUGGINE Have you killed someone?

SUFRONIO I'm afraid you must be joking, if I may say so. "Sufronio's blood will pay the debt."

TESTUGGINE I'd read on, if I were you.

SUFRONIO "It is a great wrong to kill someone who loves, and the executioner will exact the price for it. Too much love and too much hate will lead the house of Zizolieri to its downfall."

TESTUGGINE Since you always take your two little Zizolieri berries with you to the whorehouse, you're going to be in trouble.[xxiii]

SUFRONIO Oh, che intrico è questo! "Già si piantano i palchi e si suspendono le manarre, per troncar il collo a chi tronca lo stame di mia vita."

TESTUGGINE Signor Sufronio gambe in ispalla. Addio.

SUFRONIO Testuggine vien qua, dove corri?

TESTUGGINE Sento un imbroglio di ceppi, di manarre e di forche che v'impicchino, che non mi piace punto, punto.

SUFRONIO Batti a quella casa, mi voglio ben chiarire.

TESTUGGINE O di casa! Largo alla strada, che se i marangoni dalle fabriche del sabato fossero in casa, possa fuggire. O dalla casa, olà olà!

Scena Quinta
[Lidia, Sufronio, Testuggine, Orimberto]

LIDIA Oh, com'a tempo signor Sufronio veniste!

TESTUGGINE Debbe il tutt'esser all'ordine per appiccarvi, arrivederci.

SUFRONIO Eh, passa qua se tu vuoi! Signora Lidia, che modo di scrivere confuso e fastidioso è questo di Vostra Signoria? M'avete tutto posto in confusione.

LIDIA Signor Sufronio io sono stata la Sfinge agli enigmi, sarò ancora Edippo alle soluzioni; non siete voi ch'io danno, ma il sangue vostro.

TESTUGGINE Oh, l'ho intesa! Doveva questa signora aver alcun diamante di valuta, e Vostra Signoria, per farle dispetto, col sangue vostro gliel'averete spezzato; bella cosa.

SUFRONIO Doh furfante, e che il sangue mio è sangue di becco? Signora è così ridicoloso.

LIDIA Parlo del figlio di Vostra Signoria.

SUFRONIO What a tangled knot is this! "The platform is already being built, and the executioner's blade is already hanging in the air, to chop off the neck of him who cuts the thread of my life."

TESTUGGINE Master Sufronio, I'm out of here. Farewell.

SUFRONIO Come here, Testuggine, where are you running to?

TESTUGGINE I sense a trick, one involving leg irons, an executioner's axe and gallows to hang you, and I don't like it at all, not at all.

SUFRONIO Knock on the door of that house: I want to get to the bottom of this.

TESTUGGINE Is anyone at home? Leave room in the street, so that even if all the carpenters have stayed home from their workshops on Saturday, I can escape. Hello there, is anyone at home? Yoo-hoo! Yoo-hoo!

Scene Five
[Lidia, Sufronio, Testuggine, Orimberto]

LIDIA O Sufronio, you came here right on time!

TESTUGGINE Everything must be ready for your hanging: farewell.

SUFRONIO Hey, you can go this way if you want. Lidia, what is this confused and troubling style of writing of yours? You've left me quite bewildered.

LIDIA Sufronio, in my letter I was a Sphinx who posed riddles, and I will be Oedipus when it comes to answers: I damn not you but your blood.[xxiv]

TESTUGGINE Oh, now I get it! This lady must have had a valuable diamond, and Your Excellency, to spite her, must have broken it with your blood: nice job.

SUFRONIO You rascal, do you really think that my blood is as sharp as a beak? My lady, this is really ridiculous.

SUFRONIO E che le ha fatto questo figliuolo discolo? Oh traditore, indegno d'essermi figlio!

LIDIA Professa alla scoperta di volermi dar la morte, e questo perché l'amo, reputando importunità l'amore.

ORIMBERTO Oh, questa fa per me!

TESTUGGINE Non fa già per noi, se la fa per te.

SUFRONIO Sta' un poco tacito in cose di tanta importanza.

TESTUGGINE Signor io parlava con una voce, poiché non ho visto persona.

SUFRONIO Signora stupisco.

ORIMBERTO Fortuna e dormi.

TESTUGGINE Oh, se mi trovi a dormire, appiccami!

SUFRONIO Signora se n'entri, perché è tanta l'insolenza di costui ch'io mi vergogno.

LIDIA Dovrei star qui molto, e dir molto, per detestar la barbarie di questo figliuolo di Vostra Signoria indegno; non però son qui per ubbidirla, ma faccia sua cura il trovarlo e 'l riprenderlo, in modo che mi venga a chieder perdono.

SUFRONIO Or, ora io parto per una via. Testuggine, benché la testuggine sia animal pigro, vola ancor tu per un'altra via, e trovatolo a me conducilo. Non son Sufronio Giuggiolieri, s'io non vendico Vostra Signoria, non con la lingua piena d'ingiurie, ma con la mano armata di bastone.

LIDIA Vada, e vendichi una innocente; ma per ora con la riprensione sola, sola.

TESTUGGINE Il torrò ben io a cavallo, e a cul nudo gliele farem contare. Addio.

LIDIA I speak of Your Excellency's son.

SUFRONIO And what has that naughty boy done to you? O traitor, unworthy of being my son!

LIDIA He openly proclaims that he wants to kill me, and this because I love him: for he considers love a nuisance.

ORIMBERTO Oh, this one's for me!

TESTUGGINE If she's for you, then she's no longer for us.

SUFRONIO Keep quiet in matters of such importance.

TESTUGGINE Master, I was talking with a voice, since I haven't seen a soul.

SUFRONIO My lady, I'm astonished.

ORIMBERTO Good luck and good night.

TESTUGGINE Oh, if you catch me sleeping, you can hang me!

SUFRONIO My good lady, please go inside, for I'm ashamed of this fellow's insolence.

LIDIA I'd have to stay here a long while, and say a great deal, to express what I really think of the barbarity of Your Excellency's unworthy son. I'm not here to obey you, however; make it your business to find him and bring him back here so that he may ask for my forgiveness.

SUFRONIO I'm off now, by this road. Testuggine, although your namesake the tortoise is a lazy animal, you fly off by another road, and when you find him, bring him to me. If I don't revenge your ladyship with a stick in my hand rather than with a heap of insults on my tongue, then my name isn't Sufronio and I'm not the owner of those two little Zizolieri berries.[xxv]

LIDIA Go, and revenge an innocent woman; but for now, do it only by reprehending him, and no more.

LIDIA   Amor, tu vedi fra quanti strani ravvolgimenti mi ritrovo; perché Silvio mi disprezza, né più vuol passar per queste contrade, l'amore è passato al furore, e col perder l'intelletto, ma ancor da far perder la fama, col trovar questa invenzione che mi vuol dar la morte. Ma questo a due fogge s'intende: altri l'intende assolutamente che mi voglia ammazzare, e così ho caro che s'intenda; ma io sola intendo che dar mi vuol la morte con la sua crudeltà; se verrà a me tanto ch'io 'l vegga ancor, che irato mitigherò lo sdegno mio, caso che no: "Mora Sanson con tutti i filistei," donna disperata anch'io, voglio nelle mie ruine sommerger questo crudele, e con questa ferma intenzione me n'entro. Ch'a disperato cor, furore è scorta.

Scena Sesta
[Lelio, Granello]

LELIO   Amor, Granello mio, è nume troppo valoroso e possente, tutti abbatte, e però gli antichi il dipingevano col dio Pan a' suoi piedi; e perché Pan vuol dire il tutto, però in quell'atto mostravano che 'l tutto soggiogava.

GRANELLO   Certo sì che 'l pane dinota il tutto, poiché senza pane, e senza vino, non si può far zuppa; chi non fa zuppa dorme male, chi dorme male fa cattivo sangue, il cattivo sangue fa della rogna, la rogna si gratta; col grattarla cresce, crescendo si fa tutto una piaga, come sei tutto una piaga vai all'ospitale; tanto che questo vostro Amore è cagion d'una bella cosa.

LELIO   Insomma, da questo fanciulletto schermirsi non possiamo. Amore è come la tignuola.

GRANELLO   Medica, medica, non mai ti guarisce, e quel ch'è peggio ti pela tutto.

LELIO   Di che parli goffo?

GRANELLO   D'una buona tigna, e non d'una tignuola come dite voi.

LELIO   Oh semplice!

GRANELLO   E voi sarete tosto doppio, poiché amore vi farà cascar

TESTUGGINE I'll straddle his back and we'll make him count the blows on his bare bottom. Farewell.

LIDIA Cupid, you see how I find myself caught up in so many strange and torturous twists of fate. Silvio scorns me, and no longer wants to pass through this neighborhood; love has changed to fury, and although I've lost my mind, he hasn't yet lost his reputation; but I'll bring that about by claiming that he wants to kill me. This, however, can be understood in two ways: others will think that he literally wants to kill me, and it's important to me that they should think so; but I alone understand that he only wants to kill me with his cruelty. If he should come to me and I should see him again, that would appease my angry disdain for him. Otherwise, as they say, "let Samson die with all the Philistines": for I too am a desperate woman, and I want to bury this cruel man beneath my ruins.[xxvi] With this firm intention, I'll now go back inside, for rage is the escort of a desperate heart.

Scene Six
[Lelio, Granello]

LELIO My good Granello, Cupid is a god too brave, powerful, and all-conquering. The ancients painted him with the god Pan at his feet; and because in Greek "pan" means "everything," by that they showed that all are subject to Love.[xxvii]

GRANELLO Sure, in our own tongue "pane" means bread, and bread is everything, for without bread and without wine you can't make soup; without soup you sleep badly, and whoever sleeps badly has bad blood; bad blood causes scabies, and scabies gets scratched; the more you scratch, the worse it gets, and, worsening, turns into one big sore; and when you're covered with sores, you go to the hospital; so a really great thing happens, thanks to this Cupid of yours.

LELIO We can't hide from this little boy, in short: Cupid is like a woodworm who disappears for a time, only to reappear later.

GRANELLO You can treat it and treat it, but it'll never heal and, what's worse, it'll completely peel your skin off.

LELIO What are you talking about, you clown?

parte de' capelli, delle ciglia e la punta del naso, e così bisognerà rifar quegli, quelle e quell'altro, con una capigliara, con il carbone e con un pezzo di carton dipinto.

LELIO La tignuola è...

GRANELLO La tigna.

LELIO No.

GRANELLO Signor sì, mo' il latino la declina pure, nominativo hec tignola la tigna, genitivo huius tignole della tigna.

LELIO Tu mi fai ridere.

GRANELLO Et un dì la tigna vi farà piangere, state pur a vedere.

LELIO Oh che pena, tignuola tignato!

GRANELLO Vedete, et pluraliter nominativo tignatarum i tignati, et il tignato, cioè colui ch'è tutto tignoso.

LELIO E pur su questo tuo latino cavato dal vino! Io non parlo di quel male ulcerato che vien nella cotenna del capo, dal latino detta *achores*, ma della tignuola vermicciolo picciolo e rodente.

GRANELLO Ah, ah, voi parlate d'un verme et io di tigna! Oh guardate che cos'ha da far la luna con i granchi. E bene, che fa questa tignuola?

LELIO Dicesi adunque, che questo Amore è come la tignuola, la quale fa più crudel danno ne' panni fini che ne' vili; però com'egli entra in un cuor nobile, oh, che squarci!

GRANELLO Come va per isquarci, la vostra signora è innamoratissima, poiché la voce corre che Amore le abbia fatto più d'un palmo di squarcio. Amore alfin se' come la vaiuola, chi non l'ha in gioventù l'ha in vecchiaia.

LELIO È vero, è vero. E sì come la vaiuola è quella che ci cava gli

GRANELLO About ringworm, and not that worm you were going on about.

LELIO O you simpleton!

GRANELLO And you'd have to be twice as simple as I am, since Love will make some of your hair, your eyelashes, and the tip of your nose fall off; so you'll have to redo them all, using a wig, coal, and a piece of painted cardboard.

LELIO The woodworm is…

GRANELLO You mean ringworm.

LELIO No.

GRANELLO Yes sir, and you can even decline that in Latin, whether in the nominative or the *genitive*.[xxviii]

LELIO You make me laugh.

GRANELLO And one day ringworm will make you cry. Just wait and see.

LELIO Oh what a sorry sight: a woodworm with ringworm!

GRANELLO You see, sir, in the Latin plural the name for those with ringworm is "the ringwormèd" (I'm translating), and in the singular it's the same for any poor devil who's all ringwormy.

LELIO The only Latin you know is whatever you picked up in some tavern! I'm not talking about the ulcerous disease that you get on your scalp, which in Latin is called *achores*,[xxix] but about a little worm that gnaws on wood: the woodworm.

GRANELLO Ah-ha, I get it! You're talking about a *worm* and I'm talking about *ring*worm! So you want me to believe that somehow they're not related. Very well, what does this worm do?

LELIO It's said that Cupid is like a worm, for he does far worse dam-

occhi, ci deforma, ci storpia, e ci dà morte, così n'accieca dagli occhi dell'intelletto, ci deforma ne' costumi, ci storpia sovente con le malattie, e ci dà morte, poiché Amore come non consegue il suo fine divien furore; e qui i miseri o prendono esilio dalle patrie, o s'avvelenano, o col ferro o con la fame terminano i tormenti amorosi.

GRANELLO Oh bene, anzi che vi appicchiate, datemi un poco il salario di sei mesi.

LELIO Non aver paura di questo.

GRANELLO Anzi n'ho tanta che m'inspirito. Orsù ch'abbiam da fare? Volete pur tornar a pregar un sasso, non è vero? Non siete ancor chiarito, non vedete che odia tutti gli uomini?

LELIO Timone.

GRANELLO Ci vuol il timone; e non è balorda, sa ch'ogni timone non è per la sua barca, però vorrà prima vederlo, e come lo vede siete chiarito. Non vedete ch'ha della marciliana vassello da mare, così ancora com'è gran barcaccia vorrà gran timonaccio.

LELIO Siasi quello che si vuole; ho detto, quando tu dicesti ch'odia tutti gli uomini, Timone, poiché uno che odiava tutti gli uomini fu detto anticamente Timone.

GRANELLO Senz'altro costui sarebbe stato dalla vostra amata amato, poiché per questo fatto doveva esser detto quel Timon grande e crudele; però come di fama smisurato sarebbe stato a suo gusto. Io batto vedete, ma arricordatevi che non vuol non solo sentire, ma veder uomini.

age to finely woven than to rough cloth. When he enters a noble heart, how he cracks it asunder!

GRANELLO Speaking of cracks, your lady must be deeply in love, for word is going around that Cupid gave her quite a good-sized one of those. In the end love is like the pox, because if you don't get it when you're young, you'll get it when you're old.

LELIO Very true, very true. And just as the pox destroys our eyes, deforms, cripples, and kills us, so does love blind the eyes of our intellect, deform our behavior, often cripple us with illnesses and kill us; for Cupid, if he doesn't get what he wants, goes mad with fury. His poor victims must—in order to put an end to their sufferings in love—choose either exile from their homeland or death by poison, blade, or hunger.

GRANELLO Fine, but before you hang yourself, pay me some of the six months' back wages you still owe me.

LELIO Don't worry about that.

GRANELLO On the contrary, that's precisely what I'm worried about. So what're we to do? You want to go back to her and try to squeeze water from a stone, don't you? Haven't you got the picture by now? Can't you see she hates all men?

LELIO Like Timon.[xxx]

GRANELLO Did you say "tillerman?" You won't be able to sail in those waters without a good stiff tiller. And she's no fool, for she knows that not every sort of tiller will suit her vessel; she'll want to see it first, and when she gets a look at yours, she'll cry out: "abandon ship!" Don't you understand that she's like one of those broad Venetian galleys that needs a really big and really long tiller to steer her?[xxxi]

LELIO Be that as it may. When you said she hates all men, I said "Timon" because in ancient Greece there was a fellow named Timon who hated all men.

GRANELLO No doubt about it: your beloved would have loved that guy. Timon must have been known as "the great" and "the cruel" for

LELIO Molto bene il so.

GRANELLO Conciatevi in un bel gesto pietoso, così col collo torto, col viso aguzzo, col tabarro che vi caschi e con la spada che guardi col puntale alle ventiquattro ore. Oh, poverino, io batto.

LELIO Picchia una volta.

GRANELLO Voi farete che una volta v'appiccherete.

LELIO Sì, a quel bel seno di neve.

GRANELLO No, no, dico a tre bei travi di forca io; batto. O di casa, o di casa?

Scena Settima
[Florinda, Lelio, Granello, Bernetta]

FLORINDA Chi è là, chi è là, chi è là? Uh, uh!

GRANELLO È questo galantuomo signora, e non io.

FLORINDA O signor Lelio, siete sordo; che importunità insolente è questa? Andate a far i fatti vostri.

GRANELLO Buon pro vi faccia. Vedete, con queste vivande la signora vostra cuoca d'Amore v'apparecchia la tavola. Or non avete ben desinato? Lasciate far a me, che voglio un poco sbizarrirmi con dirle due parolette, che m'intenda. Corpo del mondo, duro con duro fa buon muro. O di casa.

BERNETTA Via, via, via, uomini eh, guarda la gamba!

the reason you've described, but in her eyes his fame would have been boundless. I'll knock—see?—but remember that she doesn't care for the sight or sound of men.

LELIO I know it only too well.

GRANELLO Then assume a prayerful position, with your neck twisted like this, and your face pointed like that; your cape should be falling off you, and you should be holding your sword with the tip pointing to the twelve o'clock position. All right, poor fellow, I'll start knocking.

LELIO Knock once.

GRANELLO If you keep this up, you're going to hang yourself sooner or later.

LELIO Yes, upon that snow-white bosom.

GRANELLO No, no, I'm talking about some gallows-beams. Well, here I go. Is anyone home, is anyone home?

Scene Seven
[Florinda, Lelio, Granello, Bernetta]

FLORINDA Who's there, who's there, who's there? Uh oh!

GRANELLO It's this gentleman, my lady, and not me.

FLORINDA Lelio, you're deaf: what insolent importunity is this? Go away and mind your own business.

GRANELLO A lot of good may it do you. You see with what delicacies your lady, Cupid's cook, sets the table for you. Have you not dined well? Leave it to me: I feel like having a little chat with her, so that we may come to understand one another. Put the hard with the hard to make a good wall, got it? Hello, anyone home?

BERNETTA Go away, go away, go away! Men, eh? Just watch my leg!

GRANELLO Oh, adesso vi potete andar a far appiccare, poiché in fin la serva v'ha data la stremità, e poich'ha detto tre volte: "Via, via, via," io che l'ho intesa alla prima, fo così.

LELIO Io, che farò misero? Seguirò l'orme del mio servo, per non rivolger il piede alla via della disperazione.

Scena Ottava
[Giudice, quattro labardieri, Notaio, Orimberto]

GIUDICE Iustitia est dare unicuique quod suum est. La Giustitia mi sovvien d'averla veduta dipinta col piede in terra e 'l capo in cielo, per dinotare che la giustizia è celeste, e che il ministrator di lei debbe sentenziando aver il capo nel cielo, per non esser corrotto da cose terrene, onde si dica che sia più reo di forca il condannante che 'l condannato.

ORIMBERTO E per tutte queste così fatte cose ricorsi alla giustizia di Vostra Signoria illustrissima, ch'è avvezzo a non bilanciar le sentenze con l'oro, acciochè punisca il nocente e l'innocente mandi assoluto. Sa già Vostra Signoria Illustrissima che l'ho (retiratevi un poco) avvisata di quel giovine non solo tanto inquieto con suo padre, quanto fastidioso a tutta questa città per le sue infinite insolenze; e sa che le ho detto che presume d'ammazzar una gentildonna gentilissima; sa ora quello ch'ha da fare, e a me può credere, poiché sa che amando la quiete della mia patria, d'ogni piccola cosa che si fa in quella io di segreto l'avviso.

GIUDICE Se voi non m'incontravi in questo punto, portava il caso che per questa sera non mi vedeste, poich'io vo or ora (e poco lontane son le carrozze) fuor delle porte un miglio, per un certo svaligio che s'è fatto a un gentiluomo armata mano. Notaio.

NOTAIO Signore.

GIUDICE Avete notato chi sia il giovine, di chi è figlio, la casa, i segnali d'essa e la contrada?

GRANELLO Now you can go hang yourself, sir, for this maidservant has given you the end,[xxxii] and because she said three times, "go away, go away, go away!," I'm going to do just that, since I understood her the first time.

LELIO Woe is me, what shall I do? I'll follow in the tracks of my servant, to keep my feet from taking the path of desperation.

Scene Eight
[Judge, four halberdiers, Notary, Orimberto]

JUDGE *Iustitia est dare unicuique quod suum est* [justice is giving to each that which is his]. I recall having seen Justice painted with her feet on the ground and her head in the sky, in order to indicate that justice is heavenly. Her administrator must, in passing judgment, keep his own head in the heavens in order not to be corrupted by earthly things, so that it may not be said that the judge is more worthy of the scaffold than the condemned man.

ORIMBERTO And precisely for all of these reasons I've appealed to the justice of Your Most Illustrious Lordship, who is accustomed to not balancing sentences with gold, so that the guilty are punished and the innocent absolved. Your Most Illustrious Lordship already knows I've informed him (please stand back a bit) about that young man who's not only such a rebel against his father, but vexes this entire city with his infinite insolence. And you know I've told you that this same youth presumes to kill the sweetest gentlewoman; you know now what you need to do, and you can believe me, for you know that I, who love peace in my own homeland, secretly inform you of every little thing that happens in it.

JUDGE If I hadn't encountered you here just now, the case would have been deferred, for you wouldn't have been able to see me here later on. I must travel immediately—and my carriages are waiting for me nearby—a mile outside the city walls, to deal with a certain armed robbery of a gentleman. Notary.

NOTARY Sir.

NOTAIO Signor sì, diligentissimamente ho fatto il tutto.

GIUDICE Silenzio, poi sapete, né per quanto v'è cara la libertà, che perdereste in un fondo di torre, non si nomini l'accusatore.

ORIMBERTO No vedete, che mi direbbeno lo spione; e 'l cielo sa s'è tutto per giovar alla mia cara patria, il cui amor è così dolce. Ma retiriamci, retiriamci tutti tutti fuor di strada. Signori, ecco il padre e 'l giovine tanto infame.

GIUDICE È quello che si vede colà?

ORIMBERTO Sì signore.

GIUDICE Poveri padri, affaticatevi in educar i figliuoli, fate loro delle facoltà, che quant'essi acumularono con pianto, gettano questi via con riso. Vedete come altiero parlando, ha sempre le mani con gesti irati sul viso al povero padre. Giuro al cielo che ancor non l'ho veduto, e non come giudice, ma come Latanzio io l'aborrisco.

ORIMBERTO È cattivissimo signore. Ma eccolo che ormai ragionando è qui pervenuto.

GIUDICE Retiriamoci tutti, tutti, in modo che non siam veduti.

Scena Nona
[Sufronio, Silvio, Lidia, Giudice, Notaio, Orimberto, quattro labardieri]

SUFRONIO Figlio, figlio.

SILVIO Padre, padre.

SUFRONIO Silvio, Silvio.

SILVIO Sufronio, Sufronio.

JUDGE Did you remark who this young man is, whose son he is, the house, its features, and the neighborhood?

NOTARY Yes sir, I've done everything with the greatest of care.

JUDGE Keep silent, then: know that the accuser's name mustn't be mentioned, or, no matter how dear your liberty is to you, you'd end up in a dungeon.

ORIMBERTO No, you see, because they'd call me a spy; and heaven alone knows that it's all for the benefit of my adored homeland, whose love is so sweet. But let us away; everyone out of the streets. Sirs, here are the father and his infamous son.

JUDGE Is that the man, over there?

ORIMBERTO Yes sir.

JUDGE Poor fathers, you toil to bring up your sons, and you give them all you can; yet they throw away with a laugh what you've accumulated with your tears. See how haughtily he speaks, with his hands always making angry gestures right in his poor father's face. I swear to heaven that, although I haven't yet had a close look at him, I abhor him, not as a judge, but as if I were the Governor himself of this city.[xxxiii]

ORIMBERTO He's as bad as they come, sir. But now, while conversing with his father, he's coming over here to us.

JUDGE Away, away one and all, so that they will not see us.

Scene Nine
[Sufronio, Silvio, Lidia, Judge, Notary, Orimberto, four halberdiers]

SUFRONIO Son, son.

SILVIO Father, father.

SUFRONIO Silvio, Silvio.

SILVIO Sufronio, Sufronio.

SUFRONIO Bestia, bestia.

SILVIO Poco uomo, poco uomo.

SUFRONIO Mi se' figlio?

SILVIO Mi siete padre?

SUFRONIO No 'l so.

SILVIO Né io.

SUFRONIO Non mi se' figlio, perché un arbor buona non può far frutto cattivo; tu se' cattivo, adunque non se' frutto di questa pianta.

SILVIO Signor padre, sarei vostro figliuolo ogni volta che non porgesti volentieri l'orecchio alle mormorazioni che tornano in danno mio. Ma sapete quello ch'uno disse, interrogato chi più faceva errore, o colui che mormorava, o colui che volentieri udiva le mormorazioni?

SUFRONIO Io no, che disse messer filosofo sputa sentenze?

SILVIO Disse: "Certamente io non lo so dire; so bene ch'uno ha il diavolo nella lingua e l'altro nelle orecchie."

SUFRONIO Buono, mi piace, è vero. So anch'io che nuoce una cattiva lingua e ch'è al contrario della lingua dell'orsa, poiché quella con la lingua dà vita e 'l maldicente con la lingua dà morte. Ma le tue opere, sono quelle che sclamano e t'accusano. Dimmi un poco, conosci la signora Lidia?

SILVIO Non me ne parlate, non me ne parlate. Oh, questa sì ch'è la via di far ch'io m'adiri e vi perda la riverenza!

ORIMBERTO Sentite signor Giudice.

GIUDICE Sento, sento.

SUFRONIO You animal, you animal.

SILVIO You loser, you loser.

SUFRONIO Are you my son?

SILVIO Are you my father?

SUFRONIO I don't know.

SILVIO Neither do I.

SUFRONIO You're not my son, because a good tree can't make bad fruit; you're bad, and hence you're not the fruit of *this* tree.

SILVIO My father, I would be your son—that is, whenever you didn't willingly listen to the harmful rumors circulating about me. Do you know what someone once said, when asked who made a worse mistake, the rumormonger or those who listened willingly to rumors?

SUFRONIO I don't know: what did that know-it-all philosopher reply?

SILVIO He said: "I certainly don't know what to say, for I know that one has the devil in his tongue and the other has the devil in his ear."

SUFRONIO Very good, I like that, it's true: I too know that a malicious tongue can do harm. It is quite the opposite of the she-bear's tongue, for the she-bear gives life with her tongue and the slanderer gives death with his.[xxxiv] But your own actions shout out the accusations against you. Tell me, do you know Mistress Lidia?

SILVIO Don't talk to me about her, don't talk to me about her. That's the one sure way to make me lose my temper and lose my respect for you!

ORIMBERTO Do you hear that, Judge?

JUDGE I hear it, I hear it.

SUFRONIO E perché questo? Perché ti vuol bene?

SILVIO Non voglio che lo sappiate.

SUFRONIO L'ammazzeresti?

SILVIO Io sì, perché? Sarebbe tanta cosa ammazzar una femina insolente?

LIDIA Te ne menti villan rivestito.

SILVIO Io "villano?" "Mentite" a me?

GIUDICE Ferma là, ferma là; piglia, piglia!

SUFRONIO O poveretto me, oh figlio traditore!

LIDIA Sì signore, che non solo più volte ha cercato di levarmi la vita, ma ora cacciando mano a quel pugnale m'uccideva, se 'l cielo e Vostra Signoria Illustrissima non soccorrevano questa innocente.

SILVIO Si parte dal vero, signor Giudice, questa accusatrice bugiarda.

GIUDICE E come si parte dal vero, se l'effetto v'accusa? Conducetelo [alla] prigione.

SILVIO Ah, Lidia ingannatrice!

LIDIA Ah, Silvio micidiale! Tu in prigione e io con sua licenza anderò in casa per rispondere ad ogni suo minimo avviso.

SILVIO Si saprà ben il vero.

GIUDICE Là, là; conducetelo alle prigioni. Signor Sufronio convien aver pacienza; il fuoco purga l'aria dalle infezzioni, e la prigione purga la città dall'infezzion de' cattivi.

SUFRONIO And why? Because she loves you?

SILVIO I don't want you to know why.

SUFRONIO Would you kill her?

SILVIO I surely would. But why do you ask? Would it be such a big deal to kill an insolent female?

LIDIA You lie, you peasant in disguise.

SILVIO Are you calling me a lout? Are you calling me a liar?

JUDGE Stop right there, stop right there: grab him, grab him!

SUFRONIO O woe is me, o what a deceitful son!

LIDIA Yes sir, not only has he tried a number of times to take my life, but just now he put his hand to his dagger in order to kill me, if heaven and Your Most Illustrious Lordship had not come to the aid of this innocent woman.

SILVIO Her lying accusations take leave of the truth, Judge.

JUDGE And how can they take leave of the truth, if the action accuses you? Take him to prison.

SILVIO O deceitful Lidia!

LIDIA O murderous Silvio! Go to prison, and I, with the Judge's permission, will go home, where I will comply with any and all inquiries that he might make.

SILVIO The truth will be known.

JUDGE Go on, go on, take him away to prison. Sufronio, you must be patient: as fire purges the air of contagion, prison purges the city of the infection caused by wrongdoers.

SUFRONIO Signore, s'è cattivo che si castighi, non è mio figlio. Oh, povero padre serbato in questa età grave a spettacoli così lagrimosi!

FINE DELL'ATTO PRIMO

SUFRONIO Sir, if he's bad he should be punished, for he's not my son. O wretched father that I am, who must in my old age witness such scenes that make me weep!

END OF ACT ONE

ATTO SECONDO

Scena Prima
[Lelio, Florinda]

LELIO E pur di nuovo farfalla alle fiamme, serpe all'incanto io ritorno. Parmi che 'l cuore, tacito oratore, mi persuada a parlarle, che otterrò mercede; e caso che diverso l'effetto sia dal mio desiderio, so poi quello che far mi debba, però voglio battere. O dalla casa? Amore aiutami.

FLORINDA E pur conviene che l'odiato aspetto di costui mi s'appresenti avanti gli occhi e interrompa le mie contentezze.

LELIO O Amore—o possente nume!—tu che alle cose oscure puoi dar la luce, alle fastidite grazia e alle dubbie fede; tu che gli elementi discordi insieme unisci; tu che puoi ciò che ti piace alfine, soccorso attendo. Ecco in questo amoroso steccato un tuo fedel campione, una tua mortal nemica; un amante, una ch'odia; uno che ti serve, una che ti sprezza; uno che ti segue qual Ippomene, una che ti fugge qual Atalanta; da te ardire, da te forza, da te vittoria aspetto. Vi renda il cielo felice e Amor pietosa, o signora Florinda, a chi pena per voi, a chi languisce, e sgombri dall'animo vostro quella fierezza e quella crudeltà che 'n voi nudrite. Ohimè, perché così turbata vi mostrate?

FLORINDA Perché il vedervi m'è così noioso che 'l sole m'apporta la notte, la luce mi si oscura, i miei piaceri vengono turbati, la mia quiete interrotta, per questo tal effetto in me scorgete. Ond'io mi risolvo di non mi lasciar giamai veder da voi per non turbarmi.

LELIO Se nemico fossi, se vi odiassi, se vi sprezzassi, grandissima ragione avereste; ma pur vedete ch'io vi sono amico, conoscete ch'io v'amo e scorgete ch'io v'onoro, onde però questi segni d'amistà, d'amore e d'onore, non meritano d'esser ricambiati con segni d'odio.

FLORINDA Se con segni d'odio non meritano d'esser ricambiati, meno merito io dalla vostra importunità esser molestata.

ACT II

Scene One
[Lelio, Florinda]

LELIO I'm back once again, like a moth to the flame or a serpent to the snake-charmer. It seems to me that my heart, that silent orator, is persuading me to talk with her, and that she'll have mercy on me. If the effect shouldn't be the one I desire, I know then what I must do. But I want to knock: is anyone home? Cupid, help me.

FLORINDA And so the hated countenance of this fellow appears before my eyes and interrupts my pleasures.

LELIO O Cupid, o powerful deity, I await your help, you who can shed light on dark matters, give grace to the troubled and faith to the doubtful, you who unite conflicting elements, you who can do what you please. Here, in this amorous ring, stands your loyal champion, and there stands your mortal enemy; here a lover, and there one who hates; here's a man who serves you, and there's a woman who despises you; here's a man who follows you like Hippomenes and there's a woman who flees you like Atalanta.[xxxv] From you I expect daring, strength, and victory. May heaven make you happy, o Florinda, and may it make Cupid piteous for him who suffers and languishes for you. May your thoughts be freed of the pride and cruelty that you nourish. Alas, why do you look so upset?

FLORINDA Because the sight of you is so annoying to me that the sun brings night to me, the light grows dark for me, my pleasures are disturbed, my peace and quiet interrupted: this is why you see me this way. I am therefore resolved never to let you see me again, in order to keep from being troubled thus.

LELIO If I were your enemy, if I hated you, if I despised you, you'd be completely right; yet you see I'm your friend, you know I love you and you perceive I honor you; thus these signs of friendship, love, and honor don't deserve to be rewarded with hatred.

FLORINDA If they don't deserve to be rewarded with hatred, even less do I deserve to be harassed by your importunity.

83

LELIO Non è importunità signora, è gran servenza d'Amore, e l'amore merita d'esser ricambiato d'amore.

FLORINDA   Non aspettate già da me questa ricompensa, che ve n'assicuro, il vostro amore è nemico dell'onore, e l'onor è quello che rende immortali i nomi, e a questo attendo.

LELIO   Non riporta premio d'onore chi non riama l'amante, anzi s'arroga il nome di micidiale; e l'esser micidiale non è strada per acquistarsi onore, ma biasimo e vergogna.

FLORINDA   È meglio un biasimo e una vergogna onorata, che un onor vergognoso.

LELIO   È però vergogna esser nemica alla natura e repugnar alle sue leggi; e la natura vuol quello che vuol Amore. L'Amore commanda che s'ami, e la natura vi consente. Miratelo nelle cose innanimate: l'ambra per amor a sé tira la paglia, la calamita il ferro; miratelo nelle cose animate sensibili: l'edera abbraccia il tronco, la vite l'olmo, la palma ama la palma. Che più? Ama il leone, la tigre, l'orsa, la iena, l'idra, insomma ama il tutto. E voi che del tutto siete parte non sentirete amore?

FLORINDA   Anzi sono amante, e udite quante passioni io sento per Amore. Anch'io sospiro, mi rammarico, impallidisco, arrossisco, rimango immobile e provo altri varii accidenti. Sospiro alor che penso al farmi immortale, mi rammarico dubitando di non potere, impallidisco dubitando smarrir la strada ch'a tanta felicità conduce, arrossisco di vergogna in veggendo tante onorate donne giunte nel seno dell'eternità, e rimango immobile per l'invidia che loro porto. Onde perciò mi convien dire: "O desideratissimo Amore! O fortunati sospiri! O pallor grato! O rossor di somma gioia! O immobilità colma di dolcezza!" poich'amando, sospirando, impallidendo, arrossendo, e immobil rimanendo, tutti sono mezi di farsi cari al cielo, e al mondo eterni.

LELIO   Se dadovero seguistate la strada di generosa donna, dubbio non ha ch'ancor voi rimareste eterna, rendendo la fama vostra immortale. Mirate la gran regina d'Egitto Cleopatra, che sarà nominata in eterno, e pur fu amante.

LELIO Madam, it isn't importunity, but a great fervor brought on by Cupid, and love should be rewarded with love.

FLORINDA Do not await such a reward from me. I assure you, your love is the enemy of honor, and honor is that which makes our names immortal; only this concerns me.

LELIO One who doesn't love one's lover in return receives no prize for honor, but on the contrary claims for herself the name of "murderous;" and being murderous isn't the way to acquire honor, only blame and shame.

FLORINDA Better blame and honorable shame than shameful honor.

LELIO It's shameful to be the enemy of nature and to defy her laws; and nature wants what Love wants. Love commands us to love one another, and nature consents. Look at inanimate things: amber for love draws straw to it, as a magnet does iron. Look at living, animate things: ivy embraces the tree trunk, as a vine does the elm, and the palm loves a palm. What else? The lion loves, as do the tiger, the she-bear, the hyena, the hydra. In short, everything loves. And you, who are a part of everything, do you not feel love?

FLORINDA But indeed I am a lover; listen and I'll tell you of the many passions I feel for Cupid. I sigh and regret; I grow pale or blush; I cannot move a muscle; and I display many other such symptoms. I sigh because I hope to become immortal; I grow regretful when I doubt I can do so; I turn pale with doubt about losing my way toward such great happiness; I blush with shame in seeing so many honorable women who've reached the bosom of eternity itself; I remain immobilized by my envy for them. Thus I may well say: o most longed-for Cupid, o fortunate sighs, o welcome pallor, o blush of greatest joy, o stillness so full of sweetness! For loving, sighing, growing pale, blushing, and falling still are all means for making oneself dear to heaven and eternal in the eyes of the world.

LELIO If you as a woman were truly to follow the path of generosity, I have no doubt that you would become eternal and your fame immortal. Look at Cleopatra, the great queen of Egypt, whose name will be known throughout eternity, and yet who was a lover.[xxxvi]

FLORINDA Fu amante sì, ma impudica, e se ne vive ancora la memoria, e però sbandita dal tempio dell'onore.

LELIO Sovvengavi di quella Lucrezia romana, ch'è stimata un tempio di pudicizia, e pur acconsentì al suo amante, e nondimeno nella memoria degli uomini non è vergognosa.

FLORINDA Perché col darsi la morte, pagò la pena che meritava lo scellerato Tarquinio; e volle mostrar con quell'azzione che più cara le era la morte, che la difendesse dall'infamia, che la vita, che la mantenesse in vituperio.

LELIO Se gli essempi de' mortali non ponno movervi il piede alla bella carriera d'Amore, ciò facciano gli essempi delle deità immortali. Ecco la gran madre d'Amore, la gran dea di Cipro, che pur era dea e amava; che se Amore avesse recato disonore alla sua deità, poteva non soggiacere a queste amorose passioni.

FLORINDA E perché tenuta fu concubina di Marte? Perché a beffeggiarla vi concorsero tutti gli dei? Perché s'acquistò questo nome disonorato d'impudica e di disonesta? Per accrescer maggior onore alla sua deitade? Per esser oltraggiata e vilipesa da' mortali?

LELIO E che direte della dea della castità, che pur si compiacque d'Endimione, e pur era dea, ed egli mortale? Direte che peccò? Porrete la bocca in cielo? Vorrete dar legge a' numi eterni?

FLORINDA Se gli dei soggiacessero alle leggi dell'onore, a questo i' vi risponderei che fece error grave, perciò fu confinata ne' boschi e le fu tolto il nome di Diana e attribuitole il nome di Cinzia cornuta; ma perché a me non tocca dar questa sentenza, rimetto il giudizio a voi.

LELIO Se questo a giudicar avessi, direi più tosto che fece bene, poiché essendo stimata dea nemica a fecondar d'uomini il mondo, e per conseguenza distruggitrice della natura, né volendo soggiacere a queste imputazioni ignominiose, s'elesse un amante. E se così è, vorrete voi fuggir di far quello che n'insegna l'essempio degno di tanta imitazione?

FLORINDA Quattro parole, e vi spedisco. Ha così ben piantate le

FLORINDA She was indeed a lover, but a shameless one; and if the memory of her is still alive, she is nonetheless banished from the temple of honor.

LELIO Remember Lucretia, the Roman lady esteemed as a temple of modesty, who nevertheless yielded to her lover; and yet mankind's memory of her is not shameful.[xxxvii]

FLORINDA Because, in killing herself, she suffered the fate that should have been the scoundrel Tarquin's instead; and in that act she wanted to show death was dearer to her than life, for death defended her from infamy, while life would have kept her in dishonor.

LELIO If the example set by mortals cannot move your feet along the beautiful path of Love, let the example of the immortal goddesses do so. Consider the divine mother of Cupid, that great goddess of Cyprus who was a goddess and yet loved;[xxxviii] and if Love brought dishonor to her divinity, she could have chosen not to subject herself to those amorous passions.

FLORINDA And why was she kept as the concubine of Mars? Why did all the gods together thus mock her? Why was she dishonored by being called immodest and dishonest? To bring greater honor to her godhead? To be insulted and scorned by mortals?

LELIO And what will you say of the goddess of chastity, who was attracted to Endymion, and yet was a goddess while he was a mortal?[xxxix] Will you say that she sinned? Will you presume to speak for heaven? Will you dictate to the eternal gods?

FLORINDA If the gods were subject to the laws of honor, I'd say that she made a grave mistake, for she was thereafter banished to the woods and her name was changed from Diana to Cynthia, who must wear horns; but because it isn't my place to pass judgment on her, I'll leave it to you to do so.[xl]

LELIO If it were up to me to judge her, I'd say she did well because she chose a lover. Although she was reputed to be the divine enemy of fecundating the world with men, and hence the destroyer of nature, she didn't want these ignominious accusations to be leveled at her. And, if

sue radici nell'animo mio l'immortalità, che debbo acquistarmi col mezzo dell'onore, che non trovo oggetto da elegger per amante altro che l'onore. Voi, che siete nemico di questo, mi dovete fuggire come troppo amica i' di lui. Ben è vero che v'è una sol via per compiacervi, cioè che voi diventiate un Adone e me facciate trasformar in Diana; che vi giuro, come Florinda seguace dell'onore, convien ch'io lo segua e le sue leggi adempia; sì che andate a far i fatti vostri, se mi volete far cosa cara.

LELIO Poich'altro non bramo ch'ubbidirla, mi parto. Cruda, ben vedrai a che dovrò appigliarmi per mia salute.

FLORINDA Appigliatevi alla salute dei disperati, fune e legni. Ch'io ami? E amando languisca? E amando mi distrugga? E amando, la libertà io perda? E col perder della libertà perda me stessa? Perdansi pria gli uomini tutti ch'a pentimento così grave io pervenga. Se amar Florinda dovesse, amar vorrebbe senza fatica; s'amar Florinda dovesse, amar vorrebbe uno, ch'acquistato conservar suo ad ognor potesse senza sospetto; se amar Florinda dovesse, la verginità così cara ad ognora illesa conservar vorrebbe; s'amar Florinda dovesse, unqua non vorrebbe con tiranno consorte, di libera felice, farsi cattiva dolente; e questo petto supporre al duro incarco della gravidanza, infortunio nel quale spesso la misera donna doppo aver lasciato patria, padre, madre, parenti, lascia ancor la vita.

Parmi ch'una voce m'accusi e così dica: "O folle, con tante condizioni Amor non si gusta;" alla quale anch'io ardita rispondo: "Io tutte le godo, e così vuole Amore," e ch'io non mentisca.

Questo è 'l ritratto di colui ch'adoro; e 'n questo al presente vagheggio colui che, Proteo d'Amore, s'io mesta sono, egli è mesto, se lieta lieto, e s'io piango, pur ei piange. Anzi, novella Eco amorosa, non in antro, ma in questo specchio sta nascosto colui ch'al moto solo delle mie labbra, senza pur udir picciolo suono di voce, alle mie voci risponde, e che 'l vero io discorra, imagine bella, Eco gentile, ch'io seco favelli, ch'egli cortese mi risponda. "O bella imagine di colui ch'adoro, ami pur la tua Florinda, non è così?" Ed ella col gesto dice sì. "La lascerai giamai?" Ed ella dice: "Mai." "Sarai della tua amata disamante?" Ed ella dice: "Amante." "Se l'abbandoni nel morir farà le guance smorte;" ed ella dice "Morte," cioè che non mi lascerà se non per morte. "Io baciar ti vorrei; dimmi tu voglio o non voglio." "Voglio." "Or che tu vuoi ti bacio." Oh com'è dolce! Oh come tutte le canne d'Ibla, tutte le manne

it were so, would you want to flee from following her example, which is so worthy of imitation?

FLORINDA Just a few words, and I'll send you on your way. Immortality—which I must obtain through honor—has sunk its roots so deeply into my heart and mind that I can find no object to choose as my lover other than honor itself. You are the enemy of all this, and thus should flee me because I already have a lover. There's but one way to satisfy you, and that's for you to become Adonis and to transform me into Diana.[xli] I swear to you that I, Florinda, the follower of honor, intend to respect and obey his laws: so if you want to do something nice for me, go about your business.

LELIO Since I wish only to obey you, I'll go. Cruel one, you'll soon see on what, for my own sake, I'll have to hang my hopes.

FLORINDA You can hang on the same things to which all desperate men turn: wooden beams and a rope. *I* should love? And, in loving, languish? And, in loving, destroy myself? And, in loving, lose my freedom? And, in losing my freedom, lose myself? First let all men lose these things, before I should so fully repent of my intention. If I, Florinda, must love, then I would like to love effortlessly. If I, Florinda, must love, then I would like to love someone who could keep me always as a lover without any suspicions. If I, Florinda, must love, then I would like to preserve intact my virginity, which is so dear to me always. If I, Florinda, must love, then I would never want to end up in sorrow because of my consort's tyranny, rather than remain free and happy. Nor would I willingly submit my body to the difficult task of pregnancy, an injury for which often a poor woman, having left behind her country, father, mother, and relations, also loses her own life.[xlii]

   It seems to me I can hear a voice accusing me, saying: "Madwoman, Love can't be enjoyed if you impose so many conditions." To which I answer, boldly and truthfully: "I take pleasure in all of them, and that's what Cupid wants."

   Here's the portrait of the one I adore. In it I now gaze lovingly upon this Proteus of Love: if I'm sad, he's sad; if I'm happy, he's happy; and if I weep, he weeps too.[xliii] In this mirror is hidden, like an amorous new Echo far from any cave, the one who answers me at the least movement of my lips, although my voice makes not the slightest

vengono tributarie a riversciar sovra questo specchio tutti i liquori. Questo, questo è l'Amor acquistato senza fatica, quest'è colui che perder non potrò, se non al perder della vita. Quest'è colui che leggero, in altrui non rivolgerà l'amore. Quest'è colui che amando, illeso conserverammi il fior verginale. Quest'è colui che 'l petto al mio petto aggiungendo, dall'angosce del parto mi farà viver sicura. O benedetto Amore, o fortunato modo d'amare! Dei tre diletti maggiori che 'n Amor si gusti, io tutti appieno gli godo; e s'uno di quelli è 'l mirar la cosa amata, l'altro l'udirla e l'ultimo, e il maggiore, è 'l goderla.

E io Florinda sempre miro, sempre ne' dolci moti della bocca tacita l'ascolto, e ad ognor nel seno stringendola io la godo. Abbracciami cor mio e così tiemmi stretta, che non mai t'abbandoni. In altro luogo andiamo, gridando: "Io amo, io amo!"

Scena Seconda
[Lelio, Granello, Mago]

LELIO Granello ho gittata l'ultim'ancora, detta da' marinari la speranza, nel mar d'Amore, e più che mai scorro naufragio.

GRANELLO Gittatevici dietro ancor voi, come vedete che va così male.

LELIO Ho pregato quel mar ondeggiante di Florinda, e più s'è fatto a' miei sospiri tempestoso, a mie preghiere pieno di scogli; e pur è questo amor onesto, e pur la bramo per mia consorte.

sound.[xliv] O lovely image, courteous Echo, may I be telling the truth when I say that I speak with you and that you so sweetly reply to me. "O lovely image of the one I adore, you do love your Florinda, do you not, yes?" And with a gesture she answers "yes" to me. "Would you never leave her, never?" And she says: "never." "Will you fall out of love with your lover?" And she says: "Love her." "If you abandon her, her cheeks will grow pale as death." And she says: "death": that is, she'll not leave me except in death. "I'd like to kiss you: tell me what's your want." "Want." "Since you want to be kissed, I'll kiss you." Oh how sweet it is! Oh how all the reeds of Ibla, all the manna from heaven, come to pay tribute, pouring balms of every sort over this mirror. This, this is Love that comes effortlessly, this is the one I cannot lose, except by losing my very life. This is the one who will not lightly turn to love another and who, in loving, will preserve unharmed the flower of my virginity. This is the one whose breast will be joined to mine, and who'll allow me to live safe from the anguish of childbirth. O blessed Love, o fortunate way to love! I fully take my pleasure in all three of the greatest delights that can be had from loving: first, to see the thing one loves; second, to hear it; and, last but best, to be pleasured by it.

And I, Florinda, am always gazing at that lovely image; I'm always listening to the sweet movements of that silent mouth; and, pressing it to my breast, I'm always pleasured by it. Embrace me, my love, and hold me so tightly that I can never leave you. Let us go together, crying: "I love, I love!"

Scene Two
[Lelio, Granello, Wizard]

LELIO Granello, I've cast overboard my last anchor, the one sailors call "hope," into the sea of Love, and more than ever I head toward shipwreck.

GRANELLO And throw yourself in after it, since you see how badly things are going.

LELIO I've pleaded with that rolling sea named Florinda, yet it grew all the stormier at my sighs, and all the more crowded with reefs at my prayers. Yet mine is an honest love, and I long to marry her.

GRANELLO O signore, il medico pietoso fa la piaga puzzolente. Vi dico il vero, io ne piglierei, se non si può un buon desinare, una picciola merenda, e me n'anderei, né mi porrei in quell'obligo di marito.

LELIO E perché?

GRANELLO Perché colui che piglia moglie perde la sua libertà, e si obliga come que' tali che si fanno far una fontanella entro un braccio, o vero entro una gamba, che sempre, sempre bisogna tener quel buco aperto, sera e mattina, poiché serrandosi porta pericolo che quegli umori che per ordinario vanno al basso, non vadano alla testa in un subbito.

LELIO Insomma io mi risolvo, poiché da buon soldato ho dato oggi l'ultimo assalto, di voler, non potendo averla per amor, averla per incanto.

MAGO E per incanto, o Lelio, l'avrete. Signore mandate via quel servo, che discorrer solo con Vostra Signoria io voglio.

GRANELLO Non me lo dirà più d'una volta. Addio, non tresco con diavoli.

MAGO Benché non mi conosciate, o gentiluomo, io ben conosco voi; e basta che siate amante, prontissimo sono all'aiutarvi, poiché amante sono stato anch'io. Io son colui del quale ormai è sparsa la voce per tutta la città, nomato Arfasat, venuto per cavar tesori, e così fatto venir da gran personaggi di questa vostra patria di Firenze, a' quali ho già data compiuta sodisfazione. Ora, in disparte avendo il disprezzo primo veduto che vi fece questa signora col serrarvi le porte nel viso, e avendo pur mirato l'affronto presente, mi risolsi farvi contento. Prenda però questa ghirlanda, questo libro e questa verga; aspetti la notte ch'è vicina; si trovi in questo luogo diritto la porta della sua morosa, là verso le due ore; pongasi questa ghirlanda in capo segno di trionfo, abbia questa verga nella destra, il libro nella sinistra, questa candela un servo suo la dovrà accesa tener in mano, per far lume ai sacri accenti. Legga l'incanto, e alor che li sarà portata la sua donna, la tocchi subbito con questa istessa verga, o tocchi quella cosa dov'ella sarà dentro, e poi la miri, la porti al suo domicilio e sarà contento. Né punto cercate d'estendervi in parole di ringraziamento, come so che ne siete

GRANELLO Master Lelio, the doctor who takes pity on the patient makes the wound fester. I'll tell you the truth: I'd gladly take a little snack, if a solid meal isn't possible, and then I'd go away, without getting myself tied down as a husband.

LELIO And why?

GRANELLO Because the man who takes a wife loses his freedom. He takes on an obligation, just like a fellow who has himself cauterized and bled on the arm, or rather on the leg, and must always, always keep that wound open, night and day. For if it were to close, he'd run the danger that those bodily humors, which usually flow downward, might go to his head in an instant.[xlv]

LELIO Like a good soldier today I've carried out my last assault: I'm now resolved to have her through magic, since I can't have her through love.

WIZARD And through magic you'll have her, Lelio. Sir, send away this servant, for I wish to speak with you alone.

GRANELLO He won't have to ask me twice. Farewell, I won't have anything to do with the devil.

WIZARD Although you don't know me, my good gentleman, I know you well. I stand ready to help you right away, for you're in love, and I too have been in love. My name is Arfasat, and word has spread throughout the city that I've come to find treasure here.[xlvi] I've been brought to your city of Florence for this purpose by important individuals, to whom I've already given complete satisfaction. From off to one side I saw the lady treat you with contempt when she shut the door in your face; once I witnessed that affront, I decided to fulfill your wish. Take this wreath, this book, and this staff; wait until night, which is coming soon; come to this place, here in front of your beloved's door, at around two o'clock; place this wreath on your head as a sign of victory, while holding this staff in your right hand and this book in your left hand. One of your servants will have to hold a lighted candle in hand, to shed light on the sacred verses. Read the spell, and your lady will be brought to you; with this selfsame staff, right away you must touch either her or whatever it is that she comes

facondo, perché né il tempo il ricerca, né io ne godo; al nuovo giorno, poi, caro mi sarà il vedervi. Andate felice ch'io parto.

LELIO Oh quanto savio altrottanto cortese! Mira come anch'egli, sdegnato della crudeltà tiranna di costei, perch'io vada a così fortunato acquisto, meno m'ha voluto conceder tempo ch'io lo ringrazi. Oh come lieto sono! Vedi pur Florinda, se del mio combattere ne riporto la ghirlanda. Sì, sì, ridi pure, scherza pure; ben so ch'anzi ch'addormentarti ne chiamerai a te Bernetta, e discorrendo per disprezzo di me racconterai di nuovo il chiudermi la porta in faccia, l'aver discorso d'onore e l'avermi lasciato pieni gli occhi di lagrime, la guancia di pallore, la bocca di sospiri e 'l cuor di tormenti; stanca alfine t'addormenterai. Ma che succederà poi, alor che l'ancella chiudendoti la porta ti farà più sicura? Alora più che mai mal custodita, sarai levata dal letto, della stessa casa, e portatami nelle braccia. Oh, pensa tu in quel punto, vendicator amoroso, quanti baci darò a quella bocca chiusa, che aperta cotanto m'offese! Ecco mi parto, e tosto ingolfato nelle tenebre rapisco il mio sole.

Scena Terza
[Guerindo, Coradella, Mago]

GUERINDO Coradella, io mi risolvo poiché per amor non posso aver costei.

CORADELLA Che volete far, appiccarvi?

GUERINDO Che appiccarmi; Guerindo, c'ha 'n cuor guerriero, dovrà far queste pazzie?

CORADELLA Vedete, appiccandosi delle volte l'uomo trova la sua ventura.

GUERINDO O la sua ultima disgrazia.

to you in, and then look at her; take her home with you and you'll be happy. Don't try to find the words to thank me, for I know that your speech is generous, but there isn't time and I wouldn't enjoy listening anyway; when the new day comes, however, I'll be delighted to see you. Go in peace, for I'm taking my leave of you now.

LELIO He's as courteous as he's wise. He too is indignant at the tyrannical cruelty of that woman: and in speeding me toward my long-desired goal, he didn't even want to leave me time to thank him. O how happy I am! You'll see, Florinda, if in combat I win the wreath. Yes, yes, go ahead and laugh, go on making fun of me. For I know full well that instead of going to sleep, you'll call Bernetta to you; and, speaking out of disdain for me, you'll tell her once more about shutting the door in my face, about having spoken of honor, and about having left me with my eyes full of tears, my cheeks full of pallor, my mouth full of sighs, and my heart full of woe. When you grow tired at last, you'll fall asleep. But then what will happen? When your maidservant closes the door to your bedroom, do you think that you'll be the safer for it? Quite the contrary: more unprotected than ever, you'll be taken from your bed and from that house, and brought to my waiting arms. O avenger of love, just think how many kisses I'll then give to her still-closed mouth—the very same one that, when open, offended me so greatly! Away I go, and engulfed in shadows I'll kidnap my sun.

Scene Three
[Guerindo, Coradella, Wizard]

GUERINDO Coradella, since I can't have that woman through love, I've made up my mind.

CORADELLA What do you want to do, go hang yourself?

GUERINDO Whatever are you talking about? Do you think that I, Guerindo, who have a warrior's heart, would act so rashly?

CORADELLA You see, sometimes a man finds his fortune in life by hanging himself.

GUERINDO Or his final misfortune.

CORADELLA Dico la sua principalissima fortuna io. Uditemi: un padre, antivisto la dissoluta vita del figliuolo, giunto a morte il chiamò, e disse: "Figlio, per natural debito ti lascio tutte le mie ricchezze; duolmi quello che 'n molt'anni affaticai, tu in brevi ore gittar il debbi; ti benedico e ti lascio ad un trave appeso, colà su del granaio in un vilissimo camerino, una fune ben legata ad un trave; com'hai gittato via il tutto, appiccati ancora." Così, morto il padre, in brevissimi giorni si ridusse con tanti debiti costui, che disperatissimo un giorno, se n'andò, per ubbidire il padre, del granaio nel camerino.

Or quello che disse nel premer la soglia di quella entrata, nell'alzar gli occhi, nel mirar il trave, la fune, pensatelo voi, se vi siete mai appiccato. Alfine s'attortiglia e annoda la fune al collo, montato sovra d'un alto scagno; poi, dando la volta allo stesso scagno, si lascia cader risolutissimo di morire. Or che intervenne? Oh providenza paterna, ch'induce i padri ad amar i figliuoli ancor doppo morte! Il trave era fragilissimo e vuoto, a bello studio fatto così dal padre, era colà dentro accomodato dell'argento, dell'oro, sì che nel cader che fece, la fune senza molta fatica fece ruinar il tutto, ond'egli si trovò sepolto nell'oro; sì che appicandovi ancor voi potreste farvi contento.

GUERINDO Fratello, non voglio per via di fune poggiar al cielo d'Amore, ma Florinda per incanto voglio.

MAGO E per incanto l'averete. Guerindo, chi vi amiate io non so, né men curo di saperlo al presente, basti solo ch'avendo meco stesso giuramento di consolar tutti quelli ch'hanno in amor sorte contraria, mi dispongo d'aiutarvi.

GUERINDO Questo favor a me signore? E quando giamai la potrò riccompensare?

CORADELLA Quando v'anderete ad appiccare, che vi pioverà tant'oro addosso.

MAGO Prendete questa ghirlanda, questo libro, questa verga, questa candela.

GUERINDO E di queste così fatte cose che dovrò fare?

CORADELLA I'm talking about his greatest good fortune. Listen to me. A father is on his deathbed. He has foreseen his son's dissolute lifestyle, and when he calls him to his bedside, he says: "My son, I must pay nature its due, and so I leave you all of my wealth: it grieves me to think that you'll throw away in just a few hours what I toiled for years to save; I bless you and leave to you a rope hanging from a beam, up there in a squalid little room in the granary; when you've thrown everything else away, go hang yourself." With his father dead, the son accumulated in just a few short days so many debts that, in utter despair, he went up to the room in the granary to obey his father's final wish. What did he say as he stepped across the threshold of the room, and raised his eyes to look at the rope and the beam? Now you can well imagine it, if you've ever gone and hung yourself before. In the end he wound the rope around his neck, knotting it before climbing onto a tall stool. Then, kicking away the stool, he let himself fall, firmly resolved as he was to die. But now what do you think happened? O paternal providence, which leads fathers to love their sons even after death! The beam was extremely fragile and hollow, for the father had very carefully made it so, in order to cache silver and gold in it. The son, in his fall, brought down the beam over which the rope was hung without much effort, and found himself buried in gold. So, if you go hang yourself, you too could make yourself happy.

GUERINDO Brother, I don't wish to climb into the heaven of Love by way of the rope; but I want Florinda by way of a magic spell.

WIZARD And with a spell you'll have her. I don't know whom you love, Guerindo, nor do I care to know at present. I've sworn to myself that I'll console all those who are unlucky in love, and therefore stand ready to help you.

GUERINDO Sir, you would do this for me? And when would I ever be able to repay you?

CORADELLA When you go hang yourself, and all that gold comes raining down on you.

WIZARD Take this wreath, this book, this staff, and this candle.

GUERINDO And what am I supposed to do with them?

MAGO Su le tre ore di notte, comparendo avanti la porta della vostra amata, vi porrete questa corona in capo, la verga nella destra mano, il libro nella sinistra, e la candela accesa la terrà il vostro servo; aprirete poscia il libro, e leggendo col servo dove sarà segnato, vi sarà portata l'innamorata vostra; la quale subbito, senza altro fare, la toccherete con la verga, o vero toccherete quella cosa dov'ella sarà dentro, ma avvertite non errare.

CORADELLA O signore, di grazia, non v'impacciate con quella bestia del diavolo.

GUERINDO Sta' cheto. Signore quanto le sia obligato.

MAGO Piano, piano. Io son nemico de' ringraziamenti e però fuggo. Io sto in questa casa, domani l'aspetto.

CORADELLA Cappari, questo è un galante barbaccia. Che guadagno ora?

GUERINDO Tutto quello che tu vuoi. Son così contento ch'a pena ho piedi che mi portino a tanta gioia.

CORADELLA Ormai è vicina la sera, andiamo a far amicizia con Satanasso, bench'io difficilmente li creda, ch'è sempre bugiardo.

GUERINDO Quand'è costretto è verace mal suo grado, andiamo. Oh, vedi Florinda che sarà l'uomo più nobile della donna, per l'intelletto acuto e per l'invenzioni sottili!

CORADELLA Affè, che questa volta l'uomo fatto maggiore toccherà a cavalcar la donna. Andiam via.

GUERINDO Andiamo. Stelle v'invoco, tenebre omai venite.

WIZARD At around three o'clock at night, go to the front door of your beloved's house. Put this wreath on your head, hold the staff in your right hand and the book in your left hand; your servant will hold the lighted candle. Open the book, and, with your servant's help, read the passage I've marked for you. Your beloved will then be brought to you. With the staff you must immediately, before doing anything else, touch either her or whatever it is that she comes to you in; but be careful not to make a mistake.

CORADELLA Master, I implore you, don't get yourself involved with that brute the devil.

GUERINDO Keep quiet. Sir, I'm most obliged to you.

WIZARD Not in the least… I'm the enemy of thanks and must flee from them. I'm staying in this house; I'll look forward to seeing you tomorrow.

CORADELLA Christ, this fellow and his ugly beard are full of gallantry. What'll I get paid for this?

GUERINDO Whatever you wish. I'm so happy that I can barely feel my feet moving toward this encounter with bliss.

CORADELLA Evening now draws near. Let's go make friends with the devil, although I've a really hard time believing him, because he's always such a liar.

GUERINDO When he's forced to be, he's truthful in spite of himself. Let's go. O Florinda, you'll see that man is nobler than woman, thanks to his acute intellect and cunning!

CORADELLA In faith, this time the man, who is superior, will ride the woman. Let's go.

GUERINDO Let's go. Stars, show yourselves; come now, shadows.

Scena Quarta
[Lidia, Florinda, Bernetta]

LIDIA Oh quanto mi dispiace d'aver, per soverchia rabbia amorosa, posto in pericolo il mio povero Silvio. Così commanda la disperazione alor che de' cuori nostri prende il dominio; son però così fuor di me stessa che, se la prudenza non mi servisse, per ritegno da questa finestra mi precipiterei. O povero Silvio, com'al presente tra que' ferri, tra quelle oscurità, tra que' fetori, di me querelar ti dei. Deh, almeno su l'ali de' miei sospiri giunga il grave delle mie passioni al mio tradito amante; e così intenda quant'io m'accori, e come lagrimando io mi distrugga. Ma che veggio? Quest'è la signora Florinda. Voglio star qui in disparte da me stessa piangendo, e solinga osservando.

FLORINDA Bernetta cammina veloce. Vedi se quella gentildonna amica è nella città o s'è alla villa, poiché per liberarmi da questa importunità d'uomini voglio andar a star seco, conforme il mio uso, cinque o sei giorni.

BERNETTA Che sieno maledetti questi ominacci, che tanto impero vogliono aver sopra noi. Povere donne, sanno questi traditori che siamo come la campana e come la lanterna, che non possiamo suonare, che non possiamo risplendere senza il batocchio e senza il candelotto, e per questo fanno tanto gl'intirizati. Io vo signora, state pur di buon cuore, faremo come quelli che non han cuochi, si fregheremo la padella fra noi. Addio.

FLORINDA Care sono le perle, gli ori, le cittadi, i regni, gl'imperi, le monarchie, i mondi; ma più cara di tutti è la cara libertade, ond'il poeta lagrimoso cantando così disse:
        "O cara libertà dove se' gita."
O Florinda, o Florinda mio bene, vedi s'io son constante. Pur sai che da molti colpi d'accetta percossa, cade la dura quercia; pur t'è noto ch'a' replicanti colpi di martello, l'oro s'affina, e che per continuo cader di picciola stilla, lo smisurato sasso si spezza e frange. E io più che percossa, più che pei colpi aggravata sono, più resisto, né m'indebilisco, ma più mi rinforzo, quasi palma robusta, che quanto più con ismisurato peso i suoi rami si aggravano, tanto più resiste e 'l greve peso innalza. Ma ohimè! Che veggio? Così pallida se'? Cor mio, forse temi ch'io t'abbandoni? Ah, prima che ciò sia, questa mia vita si risolva in

Scene Four
[Lidia, Florinda, Bernetta]

LIDIA How sorry I am to have put my poor Silvio in danger by acting out of overwhelming amorous rage. This is what desperation does when it seizes control of our hearts. I'm so beside myself that, if prudence did not restrain me, I'd throw myself out this window. O poor Silvio, in irons, in darkness, in that stench, you must want to see me prosecuted. May the weight of my passions at least reach my betrayed lover on the wings of my sighs. Then he'd understand how I grieve, and how, weeping, I pine away for him. But what do I see? It's Florinda. I'll stay off to one side, weeping and watching in my solitude.

FLORINDA Go quickly, Bernetta. See if that gentlewoman and friend of mine is in the city or in the country, for I'd like to go and stay with her, as I sometimes do, for five or six days, in order to get rid of these bothersome men.

BERNETTA Accursed be those nasty little fellows who want to lord it over us. Poor women: these traitors know that we're like the bell and like the lantern, for we can't ring without a clapper and we can't glow without a candle, and for this reason they act so stiffly around us. I'm going, my lady. Be of good cheer; we'll do as those who live without cooks, and between the two of us we'll stir the pot. Farewell.

FLORINDA Dear to me are pearls, gold, cities, kingdoms, empires, monarchies, and worlds, but dearest of all to me is my beloved freedom. A sorrowful poet once sang:
     "O dear freedom, where have you gone?"[xlvii]
O Florinda, o Florinda my love, you'll see how constant I am. Yet you know that even the hardest oak falls if struck enough blows with a hatchet. Yet you also know that gold is refined by the hammer's blows, and that a steady fall of little water-drops will break and shatter even an immense boulder. And I, the more I'm struck and assailed with blows, resist all the more; I don't grow weaker, but stronger, almost like a robust palm-tree which, the more its branches are burdened with great weight, resists it and indeed lifts it upward. But woe is me! What do I see? Why so pale? My love, are you perhaps afraid I'll abandon you? Ah, before that happens my life will have to end in death. Are you weeping, while I do not weep? Are you sighing, while my soul

morte. Tu piangi, e io non piango? Tu sospiri, e in sospiri l'anima io non spiro? Giuro al cielo che d'ogn'uomo io voglio far crudelissimo scempio, per consolarti, o sconsolato volto, che 'n tal guisa trafitto se' che per Florinda non ti riconosco.

Scena Quinta
[Testuggine, Lidia, Florinda]

TESTUGGINE Signora Florinda, chi ha tempo non aspetti tempo; amate prima che 'l diavolo ci ponga la coda.

FLORINDA Che diavolo? Che coda? Che sieno maledetti gli uomini e le loro code.

TESTUGGINE Ohimè ferma! Ohimè, ferma ferma! Per mia fé son Testuggine, ma hammi giovato il correr da cervo. Uh, dalli alla nemica degli uomini, che bastona gli uomini!

FLORINDA Levati di qui che giuro al cielo t'uccido.

TESTUGGINE Volete che vi presti il pugnale, che ve lo porrete sotto il grombiale per assalir gli uomini con maggior superchiaria.

FLORINDA Levati dico; se non ch'io...

TESTUGGINE Che diamberne, è spiritata, io parto, io parto.

FLORINDA Or che dici, l'effetto fu conforme la promessa? O vago, delicato viso, pur alquanto se' lieto, pare in un che tu sorrida e che tu mi dica che benissimo feci, per trar te di doglia, a bastonar colui. Credi pur che di tutti gli uomini come nemica farò crudelissimo scempio. Ma chi è costui? Ripiglio il legno.

Scena Sesta
[Granello, Florinda, Lidia]

GRANELLO Signora.

does not breathe its last with sighs? I swear to heaven that to console you, o inconsolable face, I wish to make an utterly cruel example of each and every man; for you're now transfixed in such a manner that Florinda doesn't even recognize you.

Scene Five
[Testuggine, Lidia, Florinda]

TESTUGGINE Those who have time shouldn't wait for the right time to come, Mistress Florinda; love, then, before the devil sticks his tail into things.

FLORINDA What devil? What tail? Curses on men and their tails. [*she beats him with a stick*]

TESTUGGINE Ow, stop! Stop, stop! I swear that I'm Testuggine, like a turtle, but just now it would've been better to run like a deer. Go on, give it to her, the enemy of men, the woman who thrashes men!

FLORINDA Now get out of here or I swear to heaven I'll kill you.

TESTUGGINE Do you want me to loan you my dagger, so you can hide it under your apron and assault men with even greater arrogance?

FLORINDA Get out of here, I say; otherwise I'll…

TESTUGGINE What the devil!… She's possessed… I'm going, I'm going.

FLORINDA What do you say now? Does it look like I kept my promise to you? O lovely, delicate face, however happy you may be, you seem at one and the same time to smile and to tell me I've done the right thing to ease your pain by thrashing that fellow. Believe me: as their enemy, I'll make an utterly cruel example of all men. But who's this? I must take up my cudgel again.

Scene Six
[Granello, Florinda, Lidia]

GRANELLO My lady.

FLORINDA Signora.

GRANELLO Olà, ferma, ferma. Giuro al cielo, se non foste quella che siete...

FLORINDA Che? Che dici tu?

GRANELLO Niente, niente.

FLORINDA Levati di qui or ora, che giur'al cielo...

GRANELLO Io vado, io vado signora, ma arricordatevi che mi avete ben ben verberato, per non dir bastonato.

FLORINDA Porta queste legna al tuo padrone, di' con queste il fuoco d'Amore anderà crescendo; e caso che queste tue bastonate non sieno bastanti, n'ho ancor non so quante per sua signoria.

GRANELLO Or ora fo l'ambasciata.

FLORINDA O vermigliuzzo volto, o serenati lumi, o labbra rubiconde e sorridenti, or sì che tutto quel bello col quale s'abbellisce la Bellezza istessa, è ritornato a trionfar nel seggio del tuo volto.
Ohimè, questo capello d'oro offende troppo la rosata guancia. Ma che? Non è capello, è un angue d'oro, che nel giardino del tuo leggiadro viso, tra le rose d'Amore, vigila e riposa; questo fior non è vago, forz'è ch'io te lo levi, e 'n vece di quello, questo più vago faccia ondeggiar su la tua chioma vaga; su, piglia questo ancora, e questo, e questo. Ohimè, dimmi cor mio, questo greve pendente non t'offende l'orecchio tenerello? Lascia, lascia ch'io 'l pesi. "No, no, no, non lo voglio." Orsù, poiché la mano all'orecchio tu porgi, a me segno facendo ch'hai gusto che ve 'l lasci, ecco ch'all'ubbidirti io mi dispongo. Ma qual volto qui dentro d'uomo rimiro? Giuro al cielo, se non mi fosti o specchio così caro, che gittandoti al suolo in mille parti io ti frangerei; adunque Florinda dello specchio fuori è nemica degli uomini, e colà dentro poi con gl'istessi uomini sta congiunta? Qual cappello di finissima paglia, con piume colorate, porta il tuo vago, il mio rivale? Fuggi da questo specchio, se a caso non fosti Amore, che per mirar più bella Psiche, qui dentro venuto fosti a trastullarti. Benignissimo nume, con le ginocchia a terra io t'adoro. Oh qual leggiadro viso, oh

FLORINDA My lady.

GRANELLO Hey, stop right there. I swear to heaven that if you weren't who you are…

FLORINDA What? What are you saying? [*she beats him with her cudgel*]

GRANELLO Nothing, nothing.

FLORINDA Get out of here right now, or I swear to heaven…

GRANELLO I'm going, I'm going, my lady, but remember that you've given me quite a hiding, not to say a thrashing.

FLORINDA Take the splinters out of your backside and give them to your master for me; tell him that the fire of Love will be fueled by them. If what you just received isn't enough for some reason, I've got lots more for his lordship.

GRANELLO I'll take him your message right away.

FLORINDA O ruddy cheeks, o eyes now clear again, o red and smiling lips: now all the beauty with which Beauty itself is adorned has returned to sit in triumph on the throne of your face.
    Oh my, this single golden hair offends too greatly the pink cheek I see here. What am I saying? It isn't a hair, but a golden snake, that keeps watch and rests in the garden of your graceful face, amidst Love's roses. This flower isn't lovely enough, and so I'm going to take it away from you; instead I'll set this other, lovelier one afloat on the waves of your beautiful locks; go on, take this one too, and this one, and this one. Oh my, tell me, my love, does this heavy pendant offend your ever-so-tender ear? Let me, o let me weigh it in my hand. "No, no, no, I don't want you to." Well then, since you're putting your hand to your ear, thus indicating you want me to leave it alone, I'm disposed to obey you, as you can see. But what do I see here in the mirror? The face of a man? I swear to heaven that if you, o mirror, weren't so dear to me, I'd smash you into a thousand pieces on the ground. Should Florinda be the enemy of men outside of the mirror, but instead be together with those same men when inside of it? What's that hat of finest straw

qual vago sembiante! Oh, se tali gli uomini fossero, non sarei già di loro così fiera persecutrice. Sento un benigno incendio, che di vena in vena giungendo al cuore tutto m'accende d'amoroso e inestinguibil fuoco. Ma sciocca ch'io vaneggio; quest'è d'un vago giovanetto sembianza vaga, il quale in alto sollevato, o da poggiolo o da finestra, trasfonde qui dentro la bella imagine sua, però lagrimosa. Or come è d'uomo il sembiante, più non mi curo di mirarlo, anzi perché con la bella imagine di Florinda non stia, chiudo lo specchio, e rimirando intorno, rimiro s'il veggo. [*Lidia qui si retira.*] Ma dove è questo vago e lagrimoso, ch'io no 'l rimiro? Torno di nuovo a riguardar nello specchio, poiché, se m'è tolto il vagheggiarlo qui d'intorno, mi sia conceduto rimirarlo qui dentro. [*Lidia torna alla finestra.*] E pur di nuovo il veggio, e che si asciuga gli occhi. Ohimè, questo pianto mi cava a forza dagli occhi il pianto e dalla bocca i sospiri; rimirerò d'intorno. [*Lidia si retira.*] Né cosa alcuna io veggio? Dove non giunge l'occhio giungano le preghiere almeno, e quelle sieno che ti smovano a farmi degna di fermarti alquanto, o vago giovine, al luogo ove tu eri, poiché del tuo pianto sono fatta così compassionevole, ch'io giuro novella Egeria e Aretusa trasformarmi in pianto s'io non rasciugo il tuo pianto. O misera Florinda, ottener non puoi questa così lieve grazia. Scopritevi signore qual voi vi siate, poiché dalla vostra pietà son fatta così pietosa, che 'n non potervi consolare sono la più sconsolata donna che viva. O bel volto appassionato, lagrimoso scopriti, bel viso. Aprirò questo specchio. [*Lidia torna alla finestra.*] Ah crudo, qui dentro io ti veggio, né qui d'intorno godi di lasciarti rimirare? Dove se', o bel viso? [*Lidia si retira.*] Or sì che 'n preda al pianto tutta mi getto, povera Florinda che 'l mal altrui chiama suo proprio, né potendo consolarlo sconsolata vive, e piange. Oh povera Florinda! Oh povera Florinda!

and colorful feathers that your lover, and my rival, wears? Fly from this mirror, if perchance you're not Cupid, who, to gaze upon a lovelier Psyche, has come in here to amuse yourself.[xlviii] Most benevolent deity, I adore you on my knees. Oh what a lovely countenance I see, oh what a beautiful face! If men were really like this, I wouldn't be such a fierce enemy of theirs. I feel a benign fire flowing through all my veins and running right to my heart, burning me with a loving and inextinguishable flame. But what a fool I am to rave like this. This handsome countenance belongs to an equally handsome young man: from on high, perhaps a window or a balcony, he infuses his beautiful yet tearful image into this mirror. Since this image is that of a man, I'll cease to gaze at it; in fact, I'll close up this mirror so that his image will not be seen next to Florinda's. If I look around, I might be able to spot him. [*Lidia withdraws.*] Where is this beautiful and tearful man, whom I cannot see? I'll look in the mirror again, since, if I can't see him anywhere nearby, I may at least be able to gaze upon him in here. [*Lidia returns to the window.*] Now I see him again; he's trying to dry his eyes. Oh my goodness, the force of his tears tears tears from my eyes and sighs from my mouth. I'll have a look around again. [*Lidia withdraws.*] Do I see nothing? Where my eyes cannot reach, may at least my prayers go: and I pray I may move you to consider me worthy, o handsome youth, to keep you for a while in that place where I first saw you. For I swear your tears have made me so compassionate that I, weeping, will be transformed into a new Egeria and Arethusa if I can't dry your tears for you.[xlix] O unfortunate Florinda, you can't obtain such easy grace. Sir, show yourself for who you are, for your pity has made me so piteous that my inability to console you has made me the most inconsolable woman alive. O passionate, beautiful, and tearful face, show yourself to me! I'll open this mirror again. [*Lidia returns to the window.*] Ah, cruel one, I can see you in here, yet you enjoy not letting yourself be seen anywhere else. Where are you, handsome face? [*Lidia withdraws.*] Now I'll truly collapse in tears: poor Florinda, who must call her own the suffering of others, and who lives and weeps, inconsolable, for that she cannot console him. O poor Florinda! O poor Florinda!

Scena Settima
[Bernetta, Florinda]

BERNETTA Che cos'è mia signora?

FLORINDA Oh povera Florinda! Oh povera Florinda!

BERNETTA Signora, slargatevi meco. Che cos'è? Che cos'è?

FLORINDA Non posso dirlo; ho la lingua nelle fauci annodata, e le lagrime, quando parlar potessi, mi affogherebbeno le parole su le labbra. Oh povera Florinda!

BERNETTA Oh povera Bernetta! Oh povera Bernetta!

FLORINDA In casa, in casa.

[*Qui tutte due in un tempo grideranno stridendo: "Oh povera Florinda," "Oh povera Bernetta," e Lidia comparirà in quel tempo ch'entrando diranno: "Oh povera Florinda" ecc., ed essa sbattendosi alla finestra dirà stridendo: "Oh povera Lidia, oh povera Lidia," e finirà l'atto senza accorgersi che Lidia sclami anch'ella.*]

FINE DELL'ATTO SECONDO

Scene Seven
[Bernetta, Florinda]

BERNETTA What is it, madam?

FLORINDA O poor Florinda! O poor Florinda!

BERNETTA Mistress, speak to me. What is it? What is it?

FLORINDA I can't tell you. My tongue is tied in knots, and if I could speak my tears would drown my words on my lips. O poor Florinda!

BERNETTA O poor Bernetta! O poor Bernetta!

FLORINDA Let's go inside, let's go inside.

[*The two go crying aloud at the same time: "O poor Florinda!" "O poor Bernetta!" Lidia reappears at the same time as they are going into the house crying "O poor Florinda!" etc.; she cries from her window "O poor Lidia! O poor Lidia!" The act will conclude without their realizing that Lidia is also crying aloud.*]

END OF ACT TWO

ATTO TERZO

Scena Prima
[Lidia, Florinda, Bernetta]

LIDIA E pur di nuovo alle lagrime io ritorno; e pur di nuovo a' sospiri. O Silvio, o Silvio, quanto della tua prigionia mi dispiace, poiché i tuoi duri ceppi assai più fieri legami mi vanno nel colmo di mia libertà ministrando. Ma ecco di nuovo quella gentildonna; ben sarà ch'io mi ritiri e or ch'io mi scopra, in questo modo contemperando con poca dolcezza il mar delle mie amaritudini.

BERNETTA Signora Florinda, guardiamo un poco prima ben ben qui d'intorno, perché per dirvela, e mi perdoni, ho che questo sia un umor malinconico.

FLORINDA Sì certo, che darò in tal malinconia ch'io verrò ad alcuno stravagante partito.

BERNETTA Non vi siete già innamorata.

FLORINDA No, ma del travaglio di questo tale son fatta così compassionevole, che s'io no 'l consolo mi sento morire.

BERNETTA Rimira qui d'intorno. Io non veggo cosa alcuna, crediatemi signora ch'è una vania. Aprite un poco lo specchio?

FLORINDA Eccolo aperto. [*Lidia comparisce.*] Eccolo. Vedi tu colà dentro quel bel viso? Vedi com'or si rasciuga gli occhi? O Bernetta mia, io non erro.

BERNETTA Oh, che bel visetto, mi fa pur tanta, tanta compassione; guardiamo intorno. [*Lidia si retira.*] E non si vede cosa alcuna.

FLORINDA Che ti diss'io? Oh povera, oh povera Florinda!

BERNETTA Piano signora. Caro visetto inzuccherato scopriti un poco, non far tanta carestia del tuo bello che ti prometto ch'averai caro di esserti scoperto, poiché la mia padrona tanto faconda nella lingua, quanto tu bello nel volto, ti darà tal consolazione, ch'averai carissimo

ACT III

Scene One
[Lidia, Florinda, Bernetta]

LIDIA Once again I return to my tears and my sighs. O Silvio, o Silvio, I'm so very sorry you're in prison, for, at the moment of my greatest freedom, your iron shackles begin to bind me even more fiercely than they do you. Here is that gentlewoman again: I'd better hide first and reveal myself later, so that I can temper the sea of my bitter sorrows with a bit of sweetness.

BERNETTA Mistress Florinda, first let's have a good look around here, because—if you'll forgive me for saying so—I've a feeling that this is just a melancholy fancy on your part.

FLORINDA Yes of course. I'll allow that, in my melancholy state, I might well be subject to some extravagant notion.

BERNETTA Have you already fallen in love?

FLORINDA No. Yet the suffering of that fellow has so moved me to compassion that, if I don't console him, I think I must die.

BERNETTA Take a look around here. I can't see anyone: believe me, mistress, it is only your mind playing tricks on you. Would you please open up the mirror?

FLORINDA Done. [*Lidia appears.*] There he is. Can you not see that fine face in it? Can you not see how he's now drying his eyes? O dear Bernetta, I've made no mistake.

BERNETTA Oh what a lovely little face: it makes me feel so very, very compassionate too. Let's take another look around. [*Lidia withdraws.*] I can't see anyone at all.

FLORINDA What did I tell you? O poor, poor Florinda!

BERNETTA Steady now, my lady. Dear sweet little face with sugar on top, do show yourself, and don't leave us famished for your beauty.

111

d'esserti scoperto. Poh, l'ustinato poltrone! Lasciate far a me. Allegrezza, l'ho trovata, starò nascosta là su quel canto; voi guardate nello specchio e lasciate far a me.

FLORINDA Tu di' benissimo.

BERNETTA Eh, signora, non voglio più pregar un sordo io. O tu, qual tu ti sia, se non ti vuoi discoprire appiccati, io vo in piazza, per faccende. Addio signora padrona, andate in casa.

FLORINDA Io vo. E io apro di nuovo lo specchio contentissima. [*Lidia torna.*] E pur qui dentro addolorato viso ti miro.

BERNETTA Ah ah! Io v'ho scoperto. No, no, non v'ascondete più.

FLORINDA Siete scoperta. Oh, questa è una gentildonna!

LIDIA Donna io sono, e perché il mio male è senza rimedio, per questo disperando ogni salute, fui sorda alle sue preghiere nascondendomi agli occhi suoi; ma per mostrarmi a Vostra Signoria grata, or or, ne vengo a lei.

BERNETTA Che dite padrona, son fina o no? M'è giovato nascer in piazza Padella questa volta, dove si friggono tutte le buone semenze.

FLORINDA Se tu non eri, io era disperatissima. Eccola appunto. Bernetta va' in casa, che forse non così liberamente dirà i suoi travagli essendoci tu.

BERNETTA Eh, tra noi altre donne possiam dir ogni cosa; tutte abbiamo un'istessa piaga e tutte abbiam bisogno d'un istesso cerotto. Addio.

FLORINDA Oh quanto, gentilissima signora, questo cuore addolorato si trovava alor che rimirando in questo specchio io la vedeva, così dal dolor trafitta. Giamai non provai il maggior tormento. Che vuol dir signora ch'ell'è così travagliata? Oh come disse bene il Filosofo, quando interrogato di che fosse composto l'uomo rispose: "D'altro non è composto, che di liti, e di contrasti."

I swear you stand to do well by showing yourself, for my mistress's tongue is as fluent as your face is lovely: she'll give you such consolation that you'll be delighted to have let yourself be found. Well, what a pigheaded loafer! Leave it to me, mistress. There, I've got it! I'll hide over in that corner, while you look in the mirror, and leave the rest to me.

FLORINDA Now you're talking.

BERNETTA Well, my lady, I don't want my words to keep falling on deaf ears. Hello there, whoever you are! You can go hang yourself if you don't want to show your face, for I'm going to the piazza on an errand. Farewell, my mistress: you can go home now.

FLORINDA I'm going. But first I'll be most happy to open up the mirror again. [*Lidia returns.*] And yet in it I see you, sorrowful face.

BERNETTA Ah ha! I've found you. No, don't hide yourself any longer.

FLORINDA You've been found. Why, this is a gentlewoman!

LIDIA I am a woman. Because there's no cure for what afflicts me, and because I despair of ever getting better, I was deaf to your prayers and hid myself from your eyes. Now, however, to show my gratitude to Your Ladyship, I'll come to you.

BERNETTA What say you, my mistress? Am I or am I not clever? If this time things panned out for me, it's because I was born in a part of town where all the good seed gets taken and put into the ovens.[1]

FLORINDA If you weren't so clever, I'd have been utterly desperate. Here she is then. Bernetta, go in the house, for she'll perhaps not speak so freely of her travails if you're here.

BERNETTA Ah, we women can say anything to each other: for we all have the same wound, and we all need the same bandage. Farewell.

FLORINDA Most gracious lady, how sorrowful this heart of mine was when I saw you in this mirror, pierced with pain. I've never felt any greater torment. What, madam, does this suffering of yours mean?

LIDIA E a me, s'alcuno ricercasse di che materia è composta la povera Lidia, altro risponder non saprei, che di lagrime, e di sospiri.

FLORINDA Ha remedio alcuno signora Lidia questo suo male?

LIDIA La morte sola.

FLORINDA Signora, cinque cose sono da' più savi sempre state reputate sciocche. La prima è che l'umano non dee dir cosa che provar non possa; la seconda, non dee donare quello che non può; terza, non dee chieder quello che non può ottenere; quarta, non contradire contra colui contra al quale non si può vendicare; quinta, e ultima, né lamentar si debbe di quella cosa che non ha rimedio. Se dunque il suo male è senza rimedio, sia anch'ella senza lagrime per piangerlo, senza sospiri per sospirarlo.

LIDIA Non doveva la natura, e gli occhi, e la bocca concedermi; né doveva il crudo fanciullo, che di faretra arma il fianco e di facella la mano, dalla fontana del cuore trarmi le lagrime, né da l'Eolia del petto i sospiri.

FLORINDA Sì, sì, l'ho intesa signora, voi siete amante.

LIDIA Amante sono.

FLORINDA Sì eh. Oh quanto mi dispiace di veder questa degna signora per così indegna cagione afflitta. Signora, dicesi che la più gran cosa che sia è 'l giovar altrui, però mi dispongo accorta chirurga, or ch'ho veduto e conosciuto il suo male, di sanarla.

LIDIA Certo sì mia signora che niuna cosa far si può qua giù ch'ad un uomo più si convenga, ch'esser a molti cagion di bene; poiché dal giovare, a Giove somiglianti si facciamo. Accingasi dunque a questa salutare e celeste impresa.

When asked what man was made of, the Philosopher was certainly right to say that "he is made solely of quarrels and clashes."[li]

LIDIA And if anyone wanted to find out what poor Lidia is made of, I wouldn't know what to say, other than tears and sighs.

FLORINDA Is there any cure, Mistress Lidia, for this affliction of yours?

LIDIA Only death.

FLORINDA Good lady, the wisest men have always considered five things to be foolish. First, men shouldn't say anything that can't be proven. Second, men shouldn't promise to give anything that they can't give. Third, they shouldn't ask for that which they can't have. Fourth, they shouldn't contradict anyone against whom they can't defend themselves. The fifth and last thing is that men shouldn't complain about that for which there is no cure. If, then, your affliction is without a cure, it should be without tears to weep for it and without sighs to sigh for it.

LIDIA Neither my nature, nor my eyes, nor my mouth, should have allowed me to do so. Nor should a cruel youth, armed with a quiver on his hip and a weapon in his hand, have drawn my tears from the fountain of my heart, nor my sighs from the Aeolian island of my breast.[lii]

FLORINDA Yes, yes, now I understand: you are a lover.

LIDIA I am a lover.

FLORINDA Really. How sorry I am to see this worthy lady so afflicted for such an unworthy reason. My lady, it's said that there is no greater thing than to benefit another: hence, now that I've seen and known your affliction, I put myself at your service as an able surgeon, to cure you of it.

LIDIA Certainly, madam, nothing may be done here below that is more fitting for us than to be a cause of good for many others. Indeed, we resemble God when we do good: please, then, set about this beneficial and heavenly task of yours.

FLORINDA Eccomi accinta.

LIDIA O cara signora, favelli e incominci. E qual medicamento salutifero porta al presente su la lingua, onde per l'orecchie la piaga del cuore si risani e si consoli?

FLORINDA Eccolo. Lasciate Amore, poich'Amore altro non è ch'una rabbia venerea, un veleno che si cova nelle midolle, una peste universale, una ragione insana, un'animosa timidità, un piacer noioso, una luce tenebrosa, una gloria non lodata, un'inferma sanità, un rimedio che dà pena, e un pericoloso cammino che ci guida al precipicio di morte.

LIDIA Voglio seguir Amore, poich'Amore è una sanità che non mai s'inferma, un veleno vitale, una medicina ch'ogni morbo risana, un sole che non mai tramonta, una luna che non mai s'ecclissa, un paradiso in sembianza d'inferno, e una via ch'alla perpetua vita c'invita.

FLORINDA Signora lasciate Amore, e sovvengavi che gli è dipinto fra ceppi, fra catene, fra coltelli, perché spoglia di libertà e ci dà morte.

LIDIA E pur dipingono Amore tra le Grazie, di stelle ornato, perché d'ogni grazia n'è favorevole, e dei celesti beni n'è largo compartitore.

FLORINDA Amore è pestifero tarlo, che del cuor si nutre.

LIDIA S'Amor è verme, è il sero, il quale con la picciola, ma onorata bocca, la seta ci fila.

FLORINDA Amor è un'acqua stagnante e putrida, la quale col fieto ci appesta.

LIDIA S'Amor è acqua, è 'l Pattolo, è l'Acheloo, ch'altro non fa che nel bello e translucido seno rivolger arene d'oro e d'argento.

FLORINDA Amor è un'asta avvelenata, che mortalissima t'impiaga.

LIDIA Amor è l'asta d'Achille, che se ti piaga, ti risana.

FLORINDA Amor è un aspide ch'a' discorsi ragionevoli chiude l'orecchio.

FLORINDA At your service.

LIDIA Then begin, dear lady: I'm listening. What therapeutic medication can your tongue give to me, so that my wounded heart may be healed and consoled through my ears?

FLORINDA Here it is: leave Love. For Love is nothing but venereal rage, poison that broods in our marrow, universal plague, irrational reason, bold timidity, tiresome pleasure, dark light, unsung glory, infirm health, painful remedy, and a dangerous path that leads us to the precipice of death.

LIDIA I want to follow Love, for Love is health that can never fall ill. It's vital poison, medicine that cures any disease, a sun that never sets, a moon that's never eclipsed, a paradise that looks like hell, and a road leading us to perpetual life.

FLORINDA Lady, leave Love. Do not forget that painters show us Love among prisons, chains, and knives, because it strips us of our freedom and gives us death.

LIDIA And yet painters show us Love among the Graces and adorned by stars, because Love is favorable to every grace, and shares amply in the goods of heaven.

FLORINDA Love is a pestilent worm that gnaws at the heart.

LIDIA If Love is a worm, it's a silkworm, whose small but honored mouth spins silk for us.

FLORINDA Love is a stagnant and putrid pool of water that plagues us with its stench.

LIDIA If Love is water, it's the Pactolus and the Achelous rivers, in whose beautiful translucent breast roll shifting sands of gold and silver.[liii]

FLORINDA Love is a poisoned shaft, whose wound is utterly deadly.

LIDIA Love is Achilles's spear, which, if it wounds, also heals you.[liv]

LIDIA Amor, com'aspide, la triaca forma, che d'ogni velenoso vizio ci purga e libera. Ohimè che veggio? Sostenetevi signora. Ah, ch'è veleno mortifero contra i rubelli suoi Amore; quindi avviene che d'Amor cotanto sparlasti, che per la lingua il veleno discendendo al cuore, cader ti fece nelle mie braccia, ond'or di te pietoso feretro fatta sono. O viso pallido, incenerito, com'or bram'io sotto quella guancia, rapir con baci quel fuoco d'Amore che v'ascondi, e tutto nel mio seno chiuderlo e conservarlo. Occhi belli, così chiusi par che nascondiate il sole, onde però tutto l'aere qui d'intorno sia tenebroso. O bocca dolce, dalla quale i rusignuoli apprendevano la dolcezza del canto, e le sfere celesti l'armonia celeste, com'or in silenzio rivolta, parmi che 'l mondo tutto in profondo silenzio ancor rivolto sia. Oh come al tuo cadermi nelle braccia, parmi che dal trono sia caduto Amore!

Amato peso io t'amo, e s'entro il vivo d'uno specchio rimirandomi ti movesti pietosa ad amarmi, e io nello specchio di questo essangue volto gli occhi fisando tutto ti dono il cuore, né più di Silvio ho pensiero che pensi.

FLORINDA Oh come alla vita ritornando, misera Florinda, dire e accertar sol puoi

"Che per calle d'Amore a morte vassi."

So, e come il tutto, alfine, vinca e abbatta Amore, onde ben il detto suona:

"O per tardi, o per tempo in uman cuore
vuol penetrar pur una volta Amore."

Sasselo questo cuor di ghiaccio, questo Rifeo nevoso, oggi fatto Mongibello d'amoroso fuoco. Ardo, ma l'ardor mio solo da voi, bellissimo viso, deriva; e questo incendio alor sostenni leggero ch'entro lucido vetro vi rimirai, e or io provo grave che vaga vi miro, che faconda v'ascolto. Dolgomi, perché piagata dallo strale degli occhi vostri io sono; e perché un solo bacio è 'l salutare empiastro ch'applicato delle labbra al di fuori, sana il cuor ferito al di dentro, per questo dalla vostra bocca di rose un sol bacio io chiedo.

LIDIA S'altro ch'un bacio non brama, sola medicina al suo male, uniamo petto a petto e bocca a bocca.

FLORINDA Love is a viper that turns a deaf ear to the discourse of reason.

LIDIA Love, like the viper, provides an antidote that purges and frees us of all poisonous vice. Oh dear, what's this I see? Stay on your feet, my lady. This is the deadly poison that Cupid uses on those who rebel against him: you criticized Love so outspokenly that the poison sank down from your tongue to your heart, and made you fall into my arms, turning me into your compassionate quiver. O ashen, pale face, how I long to steal with kisses the fire of Love hidden beneath your cheeks, and keep it and preserve it in my breast. O lovely eyes, so closed that they seem to hide the sun, and make the surrounding air grow dark and dim. O sweet mouth, from which the nightingales learned the sweetness of their song, and the celestial spheres their heavenly harmony, now that you've fallen silent, seemingly the whole world lies in deep silence. When you fell into my arms, o how it seemed to me that Cupid fell from his throne!

I love you, beloved burden. If, by gazing into the heart of the mirror and seeing me, you were moved mercifully to love me, and if I give you all my heart while fixing my eyes upon the mirror formed by your pale face, then I can have no further thought of Silvio.

FLORINDA O poor Florinda, in returning to life you may only say and confirm that
> "she goes to her death down the street of Love."[lv]

I well know that in the end Love conquers and defeats all. It's rightly said that:
> "in the human heart, early or late
> Love at last will penetrate."[lvi]

Strike, then, this heart of ice, this snow-bound summit, which today has become a volcano spewing flames of Love. I burn, but this burning comes only from you, most lovely countenance; and this fire, which seemed small when I gazed at you in the shining glass, now seems vast when I contemplate your beauty and listen to your eloquence. I suffer because I've been struck by the arrows of your eyes; and because a single kiss is the beneficial poultice which, when applied to my lips, heals the wounded heart deep inside of me. Hence I ask for a single kiss from your sweet pink mouth.

LIDIA If you long for nothing more than a kiss, as the only medicine

FLORINDA O mèle, o manna, ben siete amari appo quel dolce ch'oggi Florinda, ape celeste, ha succhiato da quelle rose con le quali s'inghirlanda Amore. Signora solo per lei, quando più era nemica d'Amore, serva d'Amor divenni; e mi dispongo solo per lei dolcemente languire; anzi le giuro, che in cara verginità vivendo, sprezzatrice sarò degli uomini tutti, per esser di Lidia sola seguitatrice.

LIDIA S'ella giurò per Lidia di non amar cosa ancor che bella, e io per Florinda giuro di disprezzar cose celesti ancora, diamoci la fede adunque di disprezzar tutti gli uomini e di noi sole far amorosa stima.

FLORINDA Io così con la mia cara Lidia giuro. Addio mia vita.

LIDIA Addio mio cuore, addio mio spirito, addio anima mia.

FLORINDA Addio.

LIDIA Addio, ma d'un breve addio.

Scena Seconda
[Sufronio, Orimberto, Mago]

SUFRONIO Ah, spione vituperoso, ti voglio morto!

ORIMBERTO Te ne menti, ch'io non sono spione, sono spurgator della patria. Aiuto, aiuto!

SUFRONIO Tu se' morto beccaccio.

MAGO Olà, olà? Si depongano l'armi, diasi luogo allo sdegno, se non per altro, almeno ad intercessione di colui che potrebbe accordar differenze celesti, nonché liti umane. So che voi siete insieme nemici battaglianti, perché Silvio vostro figliuolo, o signor Sufronio, è stato carcerato per accusazione fatta dal signor Orimberto.

for what ails you, then let us join breast to breast and mouth to mouth.

FLORINDA How bitter you taste, o honey, o manna, compared with the sweetness that Florinda, like a celestial bee, has sucked from the roses Cupid wears in his garland. Only for you, my lady, have I gone from being Love's greatest enemy to being his servant. And only for you am I disposed to languish sweetly. I swear to you that I'll despise all men, while holding my virginity dear to me, and will follow only Lidia.

LIDIA She swears to Lidia that she'll not love anything more lovely, and I swear to Florinda that I'd disdain for her sake even heavenly things. Let's promise one another that we'll despise all men and love only each other.

FLORINDA I swear it, my dear Lidia. Farewell, my love.

LIDIA Farewell, my heart and soul.

FLORINDA Farewell.

LIDIA Farewell, but only for a short while.

Scene Two
[Sufronio, Orimberto, Wizard]

SUFRONIO Ah, you despicable spy, I'll kill you!

ORIMBERTO You're lying: I'm not a spy, just someone who is cleansing our country. Help, help!

SUFRONIO You scum, you're a dead man.[lvii]

WIZARD Hey there, hey there! Put down your weapons and put aside your quarrel, for I'm interceding in this matter, accustomed as I am to harmonizing celestial differences as well as to resolving human disagreements. I know that you two are fierce enemies because, Sufronio, your son Silvio has been jailed after Orimberto accused him of wrongdoing.

SUFRONIO È vero signore.

MAGO Ma quello che fece, fece solo vinto da una trabocchevole passione amorosa, la qual però è degna di scusa, e non rea di biasmo.

ORIMBERTO È verissimo. Oh che grand'uomo; caro signore, chi siete voi?

MAGO Dirovvi, e sia fra noi. La professione mia è diferente da tutte l'altre, perché quanto più so, più m'ascondo. Né fo come il legista fastoso della sua tonica e 'l medico glorioso dell'eccellenza, ma opro segretissimamente facendo violenza all'aria, con adunar le nubi, cagionar le piogge, far udir tuoni, veder baleni e cavar folgori dalle mani di Giove. Fo fermare i fiumi, tremar la terra, camminar gli arbori; fermo le fugaci fere, e a dirvela signori, vi renderei or ora mutoli, ciechi, sordi e insensibili con una sol parola ch'io dicessi.

SUFRONIO Parli dunque meno, Vostra Signoria, che sia possibile.

MAGO "O—mi direte—Mago, in che consiste questa tua magia?" Vi rispondo che non è in altro che in saper la virtù primieramente delle cose naturali. Non dico l'ordinarie, come da un'erba cavarne il succo e l'olio, calcinare una pietra, cavar l'anima dai metalli e cose simili; ma il sapere a qual pianeta soggiacciano l'erbe, le pietre, i metalli; quali sieno l'ore dei pianeti, quali i loro caratteri e sufumigii, e quivi saper oprare con le materie a proposito, con le penne o d'upupa, o d'aquila, o di colomba, o d'uccelli notturni, o d'acquatici, scrivendo o 'n carta, o in embrioni, o 'n pelli non nate, o sul nero ippomane, o su le lamine, o 'n simili materie, e basta.

ORIMBERTO Signor Sufronio, che belle cose.

SUFRONIO Più bella sarebbe se vi facessi portar via dal gran diavolo.

ORIMBERTO Ci tetto io in queste cose. Ma a che servono caro signore queste ultime cose dette?

SUFRONIO This, sir, is true.

WIZARD But he did what he did only because he was overcome by an excess of amorous passion, which deserves pardon rather than blame.

ORIMBERTO Most truly spoken. What a great man you are, dear sir: but who are you?

WIZARD I'll tell you both, but it has to be kept between us alone. My profession differs from all others, because the more I know the more I must hide. I'm not like a lawyer pompously dressed in his robes, nor like a skilled doctor who revels in his renown. Instead I work in the greatest secrecy, doing violence to the very air; I gather clouds, make rain fall, cause thunder-claps and flashes of lightning; I steal lightning bolts right out of Jove's own hands. I stop rivers from flowing; I make the earth tremble and the trees walk; I stop elusive wild beasts dead in their tracks. Let me tell you, dear sirs, that with a single word I could right now strike you deaf, dumb, blind, and unconscious.

SUFRONIO Speak then, sir, as little as possible.

WIZARD You may well ask me, "Wizard, what's your magic made of?" I'll answer that it consists of nothing more than knowing the primary virtues of the things of nature. I'm not talking about ordinary things, such as how to extract the oil and essence of herbs, how to ignite stone, or how to purify metals and other things of that sort. I mean the knowledge of which planets influence herbs, stones, and metals; or which hours belong to what planets, and what are the characteristics and vapors of those planets. I mean, then, knowing how to work with these materials, and to write about them with quills made from the feathers of hoopoe birds, eagles, doves, night-birds, or water-birds, using sheets made of paper, metal, the skin of unborn animals, hippomanes, or similar things.[lviii]

ORIMBERTO My good Sufronio, what amazing things.

SUFRONIO They'd be still more amazing if they made the devil take you.

ORIMBERTO I can really get into this stuff. Tell me, dear sir, what do

MAGO Vi dirò. Servono per saper cose occulte d'un vostro nemico, d'una donna amata, d'un amico absente, d'un principe adirato, per far amarvi, per poner odi, per trovar cose nascoste, furti, tradimenti, tesori, per vie che sarà impossibile a conoscerle. Con un fumo ascendente, o rotto o sparso, un turbine di vento, un volar d'uccelli, un garrito degl'istessi, un cadimento di pietra, una persona trovata a sorte, un nome considerato, vi farò veder cose che direte: "Questi è un Pietro d'Abano, un Cieco d'Ascoli, e uno istesso Zorovastro inventor dell'arte."

SUFRONIO Sì che per ciò ancor sapete i fatti nostri, dovete ancor sapere com'ho un cattiv'animo di bastonar colui.

MAGO Cheto, cheto signore, io or ora accommoderò il tutto. Ho qui sotto il mio libro, eccolo; e 'n questo istesso ancor sono i caratteri, i pentacoli, le clavicule, gli almadel, il coltello col debito manico, e porto meco nel cuore quello, che più importa, ch'ho promesso alla Sibilla nell'alta montagna.

ORIMBERTO Siete un grand'uomo.

MAGO Fate entrambi pace, ch'io signor Sufronio vi prometto il figliuol prima che venga il nuovo giorno.

SUFRONIO Così mi promette il suo gran sapere, ecco fo la pace.

ORIMBERTO E io fo lo stesso, domandandovi perdono; i' ho ciecamente operato; cieco fui, perché cieco è ancor Amore; e quant'egli manca negli occhi, io nella lingua ho questo giorno abbondato, per accusar vostro figliuolo.

SUFRONIO Di questo più non mi ricordo, e me n'entro.

MAGO Signor Orimberto, prendete questo anello. Questo nel dito posto, ha forza di farvi benevolo a qualunque persona vi parlerà; però è d'avvertire s'avete ottone addosso, fuor che quello col quale avete serrate le stringhe.

you do with the last things you just mentioned?

WIZARD I'll tell you. They allow you to learn the secrets of your enemy, of a woman that you love, of a far-off friend, or of an angry prince. They can make you be loved, or create hatred between others, or find hidden things; they can be used to discover thefts, betrayals, or treasures; and all of this is done in ways that would be impossible to know. I'll show you things that will make you say: "Here is a very master of his art!"[lix] And all because I can interpret such things as rising smoke when it breaks up or fans out, a whirlwind, birds in flight, falling rocks, the twittering of the birds, a chance encounter with someone, or the name of a highly regarded person.

SUFRONIO Since you thus know all about our affairs, you must also know that I've a mind to beat that fellow with a stick.

WIZARD Calm down, sir, and in an instant I'll make everything right. I have here my book; there it is. This same volume contains magical characters, pentacles, *grimoires*, the *almadel*, and a knife with a specially made handle.[lx] In my heart I keep the most important thing of all, which I promised to the Sybil high in the mountains.[lxi]

ORIMBERTO You're indeed a great man.

WIZARD Make your peace. I promise, Sufronio, to restore your son to you before the new day dawns.

SUFRONIO If your great wisdom can promise me this, then I stand ready to make peace.

ORIMBERTO And, asking your forgiveness, I'll do the same. I acted blindly: I was blind because Love is blind, but if his eyes lack sight, my tongue worked all too well that day in accusing your son.

SUFRONIO I've forgotten all about it, and am going home now.

WIZARD Orimberto, take this ring.[lxii] When you put it on your finger, it has the power to make you liked by whomever you speak with. You must not, however, wear anything made of brass, except for eye-holes.

ORIMBERTO No signore.

MAGO Or andate sicuro e portatemi la risposta.

ORIMBERTO Vada felice. Quest'è un grand'uomo, e sotto il suo gran sapere, anch'io camminando, batto alla casa della mia cruda Lidia.

Scena Terza
[Lidia, Orimberto]

LIDIA E pur signor Orimberto mi venite ad infastidire. Che volete? Ho fatto giuramento di non solo non ascoltare, ma di non voler veder gli uomini.

ORIMBERTO E perché questo signora?

LIDIA Caro signore non mi rompete il capo.

ORIMBERTO La poverina non sa che or ora, mi correrà nelle braccia. Anello in tuono!

LIDIA O signor Orimberto, parlate da voi com'i pazzi, non è vero?

ORIMBERTO Signora, m'avete invitato al mio giuoco chiamandomi pazzo (così ragionando darò tempo all'anello che operi). Meglio a me sarà l'esser pazzo che savio; poiché se come savio mi scacciate, m'insegnate quasi di far il pazzo così dicendo: "Accostati, abbracciami, fa' il balordo, che spesso s'ottiene scherzando quello che giamai s'averebbe chiedendo." Così farò adunque. Signora accetto l'invito.

LIDIA Avvertite signor Orimberto, che i pazzi reali ponno esser da tutti lapidati, staffilati, bastonati e legati; là onde, se come tale farete insolenze, incorrerete in gravissimi errori, e io sarò la prima a farvi legare. Se poi sarete scoperto per pazzo vizioso, essend'io saggia e onesta, si convertirà il bastone in spada.

ORIMBERTO Anello, tu stai tanto; opera, se tu vuoi. A che dunque darmi tal consiglio addescandomi con quel nome di pazzo? Le parole di Vostra Signoria sono di donna, e le parole di donna si debbano pigliar per consiglio quando sono le prime; quind'ha che l'Ariosto

ORIMBERTO I won't.

WIZARD Now go and bring me back an answer.

ORIMBERTO Go in peace. This is a great man, and I move within the orbit of his great knowledge. I'll knock at my cruel Lidia's door.

Scene Three
[Lidia, Orimberto]

LIDIA So you've come to bother me, Orimberto? What do you want? I've vowed not only never to listen to men, but never to look at them.

ORIMBERTO And why so, my lady?

LIDIA Dear sir, don't annoy me.

ORIMBERTO The poor little thing doesn't know that she's about to fall into my arms. Ring, get to work!

LIDIA Master Orimberto, you're talking to yourself like a madman!

ORIMBERTO My lady, you've played right into my hands by calling me mad (by talking like this, I'll give the ring time to do its work). Better for me to be mad than wise. For if you reject me as a wise man, then you seem to be saying to me that I should act the madman. In fact, it's almost as if you were saying, "Come to me and take me in your arms, you big idiot: often you get by joking what you would never have gotten by asking." So that's exactly what I'll do. Madam, I accept your offer.

LIDIA Be warned, Orimberto, that true madmen can be stoned, flogged, beaten, and put in irons by anyone. If you play the insolent madman with me, you're making a very serious mistake, and I'll be the first to see you in chains. Since I'm wise and honest, if you turn out to be a dangerous madman I'll have to change my stick into a sword.

ORIMBERTO Ring, you're still here with me, right? Would you please get to work? To what end, my lady, do you tell me this, while trying to label me "mad?" Your ladyship speaks with a woman's tongue, and a

disse:

> "Molti consigli delle donne sono
> meglio improviso, che pensarvi usciti."

Dicami dunque, poiché realmente pazzo m'ha detto, che volete dire? Forse P. povero, A. amante, Z. zelante, Z. zefiro, O. odoroso?

Cioè ch'io sia povero di spirito, appresso Vostra Signoria mi conosce per A. amante Z. zelante dell'amor suo, Z. zefiro, cioè vento piacevole, che non vengo a lei con asprezza, ma qual vento O. odoroso spirante solo onestà, lealtà, fedeltà e amor degno veramente di lode.

LIDIA *"Tutto al contrario l'istoria converti."* Pazzo vuol dir P. poveraccio, A. amante Z. zotico, Z. zazaruto, O. orgoglioso. Andate in malora, m'intendete voi?

Scena Quarta
[Florinda, Bernetta, Lidia, Orimberto]

FLORINDA Bernetta, tu non vedi.

BERNETTA Uh, uh, Pasquino.

ORIMBERTO Le malore le numerano quelli che hanno il mal francese, e non persone sane com'io sono. Guardate qua come son disposto.

LIDIA Saldo, saldo.

FLORINDA Eh, ch'a questo ballo ci manca il suono, una...

BERNETTA Dua.

ORIMBERTO Ohimè signore che fate, errate signore, errate; non son io, non son io.

FLORINDA O cara signora Lidia, l'abbraccio e bacio. Bernetta serra l'uscio bene che questa notte non verrò a casa. Servitrice signor Orimberto, addio.

LIDIA Servitrice signor Orimberto, addio.

woman's words should be taken as counsel only when they're the first to be spoken. Ariosto says:

> "Much advice given by women is
> Better if sudden rather than thought through."[lxiii]

Tell me then, since you've said that I'm truly mad, what you mean by that. Perhaps you're saying: "*M.* marvelous *A.* adorable *D.* delicious?"

That is to say, that I'm marvelous and that you know me to be *A.* adorable and *D.* delicious, like a sweet treat I bring to you as proof of my honesty, loyalty, fidelity, and praiseworthy love for you.

LIDIA As Ariosto also says: "The story turned out quite to the contrary."[lxiv] So let me make myself clear. "Mad" means *M.* malodorous *A.* asinine *D.* degenerate. Now go to the devil, do you hear?

Scene Four
[Florinda, Bernetta, Lidia, Orimberto]

FLORINDA Do you see that, Bernetta?

BERNETTA Uh oh: speak of the devil.

ORIMBERTO A fine healthy fellow like me doesn't have such defects: do I look like I have syphilis or something? Look at what a great body I've got.

LIDIA Rock-hard, all right.

FLORINDA What's missing from this dance is the music. One…

BERNETTA Two… [*they beat him with sticks*]

ORIMBERTO Ow, ladies, what are you doing? You're making a mistake, you're making a mistake! I'm not the one, I'm not the one.

FLORINDA My dear lady, I greet you with hugs and kisses. Bernetta, shut tight the front door, as I'm not coming home tonight. Ever your humble servant, master Orimberto. Farewell.

LIDIA Ever your humble servant, master Orimberto. Farewell.

BERNETTA Servitrice signor Orimberto, addio.

ORIMBERTO Andate in malora brutte lupacce. Com'hanno menate ben le mani schiena mia! E pur ho l'anello, non già della benivolenza, ma della malevolenza, anzi l'anello vera calamita da bastoni.

Scena Quinta
[Mago, Orimberto]

MAGO Non è l'anello che sia privo di virtù, né la mia fronte di sapere, ma è solo perché nel vostro capo non è cervello.

ORIMBERTO Ah, per mia fé, per questo la signora Lidia mi disse pazzo.

MAGO E pazzo siete, poiché io vi domandai se altro metallo avevate addosso che quello delle stringhe, e mi diceste di no.

ORIMBERTO Ah, che avete ragione, ho il rame di quattro fontanelle, e me l'era dimenticato.

MAGO Per questo l'anello non ha operato. Orsù alle brevi, vadano queste linee al punto, corrano questi torrenti al mare; datemi l'anello, pigliate questo tulpante alla turchesca, questa veste bianca a nere lune, questo libro, e questa verga, e questa candeletta; e alor che sentirete la prim'ora di notte, ponetevi la veste e 'l tulpante, e disteso con la pancia in su per terra, leggerete alla prima carta segnata; poi verso le due ore uscite di casa, venite in questo luogo avanti la porta della vostra morosa, e leggendo in voci sonore dov'è segnato nel secondo luogo, comparsa la vostra diva, battete tre volte sopra quella cosa dove sarà, e poi conducetela al vostro appartamento che sarete contento; ma arricordatevi di percuoter tre volte quella cosa nella quale sarà Lidia. Addio.

ORIMBERTO Umilissimo servo suo. Or vederai, semplicetta Lidia, se pazzo o savio io sono. Ecco qua il tulpante, la veste a lune, il libro, la verga, la candeletta, e so benissimo quel che far debbo: all'un'ora mi vesto, mi getto con la pancia in su, leggo, mi rizzo in piedi, torno in questo luogo, leggo di nuovo; venuta Lidia, percuoto tre volte quella cosa dove sarà il mio bene, la porto a casa e l'ingravido. Notte, oh, così ti voglio tenebrosa; né mi curo io per le tue ombre dover penetrare,

BERNETTA Ever your humble servant, master Orimberto. Farewell.

ORIMBERTO The devil take you, you nasty she-wolves. My poor aching back! I have to admit they handed me quite a thrashing. Yet I've got the ring, which attracts not benevolence but malevolence. This ring is none other than a magnet for beatings.

Scene Five
[Wizard, Orimberto]

WIZARD It isn't that the ring lacks power or that I lack knowledge: it's just that you haven't got any brains in your head.

ORIMBERTO Good heavens, that's why Lidia called me mad.

WIZARD And you are mad, since I asked you if you were wearing any other metal except in the eye-holes of your clothing, and you told me "no."

ORIMBERTO You're right, I'd entirely forgotten that I have four fountains' worth of coins on me.[lxv]

WIZARD That's why the ring didn't work. Come on, let's get to the matter at hand. May these lines reach the point of intersection, may these streams run to the sea. Give me back the ring, and instead take this Turkish turban, this white robe with black moons on it, this book, this staff, and this candle. When you hear the bells ring one o'clock at night, put on the robe and the turban. Lie face-down on the floor, and read the first marked passage. Then at around two o'clock go outside, come back here to this place in front of your beloved's house, and read aloud the second marked passage. When your beloved appears, knock three times upon the thing in which you find her, and then lead her to your rooms, where you'll find happiness. Remember to knock three times upon the thing in which you'll find Lidia. Farewell.

ORIMBERTO Ever your most humble servant. Now you'll see, foolish little Lidia, if I'm wise or mad. Here are the turban, the robe with moons on it, the book, the staff, and the candle. I know exactly what to do: at one o'clock I'll get dressed, throw myself face-down on the floor, read, get up on my feet, come back here, and read again. Once Lidia

purché per quelle io pervenga al mio sole.

Scena Sesta
[Lelio, Granello]

LELIO Queste, o Granello, sono le tenebre desiderate, questo il luogo, questa la ghirlanda ch'ho in capo, questo il libro, questa la verga, e questa la candela accesa, che tu hai nella mano.

GRANELLO Signor padrone, non ho più gambe sotto questo corpo, non ho più cuore dentro questo petto; io tremo tutto; bu, bu, bu.

LELIO O privo appunto di cuore, così temi?

GRANELLO Ma sì, a chi la tocca ha bel dire! Ma io, che non ho da far nulla in questo, domine ad quid?

LELIO Alza quella mano.

GRANELLO Non ho più forza.

LELIO Alza quella mano dico.

GRANELLO E quale, che ho perduto così il cervello che non so più quante mani io m'abbi addosso.

LELIO E ch'hai le mani di Gige e di Briareo, che ti dimentichi il numero? Alza quella mano dico.

GRANELLO Non è più mano, chè un pezzo di ghiaccio, vedete com'ho freddo, bu, bu, bu. Dicono che a casa il diavolo cè un gran caldo, e io ho un grandissimo freddo; bu, bu, bu.

LELIO Se non fusse per non so che, ti vorrei con un pezzo di legno tutto scaldare.

appears, I'll knock three times on the thing bearing my beloved, then I'll take her home with me and make her pregnant. O night, I want you to be dark: I'm not afraid to penetrate your shadows, if through them I can come together with my sun.

Scene Six
[Lelio, Granello]

LELIO Granello, here's the darkness I desire, here's the place, here's the wreath on my head, here's the book, here's the staff, and here in your hand is the burning candle.

GRANELLO Master, my legs are giving out beneath me, my heart has stopped beating in my breast, and I'm shaking all over. Brrrr, brrrr, brrrr.

LELIO You coward, what are you scared of?

GRANELLO Sure, that's easy for you to say, since this is for your benefit! But since I don't have anything to do with it, I can ask: "O Lord, to what end?"[lxvi]

LELIO Raise your hand.

GRANELLO I haven't the strength.

LELIO Raise your hand, I said.

GRANELLO Which one? I've so completely lost my mind that I don't know how many hands I have anymore.

LELIO What do you think, that you've got as many hands as the giants Briareus and Gyges, and have lost track of the number?[lxvii] Raise *that* hand, I say.

GRANELLO That's not a hand but a chunk of ice. Look how cold I am: brrrr, brrrr, brrrr. They say that at home the devil gets damn hot, but I'm freezing cold instead: brrrr, brrrr, brrrr.

LELIO If it wasn't for I don't know what reason, I'd surely like to warm

GRANELLO Signore, potreste bastonar quanto voleste, perch'io non sentirei né fuoco né fiamma, poscia che per la paura ho tutta la carne morta.

LELIO Orsù sta' cheto.

GRANELLO Posso bene star cheto, ma non già restar di tremar vedete, bu, bu, bu.

LELIO Se tu non fosti obligato e sforzato a tener questa candela accesa, già t'avrei lasciato partire.

GRANELLO Oh quanto sarebbe assai meglio! Vedete, il diavolo è come la scimmia, com'ella vede che tu hai paura ti salta addosso.

LELIO Sta' allegramente.

GRANELLO Come quelli che vanno alla forca, giusto, giusto, e peggio; poich'il mio boia è 'l diavolo. Oh s'io m'innamoro mai, castratemi! Cominciate di grazia, e arricordatevi di toccar con la verga la pancia alla signora Florinda.

LELIO Quella cosa...

GRANELLO Dico ben la cosa.

LELIO Quale?

GRANELLO Quella che va toccata.

LELIO Quella cosa dove sarà dentro.

GRANELLO Signor sì, la cosa, e 'l dentro.

LELIO Lo mi ricordo. Io comincio.

GRANELLO Ohimè.

you with a piece of wood.

GRANELLO Master, you can beat me all you want to. I can't feel either fire or flame, because my whole body is numb with fright.

LELIO Come on now, keep quiet.

GRANELLO I can certainly keep quiet, but I can't stop trembling. See? Brrrr, brrrr, brrrr.

LELIO I would've already let you go if your presence wasn't required to hold this burning candle.

GRANELLO How much better that would've been! The devil is like a monkey, you know: when a monkey sees you're afraid, that's when it jumps on you.

LELIO Don't be so concerned.

GRANELLO Oh right, right, like a condemned man on his way to the gallows, and even worse, since my hangman is the devil himself. Listen, if I ever fall in love, have me castrated! Please go ahead and start: don't forget to touch Florinda's belly with the staff.

LELIO That thing…

GRANELLO I just said "the thing."

LELIO Which one?

GRANELLO The one that has to be touched.

LELIO That thing that she'll be inside of.

GRANELLO Yes sir, that thing, and what's inside it.

LELIO Now I remember. I'll start.

GRANELLO Ohmygod.

LELIO Che hai?

GRANELLO Cominciate, e non lo dite, che mi fate rinforzar il freddo; bu, bu, bu.

LELIO O Granello per antonomasiam!

GRANELLO Quasi testicolo eh, e per questo vi sto appiccato, né senza me potete far la cosa, toccar la cosa, e portar a casa la cosa, cioè questa Florinda.

LELIO Tu amor treschi, eh!

GRANELLO Eh sì, non ne ho tantino, tantino di voglia. Cominciate, perché l'andar tanto in lungo col diavolo ha del pericoloso.

LELIO   Luminose del ciel stelle fiammanti,
  che soggiacete a la possanza maga,
  favoritrici di scontenti amanti,
  per donna a l'altrui mal rigida, e vaga;
    per quanti fece Arfasat incanti
  sia di Lelio salute omai la piaga,
  portate quasi stral, quasi baleno,
  la Florinda sognante a Lelio in seno.

GRANELLO Ohimè, che terremoto, la terra mi balla sotto e' piedi.

LELIO Buon cuore, buon cuore.

Scena Settima
[Griffo e Orco, Marinari, Lelio e Granello, Florinda nella cassa]

GRIFFO Eccoci Lelio amante,
  ricevi quel, che ti portiamo avante;

ORCO Prendilo, o Lelio, tosto,
  mira il tesor che qui dimora ascosto.

LELIO What is it?

GRANELLO Go on and start, but don't tell me, because you're just going to make me feel even colder. Brrrr, brrrr, brrrr.

LELIO You're just like what your name means in Italian: a tiny insignificant little speck.

GRANELLO Sure, but don't forget my name has more than one meaning. In fact I'm also just like a bull's balls, and that's why I'm hanging so close to you. Indeed, without me you wouldn't be able to do the thing, touch the thing, or take the thing—that is, Florinda—home with you.

LELIO You're the expert in love affairs, eh?

GRANELLO Well, yes, even if my desire for it isn't much at this point. Go on and start, for there's danger in lingering too long with the devil.

LELIO   Stars of heaven burning bright,
        Who will yield to magic's powers,
        Favor a lover in his sad plight:
        A lady indifferent to his suffering hours.
                By the web of spells Arfasat once wove tight,
        Let Lelio's wound heal now, let her be ours;
        Bring Florinda like an arrow or flash of light
        Dreaming into Lelio's arms tonight.

GRANELLO Oh Lord, it's an earthquake: the earth is moving under my feet.

LELIO Be brave, be brave.

Scene Seven
[Griffon, Ogre, Sailors, Lelio, Granello, Florinda in the chest]

GRIFFON Here is Lelio the lover:
        Take what we're handing over.[lxviii]

OGRE Take it, Lelio, do not fear
        To see the treasure hidden here.

LELIO Buon cuore, son marinari.

GRANELLO Dico che son diavoli navali e acquaiuoli.

GRIFFO Orco.

ORCO Griffo che vuoi?

GRIFFO Voglio ch'al mar n'andiamo.

ORCO Lelio, addio ti lasciamo.

GRIFFO Granello, ci partiamo.

GRANELLO Quam primum. Or via, di grazia aprite; cavate voi di quella cassa coperta di ricco tappeto, quello che v'è dentro, che dai calzoni caverò poi anche io quello che ci ho posto dentro, ch'è poco poco.

LELIO Io apro.

GRANELLO Affé moroso, c'avete paura ancor voi.

LELIO Io apro.

GRANELLO Oh via finitela!

LELIO Che dici tu?

GRANELLO È che m'accorgo ben io che vi cacate addosso. Aprirò io.

LELIO Sì, sì.

GRANELLO Io apro.

LELIO Buon animo, buon animo.

GRANELLO Che dite?

LELIO Che tu apra.

LELIO Be brave, they're sailors.

GRANELLO I say they're naval or aquatic devils.

GRIFFON Ogre.

OGRE What do you want, Griffon?

GRIFFON I want us to go down to the sea.

OGRE Farewell, Lelio, we're leaving.

GRIFFON Granello, we're going.

GRANELLO Not soon enough.[lxix] Now please, go on and open it; from that chest draped in a fine carpet, take what's inside. And I'm going to take out of my trousers what I put inside them, which isn't much.

LELIO I'm opening it.

GRANELLO Forsooth, boyfriend, you're scared too.

LELIO I'm opening it.

GRANELLO Come on, get it over with.

LELIO What's that you say?

GRANELLO That I can see you're shitting in your pants. I'll open it.

LELIO Yes, yes.

GRANELLO I'm opening it.

LELIO Courage, courage.

GRANELLO What's that you say?

LELIO That you should open it.

GRANELLO Io apro.

LELIO E mai non apri.

GRANELLO E così due volte avete fatto voi giusto, giusto; oh, aprite voi se volete Florinda.

LELIO Ecco aperto; Granello.

GRANELLO Che c'è, alcun intrico?

LELIO Ecco il mio bene che dorme.

GRANELLO Oh, cacciatevi in quella cassa e lasciate ch'io vi ci serri, e poi che si svegli a sua posta c'averà un bel dir: "Lelio fatti in là." Rizziamla un poco. Oh, come dorme profondo! Vedete come sta in gesto quasi dicente:
>   "Lelio, che stai tu a fare?
>   Su, viemmi a misurare."

LELIO O Florinda mio bene, mira, mira come s'altra volta mi fuggisti, al presente come stabile se' nelle mie braccia; questa è pur quella bella bocca che livida per lo sdegno mi discacciò, e ora vermiglia nel sonno stando in bel gesto, par ch'a sé con dolci baci m'inviti. Or tu se' mia preda alfine.

GRANELLO Non tante parole; alla generazione, alla generazione, ch'io mi sento, come Granello, patire; ma voi avete tanto del granello che di me non vi curate. Serrate questa cassa, copriamla con questo tappeto e portiamla a casa nostra.

LELIO Ohimè questa cassa dai capi non ha que' manichi, o campanelle di ferro, ch'hanno l'altre, e però sarà al portarla difficile.

GRANELLO A casa il diavolo non si dee lavorar di magnano.

LELIO Granello, benché il mago Arfasat c'abbia detto che nel tempo che saremo impiegati nell'incanto non verrà persona qui d'intorno, non per questo voglio che tanto ci fidiamo. Guarda un poco.

GRANELLO I'm opening it.

LELIO But you never seem to do it.

GRANELLO And that's exactly what you did twice. Oh, open it yourself if you want Florinda.

LELIO It's open. Granello!

GRANELLO Is there some problem?

LELIO Here lies my love asleep.

GRANELLO Oh, go on, jump into the chest and let me close the two of you in there. If she wakes up she'll have a hard time saying, "Move over, Lelio." Let's straighten her out a bit. How deeply she sleeps! It almost seems as if she were trying to say with her gestures:
>Lelio, what's your pleasure?
>Come to me and take my measure.

LELIO Florinda my love, although you fled from me last time, see now how I hold you firmly in my arms. This is the same lovely mouth that, livid with disdain, drove me away. Yet now, in your sleep, it has turned scarlet red and inviting, and seems to be calling to me to come to it with sweet kisses. At last I have you at my mercy.

GRANELLO Don't talk so much. Hurry up and get to procreating, because your insignificant little Granello is suffering here. You, on the other hand, now have such bull's balls that you're not thinking about me in the least. Close the chest: let's cover it with this carpet and take it to our house.

LELIO Oh heavens, this chest—unlike most—doesn't have any handles or iron grips on its ends. It's going to be hard to carry.

GRANELLO The devil mustn't work at home as an ironsmith.

LELIO Granello, although the wizard Arfasat told us that while we were casting the spell no one would come near here, that's not a good reason for us to take him entirely at his word. Go have a look around.

GRANELLO Egli è scuro, e questo candelino fatto di graso di rana è oramai finito, e però vi do per consiglio che caviam fuor della cassa Florinda, e portarla un pezzo per uno in braccio.

LELIO Ottimo è 'l consiglio.

ORCO, GRIFFO [*Salteranno fuor così cantando e danzando.*]
      Che fate, che fate,
pensosi, pensosi,
pigliate, pigliate
i frutti amorosi.
      Non siate ritrosi,
s'avete l'amate,
nel farvi contenti
amanti dolenti,
cavate, cavate.

GRANELLO   O voce gentile,
o grate parole,
o suono sottile
qual raggio di sole;
      quello che vuole
il Mago facciamo
tra queste facelle
d'altissime stelle,
caviamo, caviamo.

LELIO Tiriamo questa cassa nel mezo di questa strada, e poscia caviamo Florinda. Ohimè, ohimè!

GRANELLO Salva, salva!

LELIO Fuggi, fuggi!

GRANELLO Corri, corri! Oh poveretto me, sono spiritato!

[*Qui salterà uno spirito fuor della cassa, dietro la scena facendosi co'piedi strepito di molti in foggia di terremoto finché tutti saran fuggiti del palco, e le cantonate tutte getteran fuoco, sì che nell'entrar degli spaventati incontrino nelle fiamme, e così sarà piacevolissimo il fine.*]

GRANELLO It's dark, and this little candle made of frog fat is used up. I'd advise that we take Florinda out of the chest and take turns carrying her in our arms.

LELIO An excellent idea.

OGRE, GRIFFON [*They leap out, singing and dancing.*]
>   What are you doing,
>   Do you need a good shove?
>   Worrywarts, worrywarts,
>   Take, take the fruits of love.
>   Don't be shy, don't doubt
>   That she's yours and no other's,
>   O suffering lovers,
>   Take her out, take her out.

GRANELLO   O kind voice,
>   O welcome word,
>   O how I rejoice
>   In what I've just heard;
>   By the Wizard's beard,
>   Now to end all doubt,
>   Amidst the light
>   Of stars in flight
>   We'll take her out, we'll take her out.[lxx]

LELIO Let's haul this chest into the middle of the street and then pull out Florinda. Oh no! Oh dear!

GRANELLO Run for your life, run for your life!

LELIO Let's get out of here!

GRANELLO Run, run! Poor me, I'm possessed!

[*Here a spirit leaps out of the chest. Behind the backdrop the others should stomp their feet on the floor to make it sound like an earthquake until the players have run off stage. The street corners will throw off flames which the panicking players will come up against, and thus the end of this scene will be most delightful.*]

Scena Ottava
[Guerindo, Coradella]

GUERINDO Era assai tenebroso l'aere, e or sono comparse nel cielo così lucide le stelle, che par ben certo che il cielo stesso apra gli occhi, vago di mirar i miei amorosi contenti.

CORADELLA Non solo vorrei che qui fossero tutti gli occhi del cielo, ma tutti quelli degli uomini, perché non saressimo noi duo così soletti, né io sarei così pieno di spavento. Alfin ci siamo.

GUERINDO Ecco la ghirlanda, il libro, la verga, e tu hai la candela. Lasciami dar principio.

CORADELLA Signor s'arricordi di toccar quella cosa dove sarà la vostra signora Florinda dentro; e questo vi ricordo perché si dice che 'l diavolo fa perder il cervello; sì che, l'incanto andando alla rovescia, non fussimo tutti maltrattati. Vedete, il diavolo non vuol amicizia d'alcuno, salvo che della diavolissima signoria sua; anzi egli è com'il gatto, il quale giuoca, giuoca un pezzo col topo, e poi li dà la schiacciata.

GUERINDO Lascia pur il carico a me dell'incanto.

CORADELLA E a me quello della paura.

GUERINDO Ecco il libro aperto, ed ecco aperta la via alle mie felicità; tien salda quella candeletta.

CORADELLA Oh, se mi disimbroglio!

GUERINDO   O dell'oscuro e paventoso regno
    gran monarca, che scettro hai di bidente,
    a questi accenti miei frangi lo sdegno,
    fammi lieto in amor, sono dolente,
        di Guerindo Arfasat l'unico segno
    li promette Florinda in mantinente,
    tu ch'ubidisci a circoli, e scongiuri,
    mandami il sol per via di nembi oscuri.

Scene Eight
[Guerindo, Coradella]

GUERINDO The night air was quite dark before, but now the stars are shining so brightly that it seems certain the heavens themselves have opened their eyes, wishing to gaze upon my amorous pleasures.

CORADELLA I wish not only that all the eyes of the heavens, but those of men as well, were pointed here. That way we wouldn't be all alone, just the two of us, and I wouldn't be so scared. At last we're here.

GUERINDO Here are the wreath, the book, the staff, and you have the candle. Let me get started.

CORADELLA Remember, sir, to touch that thing in which your lady Florinda will be. I'm only reminding you because they say that the devil makes you lose your head, and if the spell were to be cast in the wrong order, we might subject ourselves to abuse. You see, the devil doesn't want anyone's friendship other than that of his own diabolical self. He's like a cat that plays and plays with a mouse before striking the fatal blow.

GUERINDO Leave it to me to deal with the spell.

CORADELLA And leave it to me to deal with fear.

GUERINDO Here's the open book, and now the way is open to my happiness. Hold that candle still.

CORADELLA Oh, if only I could get out of this!

GUERINDO   O great lord, over the dark and fearful plain
     With your two-pronged scepter you reign.
     With these words put aside your disdain,
     Make me happy in love, for I'm in pain.
        To Guerindo Arfasat has made one sign:
     He has promised that Florinda will be mine.
     You, whom circles and exorcisms will obey,
     Send me the sun without the light of day.[lxxi]

Scena Nona
[Menippo e Cruone facchini, Lelio, Coradella, Guerindo, la Morte]

MENIPPO Ecco Menippo.

CRUONE   Ed eccovi Cruone,
che vi portano il sacco
né si tema di scherzo, over d'acciacco.

CORADELLA Chi son questi signor Guerindo? Coradella non ha più cuore.

GUERINDO Sono spiriti.

CORADELLA Se non sono aerei, non ho paura, poiché la mia navità dice ch'ho da morir in arica. Ma questo terremoto ch'ha fatto nel comparire, mi fa ancor tremar le budella.

MENIPPO   Su prendete prendete
de l'amata godete.

CRUONE   Qui Menippo e Cruone
vi lasciano all'inferno
dannati in sempiterno.

CORADELLA Signor Guerindo, ecco là il sacco per voi, ed ecco questa strada per me. Addio.

GUERINDO Olà dico io, così il tuo padrone osservi?

CORADELLA Anzi molto v'osservo, e per questo non essendo degno di star a tu per tu in gravi cose con voi, qui solo vi lascio.

GUERINDO Fermati dico.

CORADELLA Dite pur il vero, avete più paura di me, non è così?

Scene Nine

[Menippus and Cruon, porters;
Lelio, Coradella, Guerindo, Death]

MENIPPUS Here's Menippus.

CRUON And here's Cruon,
Who for you will carry the sack,
With no joking, and no holding back.

CORADELLA Master Guerindo, who are these fellows? Coradella's courage is gone.

GUERINDO They're spirits.

CORADELLA If they're not spirits of the air, then I'm not afraid, since my horoscope says that I'll die in the air. But the earthquake that spirit made when he appeared has my insides still shaking.

MENIPPUS Go on, take her, take her,
In your beloved take your pleasure.

CRUON Menippus and Cruon
Now might as well
Leave you forever
Damned to hell.

CORADELLA Master Guerindo, here's the sack for you, and there's the road for me. Farewell.

GUERINDO I say there, is that how you respect your master?

CORADELLA I respect you highly indeed, and since I'm not worthy of being your intimate companion in such serious matters, I'll leave you here alone.

GUERINDO Stop right there, I say.

CORADELLA Tell the truth: you're more scared than I am, aren't you?

GUERINDO Guerindo è nato alle guerre.

CORADELLA Ma non a quella del diavolo, che per murione ha due cornacce, tanto lunghe.

GUERINDO O vita mia, colà dentro è 'l mio bene.

CORADELLA Il ciel voglia, che non ci sia il nostro commune male.

GUERINDO Sento quella calamita di cuori ch'a lei dolcemente mi tira.

CORADELLA E io provo tutto al contrario, poich'ho una voglia di fuggire straordinaria.

GUERINDO Vengo, vengo mio bene.

CORADELLA E vien solo, ch'io non so movermi di qui.

GUERINDO Guarda se vien alcuno.

CORADELLA Guardate pur voi a quello ch'ha da uscire dal sacco.

GUERINDO La bella Venere dormiente.

CORADELLA Che non sia Rabuino vigilante.

GUERINDO Ecco disciolto il nodo. Ecco discopro quella massa d'oro arricciato. Ohimè, ohimè!

CORADELLA Salva, salva!

GUERINDO La Morte, la Morte!

MORTE Sì che son la Morte; sì, sì, sì.

CORADELLA A testa pelata! A culo senza natiche! Ohimè, ohimè! Arrivederci a casa il diavolo.

[*Qui con lo stesso ordine le strade tutte getteran fuoco, e di più quattro vestiti pur da morte usciranno al tempo di quelle fiamme, e pigliato*

GUERINDO Guerindo was born for war.

CORADELLA But not for the devil's war, for he wears a helmet with two wicked and very long horns.

GUERINDO Good heavens, that's my beloved in there.

CORADELLA May heaven grant that it not be our common evil.

GUERINDO I can feel that magnet of others' hearts sweetly drawing me to her.

CORADELLA And I feel the exact opposite, since I've got an extraordinary desire to get out of here.

GUERINDO Come to me, come to me, my love.

CORADELLA And come alone, because I can't move from this spot.

GUERINDO See if anyone's coming.

CORADELLA And you mind what you're supposed to take out of the sack.

GUERINDO She's the goddess Venus asleep.

CORADELLA As long as she's not Satan awake.

GUERINDO I've undone the knot. I'm uncovering that mass of curly gold. Oh no! Oh Lord!

CORADELLA Run for your life, run for your life!

GUERINDO It's Death himself! Death himself!

DEATH Yes, it's me all right: yes it is, yes it is.

CORADELLA That hairless head! That butt without buttocks! Ohmygod! O woe! Until we meet again, at the abode of the devil himself.

[*Here flames will flare from all the streets in the same manner as before.*

di peso Coradella il porteran via, ond'egli dirà quell'ultime parole: "Arrivederci a casa il diavolo."]

Moreover, four players also dressed as Death will appear together with the flames, pick Coradella up and carry him off as he speaks the scene's final line: "Until we meet again, at the abode of the devil himself."]

Scena Decima
[Orimberto, Griffo, Orco]

ORIMBERTO Ecco la notte, ecco le stelle, che innamorate anch'esse tutte con occhi lucidi mi rimirano; ecco il tulpante, la veste a lune, il libraccio e la verga.

Oh quanto si fa per Amore! E benché picciolo, per lui si fa cose grandi; egli è fanciullo e tira a' vecchi; egli è nudo, e fa che gli uomini per piacere alla cosa amata si vestono de' più be' panni; egli è nudo, e spesso ci fa armare per combattere per l'idolo adorato; e ci fa vestir a questo modo, per farci aver più dello spiritato che dell'innamorato. Orsù ci sono; e qui con un cor tricorde bisogna veder d'ottener l'intento suo, prima che la candeletta fatta di grilli pestati si finisca. Oh quanti cuori ho in questo sol petto! Oh quanti piedi ho sotto queste due sole gambe! Una lingua mi parla, e dice: "Fuggi;" l'altra mi sgrida, e dice: "Fermati;" a talché, tra questi duo F mi par d'esser su le forche; alfin voglio, poich'ho fatto tanto, seguire ancora.

ORCO Farai bene.

ORIMBERTO Ohimè, chi è colui che parla? E niun più mi risponde. Orsù, apro.

GRIFFO Finiscila.

ORIMBERTO Oh non fussi in questo intrico! Tutto tremo, e la voce nelle fauci mi annodo.

ORCO Odo.

ORIMBERTO Oh canchero, è l'eco e io aveva paura. Buon cuore, buon cuore. Or sì che sei il Re Molorco.

ORCO Orco.

ORIMBERTO L'orco è una cativa bestia; e per liberarmi da lui ci vorrebbe Astolfo, e l'Ippogriffo.

GRIFFO Griffo.

Scene Ten
[Orimberto, Griffon, Ogre]

ORIMBERTO Here's the night. Here are the stars: they too are in love, and gaze on me with shining eyes. Here are the turban, the robe with its many moons, the book, and the staff.

How much we do for Cupid! Although he's just a small boy, great things are done in his name. He's but a child, and yet he has sway over the old. He's naked, and yet he makes men dress in their finest garb to please the one they love. He's naked, and yet he often makes us arm ourselves for combat for the sake of our adored idol. And he makes us dress like this to make us seem more like madmen than lovers. Well now, here I am: and with my heartstrings taut I must try to do as the Wizard said, before this little candle made of ground crickets burns out. How many hearts I seem to have in this breast of mine! How many feet I seem to have beneath these two legs of mine! One of my tongues tells me: "Fly from here," and another yells at me: "Freeze right there." Between these two F's I feel as though I am hanging from the gallows.[lxxii] In the end, though, I've come so far that I want to keep going.

OGRE You'll do quite well.

ORIMBERTO Oh heavens, who said that? No one seems to answer me. I'll go ahead and open it.

GRIFFON Cut it out.

ORIMBERTO If only I weren't in this mess! I'm shaking all over, and my voice is stuck in my throat.

OGRE So I note.

ORIMBERTO Bloody hell, it's an echo. And to think that I was afraid. Courage, courage. You, my man, should be king the world over.

OGRE "Ogre."

ORIMBERTO The ogre is a wicked beast; and for me to be rid of him I'd need the help of Astolfo and the Hippogriff.[lxxiii]

ORIMBERTO Sarà meglio, poiché l'eco e d'Orco e di Griffo mi parla scherzando, ch'io dia principio all'incanto.

ORCO Canto. [*Orco e Griffo cantano cantando.*]
    Siam duo spirti marinari
    Orimberto mio gentile,
    che del Mago ha l'alto stile
    t'apprestiam tesori cari
    siam duo spirti marinari.

ORIMBERTO Oh poverino me, sono duo spiriti, e io pensava loro l'eco. Oh 'l cielo me la mandi buona; ma, perché debbano esser pronti a portarmi il mio bene, io non voglio far loro indugiare.
    Sulfarat, Ruspicano e Tiberino,
    Ignicolo, Gelonio e Serpicante,
    tutti al magico stile anzi divino,
    messagiero infernal giunga volante.
    Or mentre a Pluto umil ginocchio inchino
    perché d'amor ha sospirato amante,
    datemi voi la mia sognante Lidia
    che s'al cor l'ho dipinta Amor è Fidia.

ORCO   Ecco pronti i marinari,
    ecco i rari,
    di fals'onda cittadini,
        che i divini
    portan doni, singulari
    già se n'vanno i marinari.

ORIMBERTO Quel ch'i' mi faccia non so. Vennero cantando i marinari e lieti partirono. Ben so che sono spiriti, ma spiritello ancora è Amore. Oh che bella cassa, è così ricca d'oro, e di gemme rilucente, che forse nell'inferno Proserpina colà dentro tener debbe le sue reali spoglie; ma che tale esser forse non doveva chiudendo Lidia, uno de' maggiori tesori ch'abbia nel regno suo Amore? Oh che bell'invito, voglio aprirla, non ho più tema, ho più cuore d'un bue, d'un elefante. Oh caro il mio bene! Non par giusto la bella Psiche, che attenda dormendo Amore? Sì cor mio, che se'. Ecco io la sollevo, ecco che pur la stringo, e bacio, e ribacio; orsù torno a corcarla, e chiudo la cassa così ricca d'oro e di gemme. Oh se i marinari me la volessero portar fino a

GRIFFON "Griffon."

ORIMBERTO Because this echo keeps joking about ogres and griffons, I'd best start with the spell, right or wrong.

OGRE Not "wrong" but "song."
[*Ogre and Griffon sing.*]
> Two sailor spirits are we:
> The Wizard's style is yours, we're sure,
> So, Orimberto, with pleasure
> we're bringing you great treasure.
> Two sailor spirits are we.

ORIMBERTO Poor me! These are spirits, and I thought they were an echo. May heaven favor me now. Because they must be ready to bring my beloved to me, I don't want to keep them waiting.
> Demons of hell, hear me well:
> Fly now in style magical,
> as messengers to Him below.
> I bend my knee before Pluto,
> Who, as a lover, sighed for love.
> Give me my Lidia dreaming:
> If her painted portrait's gleaming
> In my heart, it must be because
> Cupid's the artist here above.[lxxiv]

OGRE
> We're two sailors,
> We're rare fellers,
> We're sure not
> city-dwellers.
> The gods bring gifts,
> So look at this!
> And now the time is here
> For sailors to disappear.

ORIMBERTO I don't know what to do. The sailors came singing and left happy. I know perfectly well that they're spirits, but so is Cupid a sprite. What a gorgeous chest, and how richly decorated with gold and glistening jewels. Perhaps in the underworld Persephone keeps her royal robes in it.[lxxv] But wasn't such a thing supposed to have Lidia in

casa! Ma il cielo sa dove sono andati. Orsù un buon animo, lascia qui la cassa, e portela in braccio. Ma qual error fo grave a lasciar qui tanta ricchezza? Amor mi dà Lidia per goderla, Plutone il tesoro per mantenerla; l'anderò così trascinando alla meglio. Ohimè che fuoco! Ohimè, che spiriti! Ohimè, che morti! Oh povero me! Salva, salva! Fuggi fuggi! Aiuto, aiuto!

[*Qui fuor della cassa usciranno fiamme seguenti, salteranno fuora cinque morti, tre spiriti, dui facchini, li duo marinari, e tutti correranno e circonderanno Orimberto qual criderà immoto, ed essi l'infarineranno, l'incarboneranno e bastoneranno, e alor che vorrà fuggire da tutte le parti, gettando fuochi il teatro raccoglierà bene spesso, nelle fiamme, e spiriti e morti e Orimberto.*]

FINE DELL'ATTO TERZO

it? And isn't she one of the greatest treasures Cupid has in his realm? It's so inviting; I want to open it. I'm no longer afraid; I have the heart of an ox, of an elephant. My beloved! Does she not seem just like the lovely Psyche, who sleeps while awaiting Cupid to come to her? Yes, my love—for that's what you are. Now I'm lifting her up and embracing her, and kissing her over and over again. Now I'll put her back down, and close the lid of this chest studded with gold and gems. If only the sailors would carry her to my house for me! Heaven only knows where they've gone. Come on, steady now: I'll leave the chest here and carry her in my arms. But what a grave mistake I might be making to leave such wealth here. Love gives me Lidia for my pleasure, and Pluto gives me this treasure to keep her in style. I'll try to make it home by dragging the chest as best I can. Oh heavens, what are these flames, these spirits, these corpses! O poor me! I must run for my life: run away, run away! Help, help!

[*Out of the chest leap flames, five dead men, three spirits, the two porters, the Griffon, and the Ogre. They chase Orimberto and surround him, while he shouts for help but is immobilized by fear. They cover him with flour and coal dust, and then thrash him with sticks. He tries frantically to escape: but Orimberto, the spirits, and the dead run in and out of the flames on stage until the curtain falls.*]

END OF ACT THREE

ATTO QUARTO

Scena Prima
[Sufronio]

SUFRONIO Questa notte m'è parsa composta di cento notti, tanto m'è paruta lunga e fastidiosa; e se la mia casa fosse stata senza tetto, mi sarebbe dato l'animo di annoverar tutte le stelle, poiché non mai ho dormito, aspettando il giorno, per andar alle prigioni, a far liberar Silvio mio figliuolo. L'amor de' figli, eh, è troppo grande, e ben tale bisogna che sia, essendo materie di questa carne, di quest'ossa e di questo sangue; che però nelle Sacre Carte leggiamo che fu imposto al figlio amar il padre, poiché la propria natura insegna al padre ad amar il figlio. Oh, se amiamo un innesto fatto dalla nostra mano, se ad ognora l'andiamo a visitare, se ogni germoglio che getta ne fa rallegrare, e nato il frutto poi, e si fiuta, e si mira, e si dona, e si conserva; quanto maggiormente questi figli, queste radici, che sono piantate ne' nostri cuori, questi tronchi, questi rami, queste frondi, questi fiori, questi frutti, ne debbano esser cari e custoditi, e tanto più quando un sol figlio abbiamo. Sento sopra di questo, alcuni che dicono: "Chi ha un sol figlio non ha niuno," e che perciò sia poco il gusto; e io argumento al contrario e dico ch'è meglio averne un solo che molti; non perché i figli molti diano travagli molti, ma perché le cose più singolari furno create sole. La Fenice è sola; il mondo fu un solo, il sole è solo, la luna sola; né di molti figli si compiacque il Sommo Padre, ma d'un solo; però anch'io d'un sol figlio mi glorio, e questo solo per mantenere, spargerò tutto il sangue con doglia, se per generarlo lo sparsi con diletto. Ma voglio lo stesso che l'accusò, lo stesso aver meco, avendomi il Mago fatta far la pace. O dalla casa.

Scena Seconda
[Orimberto e Sufronio]

ORIMBERTO Ohimè, ecco un diavolo diurno che batte alla mia porta; non m'affaccerò già io né a finestre, né a porte.

SUFRONIO O dalla casa, signor Orimberto.

ACT IV

Scene One
[Sufronio]

SUFRONIO Last night was so long and so troubling that it seemed to me like a hundred nights. If my house had no roof, I could've tried counting all the stars in the heavens, for I never slept a moment while awaiting daybreak, when I could go to the city jail and free my dear son Silvio. Our love for our children is too strong, alas, although that's the way it should be, for they are made of our own flesh and blood. In the Holy Scriptures we read that the son had to be required to love his father, whereas it was in the father's own nature to love his son. Oh, if we love a plant grafted by our own hand and go to visit it all the time; if every new shoot that it produces makes us happy, and, when it bears fruit, we sniff it and look at it, and we give it as a gift or keep it; how much more so these children of ours, these roots which are planted in our hearts, these trunks and branches, these leaves, flowers, and fruits, ought to be dear to us and cared for by us. All the more so when we've but one child. I've heard some say that "those who have only one child have none at all" and therefore that an only child can scarcely be enjoyed. I'd argue the opposite, and say that it's better to have only one instead of many; not because many children bring many problems, but because the most unusual things were created alone. There's only one phoenix; there's only one world; there are only one sun and one moon; our Heavenly Father didn't choose to have many children, but only one. I too take pride in having but one son, and just to keep him well I'd suffer to shed every last drop of my blood, as I once took pleasure in sowing my blood in order to generate him. But now I want to have with me the same man who was his accuser, since the Wizard made me make my peace with the fellow. Is anyone home?

Scene Two
[Orimberto, Sufronio]

ORIMBERTO Oh no, there's a daytime devil knocking at my door. I won't show myself at the window or the door.

SUFRONIO Are you home, Orimberto?

159

ORIMBERTO Oh che traditore, per ingannarmi finge la voce del signor Sufronio. S'io lo so che t'apra.

SUFRONIO Che domine ha questo pecorone? M'udite, o non mi udite, o non mi volete udire?

ORIMBERTO Non ti voglio udire.

SUFRONIO Questa bestia sarà restia in questo punto.

ORIMBERTO Mi voglio pur affacciar alla finestra. Oh guarda, com'il demonio è gran fingitore! Che scoltori, che pittori, che nature! Ecco là un corpo fantastico tutto, tutto, Orimberto.

SUFRONIO Che dite voi di natura, di pittori e di scultori?

ORIMBERTO Ah, spirito vizioso, tu sa' ben quello ch'io dico; ma t'infingi!

SUFRONIO Io son Sufronio.

ORIMBERTO Te ne menti, inventor della bugia.

SUFRONIO O Orimberto, per chi mi tieni tu?

ORIMBERTO Per colui, che indegno del cielo fu condannato all'inferno.

SUFRONIO Doh becco cornuto!

ORIMBERTO Ora mi conosco d'esser uomo da bene, poiché, se il diavolo dice sempre la bugia, m'ha detto becco, ergo non sono.

SUFRONIO Costui è diventato pazzo.

ORIMBERTO Meglio è l'esser pazzo che spiritato. Levati di qui, torna a malebolge.

ORIMBERTO Oh what a traitor! With that fake voice he's trying to trick me into thinking that he's Sufronio. Just wait and see if I'm going to open that door for you.

SUFRONIO What's gotten into that mutton-head? Can you hear me or not, or don't you want to hear me?

ORIMBERTO I don't want to hear you.

SUFRONIO I must be making this ass nervous.

ORIMBERTO I do want to show myself at the window after all. Look at what a great faker the devil is! Sculptors, painters, and nature itself can't match him! That's a 100 percent imaginary body, Orimberto.

SUFRONIO What are you saying about nature, painters, and sculptors?

ORIMBERTO Ah, wicked spirit, you know quite well what I'm talking about: you're just pretending not to!

SUFRONIO It's me, Sufronio.

ORIMBERTO You're lying! You're the one who invented lying!

SUFRONIO Orimberto, just who do you think I am?

ORIMBERTO You're the one who was unworthy of heaven and was damned to hell.

SUFRONIO And you're a damn cuckold!

ORIMBERTO Now I know that I'm a respectable man, for the devil always lies, and if he says that I'm a cuckold, then that's not what I really am.

SUFRONIO This fellow has gone mad.

ORIMBERTO I'd rather be mad than possessed. Get lost, go back to hell.

SUFRONIO Costui s'è levato dalla finestra e mi crede uno spirito. Non credo già d'aver posto questa notte le corna; non le ho già s'io non l'avessi come parte degli altri maritati, che l'hanno invisibili. O di casa, signor Orimberto, signor Orimberto.

ORIMBERTO E può una bocca maledetta, con nomi battezzati chiamarmi? Veh, mi trovo in su la porta, sta' lontano ch'ho l'acqua benedetta vicina, veh.

SUFRONIO Vi dico ch'io sono il vostro amico Sufronio.

ORIMBERTO Fatevi un poco il segno del cristiano?

SUFRONIO Farò tutto quello che volete.

ORIMBERTO Come dice così è segno che lo puol fare, come il può fare è cristiano, com'è cristiano è uomo, com'uomo ha corpo, com'ha corpo non è spirito, come non è spirito è palpabile, com'è palpabile è il signor Sufronio.

SUFRONIO Miratemi, palpeggiatemi, Sufronio io sono.

ORIMBERTO Al viso, al tatto, al tutto voi siete Sufronio; ovvero, che la natura vi ha fatto così a Sufronio simigliante, che si può dire che voi abbiate tutta la grandezza della natura, e l'istessa natura nel volto.

SUFRONIO Potren far generazione, poiché s'io ho tutta la natura nel volto, e voi tutto ci avete quel naturale ch'alla natura piace; ma perché tutti ritornelli a questa gagliarda, perché non ballar alla libera uscendo in strada?

ORIMBERTO Dovrei aspettar in capo i nove giorni a dirlo, per non pelarmi. Ma perché s'usano al presente le zazzere alla francese, così delicatamente fatte che par ch'abbiate una capigliara posticcia, io ve la dirò.

SUFRONIO Andiam verso al Palazzo per liberar mio figliuolo, e così camminando dir lo potrete.

ORIMBERTO Guardate ch'io non vi spiriti mentre lo racconto.

SUFRONIO He has left the window, thinking me an evil spirit. I don't think that I sprouted horns during the night. The only ones I've got are those invisible horns that all husbands wear. Yoo-hoo Orimberto! Is anyone home?

ORIMBERTO If he calls me by my Christian name, can he really be a demon? Here I am at the door: but stay back, I say, for I've got holy water close at hand.

SUFRONIO But I'm telling you that I'm your friend Sufronio.

ORIMBERTO Let me see you make the sign of the cross.

SUFRONIO I'll do whatever you ask.

ORIMBERTO If he says that, it's a sign he can really do it; and that means he's a Christian; and therefore if he's a Christian he's a man; and therefore if he's a man he has a body; and therefore if he has a body he's not a spirit; and therefore if he's not a spirit I can touch him; and therefore if I can touch him he's Sufronio.

SUFRONIO Look at me, touch me: I am Sufronio.

ORIMBERTO My eyes, my hands, and everything else confirm that you're Sufronio. Or rather, nature has made you resemble Sufronio so closely that it may be said you have the very greatness of nature in you, and display nature itself in your face.

SUFRONIO Then we are one and the same. For if I've all of nature in my face, you're utterly and completely natural in the way that nature likes. But why are we doing this song-and-dance routine? Why not step out into the street and let your feet go free?

ORIMBERTO I ought to wait a whole nine days before talking about it, in order not to get scalped. But since these days it's fashionable to wear long hair in the French style, with such delicately done tresses that it looks like a wig, I'll go ahead and tell you.[lxxvi]

SUFRONIO Let's go to the Governor's palace to free my son; you can talk while we walk.

SUFRONIO Se questo credete non lo dite. Ma che? S'io non m'ispirito nel mirarvi, meno sarà questo nell'ascoltarvi. Andiamo.

ORIMBERTO Andiamo, e or incomincio, Signor Sufronio. Saprà Vostra Signoria come questa notte...

Scena Terza
[Bernetta, Lidia, Florinda]

BERNETTA Uh, egli è pur la maledetta cosa il dormir sola quand'è passato il tempo per la femmina di quegli anni primi. Certamente la donna tanto dovrebbe star soletta quanto sta nelle fasce; uscita poi subbito, subbito dovrebbe esser accompagnata, perché la nostra natura il ricerca. È troppo spaurosa la donna; d'un picciolo topo si sgomenta, e se lo vede, perché sa ch'è amico delle fessure, tutta si tura; talché s'ha uno seco che possa spaventar il topo, e accorrendo turar loro ancora i luoghi sospetti, non è se non bene; poiché la lor natura è come quella del cane, com'hanno paura, subbito si tirano la coda fra le gambe. Voglio andar a chiamar la signora Florinda. Poverina, credo pur che queste due giovinette abbiano fatta insieme questa notte male, poiché si dice che la donna è come la pietra focaia, che la natura ha posto in lei tanto fuoco, che non potendo aspettar l'acciaiuolo che loro percuota, se si batteno insieme d'ogni intorno sfavillano; così averan fatte queste poverine; ma che questo fuoco sarà stato gittato al vento, poiché non ci sarà stato l'esca, il zolfanello e 'l candelotto da impicciare. O dalla casa? Signore è Bernetta, la vostra serva, ch'è così stata male soletta, come ancor malissimo voi accompagnate.

FLORINDA Signora Lidia, mia signora, temp'è ch'io mi diparta, e ch'io l'abbandoni; questo giorno poi a lei ne ritornerò, rimanga felice.

LIDIA E Vostra Signoria felicissima parta; e sigillo sia del suo ritorno questo bacio, e questo, e questo.

ORIMBERTO Take care not to become possessed as I tell you my tale.

SUFRONIO If you think it possible, then best not to tell me anything. But what am I talking about? If I haven't become possessed just by looking at you, then it's even less likely to happen by listening to you. Let's go.

ORIMBERTO Let's go, Sufronio, and I'll get started. As Your Excellency knows, last night…

Scene Three
[Bernetta, Lidia, Florinda]

BERNETTA Well, it's a terrible thing for a woman to sleep alone when her youth is over. Without a doubt every woman needs to be alone when she's still in her swaddling clothes; once she's out of them, though, she immediately must have her mate, because it's in her nature to want it. Woman is too timid: she's frightened by a little mouse, and, if she sees one, she seals everything up tight, because she knows that mice are fond of cracks. If she has someone with her who can frighten off the mouse, and fill up all of those places in question, so much the better. A woman's nature can be likened to a dog's, for as soon as they've taken fright, they'll both pull the tail between their legs. I want to go call my mistress Florinda. The poor thing! I think those two young ladies have done wrong together this past night, for they say woman is like flint: nature has placed so much fire in her that, not always being able to wait for the steel to strike, if two of them are rubbed together they throw off sparks all around them. That's what those two poor creatures must have done. But those sparks must have been cast to the winds, since there was no tinder, no match, and no candle to light. Is anyone home? It's your servant Bernetta, ladies; if I did badly by being all alone last night, you did far worse by being together.

FLORINDA Lidia, my lady, it's time for me to go, and to leave you for now. I'll return to you later today, so be happy.

LIDIA May Your Ladyship leave most happily. Let's seal your return with this kiss, and this one, and this one.

BERNETTA Poverine, la cosa passa in baci, e non plus ultra.

FLORINDA Bernetta, se' qui, t'abbiam sentita; hai fatto bene a venir per tempo. La signora Lidia gentilissima voleva uscir meco su la strada, e io non ho voluto, e le ho fatto violenza con un essercito di baci.

BERNETTA E bene, come l'avete passata? Da qui in su benissimo, nel toccar tette, petto, gola, nel dar baci, nel cicalare; ma da qui in giù poi, non andò mai peggio; o pur avete fatto come i buoni sonatori di liuto, che tanto più sono eccellenti quanto più fanno delle scorse fino alla rosetta.

FLORINDA Tu se' maliciosa e licenziosa, e però col silenzio ti darò risposta e mortificazione.

BERNETTA Avete ragione, non siete state né liuti né sonatori, ma lire, le quali tanto suonano dolci, quanto l'archetto passeggia loro in giù e in su su la pancia; per questo dite di tacere, e tacer dovete, perché siete stata lira senza archetto.

FLORINDA Oh vedi se tu se' balorda! Questa notte tutta l'abbiam passata in dir mal degli uomini.

BERNETTA E questo perché vi trattavano così male, per non ve n'esser intanto vostro bisogno, pur un mez'uno.

FLORINDA Ti dico, odiamo tanto questo sesso.

BERNETTA Sì vestito; ma ignudo non vedeste giamai la più bella cosa; e per questo, com'un pittore fa una figura ignuda, e tocca bene quelle tenerezze delle parti di mezo, è glorioso.

FLORINDA Nel mezo consiste la virtù, e la virtù è fuggir il vizio, però somma virtù sarà il non ascoltarti, essendo tu viziosissima. Entriamo.

BERNETTA Tutto quello che volete sono. Scherzo signora, perché so che questa notte sarete stata molto di mala voglia.

FLORINDA E pur ci torni su questi scherzi. Andiamo.

BERNETTA The poor things! They can't go beyond kissing.

FLORINDA Bernetta, you're here and we've heard you. You did well to come on time. Mistress Lidia most kindly wanted to go out with me into the street, but I didn't want her to, and I ravaged her with an army of kisses.

BERNETTA Well then, how did the night go? From here up, very well indeed: in touching breasts, chests, and throats; in kissing and in chatting together. From here down, however, it couldn't have gone any worse: or else you were like good lutists, whose skills are best displayed the more they run their fingers all the way to the rose.[lxxvii]

FLORINDA You're malicious and licentious; I'll answer you with silence and put you in your place.

BERNETTA You're right. You were neither lutes nor musicians, but lyres, whose sounds are so sweet when the bow is passed up and down at the waist. This is why you say you'll keep silent, and so you should, because you were lyres without bows.[lxxviii]

FLORINDA What an idiot you are! We spent the entire night speaking ill of men.

BERNETTA And that's because they treated you both so badly by not meeting your needs, not even half a need.

FLORINDA I'm telling you, we greatly hate the other sex.

BERNETTA When men are dressed, yes. But when they're naked, you've never seen anything so lovely! A painter, in executing the figure of a nude, touches up with care those sweet little private parts, just because they make men glorious and not mean.

FLORINDA Virtue consists in the golden mean, not any other, and virtue always flees vice. Thus the greatest virtue is to be found in not listening to you, because you are chock-full of vice. Let's go in.

BERNETTA I'll be whatever you wish. If I've been jesting, my lady, it's because I know that last night you must have found things most

BERNETTA Vengo signora.

Scena Quarta
[Eugenio]

EUGENIO Io non so tanti discorsi d'armi e di lettere, so che la spada punge e la penna tinge, l'una si bagna nel sangue, l'altra nell'inchiostro, questa nacque per gloriosi eroi, quella per miserabili letteratucci, le spade si portano fastose e dorate al fianco di mille cavalieri, e le penne tinte e bistinte ne' pennaruoli, sepolte, di mille e mille pedagoghi; delle spade s'ergono trofei in vita e 'n morte, e delle penne si caricano i bambocci in tempo di carnovale, quando per baccanali si portano simili imbrogli trionfanti per mano di mascherati fanciulli; delle penne s'empiono letti, capezzali, e dell'armi se ne adornano gli arsenali e le armerie di principi e di regi; queste penne sono d'oca, animale vile e amato dal giudaesmo, e le piume degli struzzi, animale famosissimo e dagl'Indiani amato, servono in fronte a ventilar leggere e colorate a mille animosi guerrieri. Non voglio io ingolfarmi in cose gravi, ma far come colui che mangiando una torta per aver del gentile, van dietro gli orli. Queste ragionette mi piacciono, come colui che nemico de' libri non va mendicando se non quello che l'intelletto li porge. Dica chi vuole, dicendo che la spada senza la penna non val un zero, poiché quanto fa la spada la penna il racconta, e quanto l'una dà morte l'altra dà vita; dica pur che i Troiani anzi ch'entrar in battaglia andassero a far preghiere alle Muse, come lo strepito dell'armi abbiano dell'armonia di queste qui fuore necessità gradissima, nulla giovando fatto senza racconto; ch'io per me apprezzo più un corsaletto del più misero soldato ch'una toga del maggior letterato. Oh quanto riscaldata la mente potrebbe per ordine quello ch'ora in confuso ho qui accennato! Ma perché, se fossero cose tanto laborate, averebbeno dello studioso, sapendo da lucerna, io che voglio aver del bellicoso e puzzar da moschetto, per questo in così fatta guisa voglio parlare; concludendo, che le lettere son parole, e l'armi son fatti; e s'è vero che proverbio non erra, dicesi che le parole son femmine e i fatti son maschi. Or quanto è più nobile il maschio della femina, tanto ancora è più nobile l'essercizio militare che l'arte della scienza, l'una insegnata per valor nel cielo, l'altra ritrovata per la necessità in terra; e poi il Sommo Fabro fu detto Dio degli esserciti, e però amator de' soldati, e non Dio delle librerie, osservator di letterati.

frustrating.

FLORINDA Yet you keep on joking. Let's go.

BERNETTA I'm coming, my lady.

Scene Four
[Eugenio]

EUGENIO I don't know many speeches about arms and letters. I know the sword pricks and the quill dips; the sword is bathed in blood and the quill in ink; the sword is born for glorious heroes, while the quill is for impoverished scribblers; swords are worn, splendid and shining, at the side of a thousand knights, while quills are dipped over and over again in inkwells, buried there by thousands of pedagogues; swords are raised as trophies in life and in death, while effigies are covered with quills at Carnival time, when such tricks are carried in triumph through the streets by masked youths during the revels; beds and bolsters are filled with quills, while arms adorn the arsenals and armories of princes and kings; such quills come from the goose, a vile animal beloved by the Jews,[lxxix] while the bright and colorful feathers of the ostrich, that most famous animal beloved by the Indians, wave on the foreheads of a thousand brave warriors. I don't want to get bogged down in serious matters; I'd rather be like someone who, when eating cake in order to be polite, rolls back his cuffs.[lxxx] I like these thoughts of mine, however, like someone who, as an enemy of books, only begs for what his own intellect gives him. Let them say that the sword without the pen is worth less than zero, because the pen narrates what the sword does, or that the pen gives life while the sword gives death. Let them say that the Trojans went to pray to the Muses rather than go straight into battle, for the din of arms was greatly in need of their harmony, since deeds left unsung were of no use. As for me, I prefer the breastplate of the humblest soldier to the gown of the greatest man of letters. If my mind were running at full speed, surely it would put in order the jumble of things that I've just said! But I want to be warlike and smell of powder, and that's why I've been speaking like this; if my thoughts were too carefully arranged I'd sound like a scholar reeking of lamp-oil instead. In short, letters are just words, while arms are deeds. If it's true that proverbs are never wrong, then it is rightly said that words are feminine and deeds are masculine. And

Scena Quinta
[Orimberto, Eugenio]

ORIMBERTO Infine, per cominciar dal fine, se la signora Lidia non vien al Palazzo, cosa di liberar Silvio anderà in lungo; poiché lo stesso Silvio dice che quello ch'ha detto circa l'ammazzarla, ha detto come uno che parli in un certo modo, disprezzando per grande importunità una persona; e però Sufronio m'invia a lei, perché mossa a pietà se ne vada al Palazzo a dir il vero.

EUGENIO Costui fa un gran parlamento da sé, debb'esser letterato, e perché ogni letterato ha del pazzo, per questo così solitario discorre. Oh, m'ha veduto; e che diavol ha, che mi guarda così fisso. Oh, oh s'avvicina! Sarà pittore, e mancandogli alcuna cosa particolare, or s'avanza, or s'arretra per rubbarla; e pur torna. Che guardate galantuomo?

ORIMBERTO O cor mio, guardo voi.

EUGENIO "Cor mio guardo voi;" costui non solo è letterato, ma filosofo; nemico delle donne. Voglio secondar l'umor falso.

ORIMBERTO Sono state più di cento bastonate una miglior dell'altra, e tutte per mano di Rabuino. Oh, se Vostra Signoria m'avesse veduto! Io pareva il gran Turco, aveva un tulpante, una vesta lunata, un libraccio, una verga, la qual si convertì in un baston grosso, che me ne diede tante che ancor le numero; né giamai quel diarbene di quel legno si ruppe.

as the male is more noble than the female, so the martial arts are far more noble than the arts of knowledge: the former are taught in the heavens by valor, while the latter have been invented on earth out of mere necessity. Our Maker himself was called "God of armies," and thus is devoted to soldiers. No one would refer to him as the "God of bookshelves," who watches over men of letters.[lxxxi]

Scene Five
[Orimberto, Eugenio]

ORIMBERTO To sum things up, if Mistress Lidia doesn't come to the Governor's palace, it's going to take a long time to get Silvio out of jail. Silvio himself now says that when he talked about killing her, he was speaking like a person who uses his words in a certain way to heap scorn on someone really annoying. Sufronio has nonetheless sent me to her, so that—moved by pity—she might go to the Governor's palace and tell the truth.

EUGENIO This fellow certainly talks to himself a lot. He must be a man of letters and, because every man of letters has some madness in him, he therefore goes on speaking while alone. Oh, now he's seen me! What the devil has gotten into him? Why is he staring at me like that? Uh oh, now he's coming over to me. Perhaps he's a painter in need of some detail or other, and has to step forward and backward in order to capture it. What are you looking at, good sir?

ORIMBERTO Oh my darling, I'm looking at you.

EUGENIO "Oh my darling, I'm looking at you": this fellow is not only a man of letters but a philosopher, and therefore an enemy of women.[lxxxii] I'll humor his strange mood.

ORIMBERTO I took more than a hundred blows, one better than the next, and all of them came from the devil himself. Oh if only Your Ladyship had seen me! I looked like the great Turk with a turban, a robe with many moons on it, a thick book, and a staff that eventually turned into a big stick with which he beat me so soundly that I'm still counting the blows. Nor did that damnable piece of wood break across my back.

EUGENIO Poverino, quanto mi dispiace; seguitate.

ORIMBERTO Mi foste portata entro una cassa, dove si conservavano quelle bastonate così cotorre; le parlai mentre dormiva; ma nel volervi levar fuor di quella, saltò dalla stessa tanta marmaglia infernale che poco meno mi portarono a casa calda. Io vi ho voluto gran bene, perché mi andate a capriccio; ma ora non voglio più questo amore, poiché per quello il diavolo m'ha voluto abbrucciare.

EUGENIO Lasciatelo, perché quello che non ha fatto il diavolo farallo il carnefice.

ORIMBERTO E che parlar è questo, mio bene?

EUGENIO E che amor è 'l vostro, mio galantuomo?

ORIMBERTO Di quell'amore che piace ai veri galantuomini.

EUGENIO E chi son io?

ORIMBERTO La signora Lidia, che per aver fatto cacciar a torto prigion il povero Silvio il giovinetto, s'è vestita in questi panni per sottrarsi alla giustizia. Non vedete, che in que' calzoni storpiate la natura femminile, e che la stessa natura patisce?

EUGENIO Galantuomo, or che mi sono un pezzo pigliato scherzo de' fatti vostri, tempè ch'io vi dica che non son Lidia, ma Eugenio, non donna, ma uomo. Io non so di Silvio, né di giustizia, né mi diletto d'Amore, ma di Marte.

ORIMBERTO Sì, sì, ogni mese per far tanto sangue in battaglia.

EUGENIO Signor sì; quel sangue ch'io cavo dal naso con le pugna agl'insolenti pari vostri.

ORIMBERTO Sì? O vedete qua il viso, dateli un poco sopra.

EUGENIO Ecco.

EUGENIO Poor fellow, I'm so sorry to hear that. Do continue.

ORIMBERTO You were brought to me in a chest, which also contained a blistering beating for me. I spoke to you while you slept; but when I tried to lift you out of the chest, out came a hellish horde of rowdy rabble that nearly managed to take me home with them to the underworld. I loved you so well, because you captured my fancy; but I don't want this love anymore, since it was the reason that the devil wanted to roast me.

EUGENIO Forget about it, for the executioner will do whatever the devil doesn't.

ORIMBERTO And whatever are you talking about, my sweet?

EUGENIO And what love do you profess, my good gentleman?

ORIMBERTO The love that true gentlemen like.

EUGENIO And who am I?

ORIMBERTO You are Mistress Lidia: you're dressed that way because, having wrongly sent to prison that poor youngster Silvio, you're now on the lam from the law. Don't you see that you're maiming your feminine nature by wearing those pants, and that that same nature is suffering?

EUGENIO My dear sir, now that you've given me a good laugh for a bit, it's time to tell you that I'm Eugenio, not Lidia. I'm a man, not a woman. I don't know anything about Silvio, or about the law; nor does Venus delight me; I prefer Mars.

ORIMBERTO Sure, sure… you draw blood in battle every month.

EUGENIO Yessir: the same blood that I'll draw with my fists from the nose of an insolent fellow like you.

ORIMBERTO Oh yes? You see my face here; go ahead and give it to me.

ORIMBERTO Un altro schiaffo.

EUGENIO Pigliate.

ORIMBERTO Oh, cappari, voi andereste seguitando tutt'oggi, dite il vero.

EUGENIO Oh, se il dare è mia professione.

ORIMBERTO O date un poco a me di quello ch'io desidero da voi.

EUGENIO E che desiderate?

ORIMBERTO Un bacio per duo schiaffi datimi.

EUGENIO Oh che bestia gomorristica; voglio servirlo. Venite a torlo, venite.

ORIMBERTO Me lo darete?

EUGENIO Come, cor mio, altro non bramo.

ORIMBERTO Certo.

EUGENIO Certissimo, e questo per ristoro di que' vostri diabolici spaventi.

ORIMBERTO Sì ch'ora conosco che dite da vero mio bene. Non sarem poi marito e moglie?

EUGENIO Certissimo.

ORIMBERTO Poverina, come l'allegrezza le fa dir delle parole lunghe. Vengo adunque, il mio bene.

EUGENIO Venite, né più indugiate bene mio, dolcissimo. Tura alla malora, vigliacco indegno, che s'io pongo mano, per questa spada ti farò conoscere chi mi sia; pedagogo presentuoso e vizioso.

ORIMBERTO Signora Lidia, signora Lidia, dove, dove? Non s'avvede

EUGENIO Here you go.

ORIMBERTO Another slap!

EUGENIO Take that too.

ORIMBERTO Good heavens, you'd go on doing this all day, if the truth be told.

EUGENIO My profession is giving to others.

ORIMBERTO Then give me a little bit of what I want from you.

EUGENIO And what do you want?

ORIMBERTO Give me a kiss for those two slaps in the face.

EUGENIO [You sodomitic beast!] I'm your servant: come and get it, come on.

ORIMBERTO You're going to give it to me?

EUGENIO Of course, my darling; I desire nothing else.

ORIMBERTO Indeed.

EUGENIO Most certainly, and may it make amends for the fright those demons put into you.

ORIMBERTO Now I see that you're speaking the truth, my love. Won't we be husband and wife afterward?

EUGENIO Unquestionably.

ORIMBERTO Poor little thing, it must be her happiness that makes her say such long words. I'm coming then, my love.

EUGENIO Come, then, and tarry no longer, my sweetest darling. Shut your damn mouth, you unworthy coward: with this sword I'll teach you who I am, you conceited and depraved schoolmaster!

che quella è la strada del bordello? Oh che frenetico umore è quello ch'ha assalito questa povera giovanetta? Signora Lidia, signora Lidia! Sì, sì, ella è oramai così lontana che più non mi può udire. E come cammina disposta, come se fosse avvezza a portar il petto e la picca. Eh, so ben io che m'era appigliato ad amar cosa di merito, ma la fortuna non m'ha voluto esser favorevole. O casa di Lidia, si vede bene che mentre ci dimorava il tuo sole eri piena di luce e ti potevi chiamar oriente di raggi, e ora che non c'è più se' fatta occidente di tenebre. Questa è pur quella porta dalla quale tu uscivi amorosa e più bella ch'uscir non suole l'Aurora cinta di rose dalle porte luminose del cielo. Oh Lidia, oh Lidia, oh Lidia!

Scena Sesta
[Lidia, Orimberto]

LIDIA Chi è là, chi mi chiama?

ORIMBERTO Ohimè che veggo? Sono ancor tra le Furie o tra le Grazie? Nell'Inferno o 'n Paradiso?

LIDIA Parla da sé.

ORIMBERTO Signora, a queste stravaganze mi volgo, veggendo or Lidia uomo o donna, or partir per le strade or tornar per le case, e ben convien ch'io dica che queste sieno apparenze diaboliche, e che 'l diavolo scherzi ancor meco. Ma s'io guardo a quel bel viso, mi convien dire che i demoni sotto angeliche bellezze ammantarsi non possono; pur si dice che in angelo di luce, l'angelo tenebroso ancor si muta per ingannare.

LIDIA Signor Orimberto, se noi facessimo una commedia, non averebbe punto di decoro il lasciarmi così sola in un canto, e voi dir tante chiacchiere solo; e se la comedia è una imitazion del vero, meno sarà dicevole che voi mi lasciate a questa foggia qui retirata com'un termine, e se Vostra Signoria non mi chiamerà, né parlerà meco, né io con voi, e me n'entrerò in casa.

ORIMBERTO Mistress Lidia, Mistress Lidia, where are you going? Don't you know that's the street where the whorehouse is? Oh what a dreadful mood this poor young girl is in. Mistress Lidia, Mistress Lidia! Ah well, by now she's so far away that she can no longer hear me. And look how she walks, as if she were used to wearing a breast-plate and carrying a pike. Well do I know that I've undertaken to love someone worthy of me, but fate hasn't looked kindly on me. O Lidia's house, it's clear that while your sun was dwelling there you were full of light and could be called the Orient of light-rays; but now that she's gone, you have become the shadowy West. Here's the door through which you used to come, in love and more beautiful than Aurora herself when she steps out, girt with roses, through the glowing doors of the heavens.[lxxxiii] O Lidia, o Lidia, o Lidia!

Scene Six
[Lidia, Orimberto]

LIDIA Who's there? Who's calling for me?

ORIMBERTO What do I see? Am I among the Graces or still with the Furies?[lxxxiv] In hell or in paradise?

LIDIA He's talking to himself.

ORIMBERTO My lady, I act so strangely because I see Lidia first as a man, and now as a woman; I see her first heading off through the streets, and now back in her house. It'd seem these are demonic apparitions, and the devil himself is still toying with me. But when I gaze upon your lovely face, I must instead admit that demons can't cloak themselves with angelic beauty, even though it's said that the prince of darkness can transform himself into an angel of light in order to deceive men.

LIDIA Orimberto, if we were putting on a comedy, it would be very poor stagecraft to leave me alone and off to one side while you go on blathering by yourself. And if comedy is an imitation of the true, it's even falser for you to leave me here alone in this manner, as if I were made of stone; so if Your Excellency isn't calling for me, or talking to me, nor I with you, then I'm going back in the house.[lxxxv]

ORIMBERTO Signora, ha grandissima ragione; ma quando sarà a parte di questo, mi terrà più tosto sensato che ignorante. Signora, questa notte io la voleva per incanto, ma io stesso per simile affare ho dovuto inspiritarmi; ma per ora transeat, ne diremo in altro tempo. Vengo a quello che più m'importa, ed è questo: che se Vostra Signoria non viene or ora al Palazzo, potrebbe il signor Silvio aver de' fastidi. Ha già detto che per martello Vostra Signoria ha detto quello che ha detto, ond'egli andò prigione; confessa che cacciò mano per isdegno, ma che non mai le avrebbe fatto oltragio. Lidia supplica pertanto a venirne alle prigioni a dir il vero, perché non può patire. Circa poi se Vostra Signoria è Lidia o no, io per Lidia la tengo, ma è così concentrato nel cuore la paura, e le forme stravaganti ho così ad ognora negli occhi, ch'io m'inganno, avendo credutola vestita d'uomo andar per le strade, e 'n abito di donna e fuor della casa holla pur vista uscire.

LIDIA Signor, mi duole che mia colpa, li sia intervenuto diabolici accidenti. Glorisi almeno, che s'io non amo lei, non amo altrui; parlo d'uomini, poiché amo così di cuore la signora Florinda che amarla più non so, né posso. Pur essendo per mio inganno Silvio prigioniero, è dovuto ch'io lo tragga da que' ferri. Or lasciate ch'io addimandi un mio paggetto e una mia serva.

Scena Settima
[Melina, Peruccio, Lidia, Orimberto]

MELINA Peruzo, quarda chi batte.

PERUCCIO Melina, sarà la signora padrona.

MELINA Te me faris benedir; guarda un pocolin!

PERUCCIO Sarà certissimo.

LIDIA O di casa, dico io.

MELINA Tuo', tuo', tuo', ti è anca chi bardassol!?

ORIMBERTO You are quite right, my lady. Once you hear what I have to say, however, you'll consider me sensible rather than ignorant. Madam, last night I wanted to have you under my spell, but I myself was bewitched in the process. I'm going to gloss over the details for now; we can speak of it another time. Let me get to the most important point, which is this: if Your Ladyship doesn't go to the Governor's palace right away, Silvio may be in some trouble. He's already explained that Your Ladyship said what you said in a fit of passion, and that's how he ended up in jail. He confesses that his indignation led him to lay a hand on you, but that he would never have harmed you. He therefore begs Lidia to come to the jail to tell the truth, because he can't take it anymore. As to whether or not you are Mistress Lidia, I'm going to take you to be her; but since great fear still crowds my heart and I still see those weird figures wherever I look, I could be deceiving myself. After all, I thought I saw you dressed as a man walking down the street, yet I also saw you come out of your house over there dressed as a woman.

LIDIA Good sir, I'm sorry if it's my fault that you were set upon by demons. At least you may console yourself with the thought that if I don't love you, neither do I love anyone else. I'm talking about men, because I love Florinda with all my heart; I don't know how, or if, I could love her any more than I already do. But since Silvio is in jail because of the deceit that I practiced, it's up to me to get him out of irons. Let me just speak with my pageboy and serving woman.

Scene Seven
[Melina, Peruccio, Lidia, Orimberto]

MELINA[lxxxvi] Peruccio, look who's knocking.

PERUCCIO Melina, it's our mistress.

MELINA You're gonna get me into trouble: just look at me!

PERUCCIO No question about that.

LIDIA I say, isn't there anyone home?

MELINA Take that, and that, and that! Are you still here, you wicked lad?

PERUCCIO Doh, vecchia poltrona!

LIDIA O di casa.

MELINA Chi è quel; guarda un pocolin sto ragaz, se l'è ustinà com'un mul.

PERUCCIO Se fussi tuo figliuolo sarei un mulo, cavallaccia poltrona.

MELINA O to' sto ganasson, bestiol.

PERUCCIO To' ancor tu questo pugno.

LIDIA O di casa, o della casa.

MELINA To'!

PERUCCIO To'!

MELINA To'!

PERUCCIO To'!

ORIMBERTO Signora Lidia, s'ammazzano costoro. Eccoli, eccoli.

PERUCCIO Signora padrona, costei m'ha dato uno schiaffo.

MELINA Signorina cara, patronzina dolza, el m'ha da' anca mi un smascelon che 'l m 'ha squas buttà un masselar in gola; e no guardé che sippa una massara, perché anca mi, potta de zuda, e son de carne, e de nierv.

LIDIA Altro tempo ci vuole a questa lite d'una vecchia pazza e d'un ragazzo troppo spiritoso. Su, con la chiave serra la porta, e tutti venite meco.

MELINA Vedi, vedi signora: Peruz m'ha fat una smorfia.

LIDIA Oh Melina! Chi ha più cervello il mostri; e tu furfantino, se non lasci star Melina vedrai come t'andrà.

PERUCCIO You lazy old bag!

LIDIA Hey, is anyone home?

MELINA Who's that? If this boy isn't as stubborn as a mule!

PERUCCIO I would be a mule if I was your son, you lazy old mare.

MELINA Here's the back of my hand for you, you beast!

PERUCCIO And here's a fist for you!

LIDIA Hey, is anyone home? Anyone in there?

MELINA Take that!

PERUCCIO Take that!

MELINA And that!

PERUCCIO And that!

ORIMBERTO Mistress Lidia, they're killing each other. Here they are, here they are.

PERUCCIO Mistress, she slapped me.

MELINA Dear miss, sweet mistress, he gave me such a smack that he almost knocked my teeth down my throat! And never mind the fact that I'm just a servant, because I'm made of flesh and blood too, goddammit!

LIDIA It'll have to keep for another time: then I'll deal with this quarrel between a crazy old woman and a boy who's too full of beans. Come on, lock the door with the key, and everyone come with me.

MELINA Did you see that, my lady? Peruccio made a face at me.

LIDIA Oh, Melina! If you have more brains than he does, show it. And as for you, you little rascal, if you don't leave Melina alone you'll

PERUCCIO Signora, quanto formaggio mi trova nelle saccocce, tutto, tutto, se lo mangia.

LIDIA Cheto, là dico.

ORIMBERTO Cheta, cheta madonna Melina; Peruccio poi è fanciullo e tutti siamo stati fanciulli; dovereste pur esser consimili, voi Melina diminutivo di mela grande, e lui Peruccio di gran pero lo stesso; e siete così discordi.

LIDIA Là dico. Va' Peruccio avanti, e sta' con creanza; e tu Melina, or ch'ho serata la porta, seguitami, che 'l signor Orimberto, grazia sua, sarà il mio onorato sostegno.

ORIMBERTO Così l'avess'io potuta sostener questa notte in braccio e portarla alle mie stanze, com'or m'è conceduto il servirla.

LIDIA Eh, eh, eh, Vostra Signoria mi fa ridere. Non voglio, né posso amare, tanta cattiva fortuna ho scorso in amore. Andiamo, che per lo cammino discorrer potremo di questo. Peruccio.

PERUCCIO Signora.

LIDIA Allunga il passo. Melina.

MELINA Patronzina, a viegn, potta de zuda mo' che farà signorina?

FINE DELL'ATTO QUARTO

see how things will turn out for you.

PERUCCIO My lady, if she finds any cheese in my pockets, she eats it all—all of it, all of it.

LIDIA Keep quiet, I'm warning you.

ORIMBERTO You keep quiet too, Melina. Peruccio's just a boy, and we've all been young ourselves. You two ought to be like one another—for if your name means "little apple," his means "little pear"—and yet you're opposites instead.

LIDIA Over here, I say. Peruccio, you walk ahead, and behave yourself. And now that I've locked the door, you follow me, Melina; Orimberto will instead be my honored escort.

ORIMBERTO If only I'd been able to escort her in my arms to my rooms last night, just as now she's letting me serve her here.

LIDIA Ha, ha, ha: Your Excellency makes me laugh. I neither want to, nor can, love again, for I've had such bad luck in love. Let's go, and as we walk we may speak of this further. Peruccio.

PERUCCIO My lady.

LIDIA Get moving. Melina.

MELINA I'm coming, my little mistress. But goddammit, what's that girl going to do?

END OF ACT FOUR

ATTO QUINTO

Scena Prima
[Coradella e Granello]

CORADELLA Oh povero Coradella!

GRANELLO Oh poverissimo Granello!

CORADELLA E che, dobbiam noi andar con questi duo fastelli d'erbe varie tutt'oggi al collo, facendo rider i fanciulli?

GRANELLO Non sai tu s'ha detto quel grand'uomo ch'è dovuto far questo per non s'inspiritare, poiché son erbe che pongono in fuga gli spiriti.

CORADELLA Ohimè, son pur lasso, fiacco, e tanto ho nelle fauci asciutta la lingua ch'io non posso né sputare, né parlare.

GRANELLO O caro fratello, non ti dico nulla, io sono così fuori di me che per diece anni Granello più non saprà trovar Granello.

CORADELLA Spiriti, eh!

GRANELLO Amori, eh!

CORADELLA Sia pur maledetto chi più s'innamora.

GRANELLO Ma se pur ci fosse accaduto questo per nostre innamorate, ma per le altrui, troppo mi pesa.

CORADELLA Guarda guarda.

GRANELLO Ohimè, dov'è lo spirito?

CORADELLA È una lucertola ch'è corsa nel buco.

GRANELLO Mago traditore; oh, di' che 'l padrone mi commandi ch'io vada solo a cavar il vino, s'io lo so.

ACT V

Scene One
[Coradello, Granello]

CORADELLA O poor Coradella!

GRANELLO O even poorer Granello!

CORADELLA Are we supposed to go around all day with these two bundles of assorted herbs around our necks, making all the kids laugh at us?

GRANELLO Don't you know what the great man said? He had us do this in order not to be possessed, since these herbs drive away evil spirits.

CORADELLA Alas and alack, I'm so weary and weak, and my tongue's so dry in my mouth that I can neither spit nor speak.

GRANELLO Oh dear brother, I can't talk to you: I'm so completely out of my mind that for the next ten years I'll be looking for myself. Granello will be trying to find Granello!

CORADELLA Spirits, eh!

GRANELLO Loves, eh!

CORADELLO A curse on whoever falls in love again.

GRANELLO It would be bad enough if all this had happened to us for our own sweethearts' sakes, let alone for someone else's.

CORADELLA Look, look!

GRANELLO Ohmygod, where's the spirit?

CORADELLA It's just a lizard running into a hole.

GRANELLO Rotten wizard! Hey, next you'll tell me that the master

CORADELLA E che ti pensi che dovrò far io? Ma ecco i nostri padroni. Oh come sono smorti! Oh com'hanno i nasi affilati! Ti so dir che si hanno avuta una che dice venti.

Scena Seconda
[Lelio, Guerindo, Granello e Coradella]

LELIO Ecco il mio servo Granello.

GRANELLO Ecco il malanno che mi pigli.

GUERINDO Oh povero Coradella!

CORADELLA Sì di grazia, ditemi povero Coradella, e come state voi?

GUERINDO Male fratello.

LELIO E io malissimo.

GRANELLO È una grà conversazione quella dell'avversario, non mai più mi c'intrico.

LELIO Ti giuriamo che nè così uscito Amor del capo, che non più vogliamo per donna sospirare, né far di quelle pazzie che fatte abbiamo. Ma non sai che pur il signor Guerindo amava Florinda, ora né lui né io vogliam sentirne parola.

Scena Terza
[Orimberto e Lelio, Guerindo, Coradella, Granello, Mago]

ORIMBERTO E dove lasciate me? S'io mai più m'innamoro, non poss'io giamai disnodarmi le stringhe alor ch'avrò tolto medicina, onde Amor essendomi addosso possa ammorbarlo. Questa notte per la signora Lidia ho avuto andar in Numidia per le poste.

LELIO E che sì, che sì, che 'l Mago averà parimente burlato il signor Orimberto?

has ordered me to go alone to get the wine from the cellar.

CORADELLA What do you think, that I'm supposed to do it? But here are our masters. They look half-dead: just look at their drawn cheeks! I can tell you that they've bitten off more than they can chew.

Scene Two
[Lelio, Guerindo, Granello, and Coradella]

LELIO Here's my servant Granello.

GRANELLO Here's misfortune come back to get me.

GUERINDO O poor Coradella!

CORADELLA Yes, thanks, please do call me "poor Coradella": and how are you?

GUERINDO Not well, brother.

LELIO And I'm most unwell.

GRANELLO The evil one makes only wicked conversation, and I'm never getting mixed up in it again.

LELIO We swear to you that Love is so completely gone from our thoughts we'll never want to sigh for a woman again, nor do those crazy things we did. Wouldn't you know that Guerindo also was in love with Florinda! Now neither he nor I want to hear another word about her.

Scene Three
[Orimberto, Lelio, Guerindo, Coradella, Granello, Wizard]

ORIMBERTO And where does that leave me? If I ever fall in love again, even before I've gotten my laces untied I'll have swallowed a remedy so that when Cupid is upon me I'll poison him. Last night, for the sake of Mistress Lidia, I went to the ends of the earth the hard way.

LELIO Can it be so? Did the Wizard also trick Orimberto?

ORIMBERTO Certo ch'Orimberto la berta ha dal Mago ricevuta, ma, vedete, solenne. Credo certo s'io tiro forte, che 'l pelo se ne viene dal capo.

GRANELLO Non solo s'io tiro vien il pelo, ma s'io mi stropiccio ancor che piano, tutta la pelle se ne viene.

CORADELLA E a me, che stanno le polpe per cadermi dalle gambe, e le chiappe dell'eccetera dove stanno appese?

GUERINDO Certo chè dovuto volger lo sdegno contra il Mago, né curando i suoi diabolici incanti far che sia discacciato da questa città, nonché da questa contrada.

MAGO Voi, voi tutti dovreste dalla città esser discacciati, come quelli che non conoscendo la virtù siete rei di star fra le selve, come que' vostri servitori alle mandre.

GRANELLO E che n'ha per porci costui?

MAGO Ditemi un poco, alor ch'io vi diedi il libro, la verga, la candela, che vi dissi?

LELIO Molto dicesti, molto facemmo; ma poco giovò.

MAGO Se rettamente aveste operato, sareste tutti contenti. Ditemi, s'io v'apparecchio un fuoco mentre gelati siete, non vi do un grandissimo ristoro? Certo sì. S'io di più, vi do legna onde maggiormente duri l'incendio, non vi fo cosa grata? Non si può negare. Or se da voi stessi vi private di tal bene, col gittar su le fiamme dell'acqua e spegner il fuoco, qual colpa è la mia? O stolti, e perdonatemi, così per l'appunto avete fatto voi altri nell'incanto. Il tutto v'era favorevole, e chi d'ogni bene v'ha spogliato? Il gittar l'acqua sopra il fuoco.

GUERINDO Ma non avevamo già acqua noi, ch'era tutto fuoco, e del buono; e ancor puzzo da brustolato ch'ammorbo.

MAGO Toccò alcuno di voi con la verga la cosa nella quale era la vostra amata?

ORIMBERTO You bet. I was not only tricked, but utterly fooled, by the Wizard. I think that, if I pull hard, the hair will come right off my head.

GRANELLO Not only does my hair come off if I pull it, but if I rub myself even a bit faster than usual, all my skin comes off.

CORADELLA And what about me? The flesh is about to fall off my legs, and where did someone hang my butt?

GUERINDO We're surely right to be angry with the Wizard. We should disavow his diabolical spells and see to it that he's driven from this city, not to mention from this neighborhood.

WIZARD All of you should be driven from the city: you are guilty of acting like savages who know nothing of virtue, just as those servants of yours are good only for herding swine.

GRANELLO And just what does this guy have against pigs?

WIZARD Tell me: what did I say to you when I gave you the book, the staff, and the candle?

LELIO You said a lot, and we did a lot; but it didn't do us much good.

WIZARD If you'd acted correctly, you'd all be happy right now. Answer me this: if I prepare a fire for you when you're freezing, do I not provide you with great relief? Of course I do. And if, furthermore, I give you firewood to keep the the fire blazing longer, do I not do you a welcome favor? Undeniably so. Now, if you deprive yourselves of this good, by throwing water on the flames and putting the fire out, why is that my fault? You fools—and forgive me for saying so—did exactly that in saying the spell. Everything was in your favor, and who took it all away from you? Whoever threw water on the fire.

GUERINDO But we didn't have any water. There was fire everywhere, and what a fire! I still stink of the smoke.

WIZARD Did any of you touch with the staff that thing in which your beloved lay?

ORIMBERTO Toccastela voi signor Lelio?

LELIO Io no certo.

GUERINDO Né io.

ORIMBERTO Né men io.

CORADELLA Al corpo di me chè vero; e pur l'arricordai.

GRANELLO E io così feci.

MAGO Incolpate dunque voi stessi, né ponete la bocca in cielo spar-
lando d'uomo celeste, siami lecito tanto dire. Ma perché siete amanti,
vi perdono, il proprio mio essendo di favorir simili oppressi. Tutti
venite meco, che levandovi l'amore, infondervi i' voglio spirito guerriero, che insegnandovi a disprezzar l'amate, vi faccia per sempre della
guerra amanti.

LELIO Quanto vuol uomo così famoso, tanto voglio anch'io, e tanto
credo che voglia Guerindo ancora.

GUERINDO Altro non desidero.

CORADELLA E noi vogliamo quello che i nostri padroni vogliono;
chè un pezzo ch'a questo modo ci siamo accordati.

GRANELLO È vero.

ORIMBERTO Io signor non son nato per la guerra, ma sarò quello
che stando nella città scriverà questo fatto guerriero.

MAGO Io mi contento, entriamo. Seguitatemi signori, e perché non
usino ceremonie io sarò il primo a far la via, ciascuno seguiti.

LELIO Andiamo signori.

GOVERNATORE Tutti vi seguitiamo signor Lelio.

ORIMBERTO E io pur vengo.

ORIMBERTO Did you touch it, Lelio?

LELIO Indeed I did not.

GUERINDO Nor did I.

ORIMBERTO Neither did I.

CORADELLA I'll be damned if it isn't so; and yet I remember it.

GRANELLO And I did the same.

WIZARD You're putting the blame on yourselves, then, and, if I may be allowed to say so, you shouldn't bite the hand that feeds you. But I forgive you all, because you're in love. It's in my nature to want to help those who are oppressed in this way. Come with me now, all of you, and I will draw love out of you in order to fill you with the spirit of the warrior instead. By teaching you to despise your beloved, I'll turn you into lovers of war.

LELIO Whatever such a famous man wants is what I want too; and I think this is what Guerindo wants too.

GUERINDO I desire nothing more.

CORADELLA And we want what our masters want. For some time now this is the way we've all been able to agree with each other.

GRANELLO True enough.

ORIMBERTO I, sir, was not born for war, but I'll remain in town to write about their great deeds of valor.

WIZARD That's good enough for me. Let's go in: follow me, gentlemen, and, so as not to stand on ceremony, I'll lead the way; each of you in turn should come after me.

LELIO Let's go, gentlemen.

GUERINDO[lxxxvii] We'll all follow you, Lelio.

GRANELLO E noi senza dir altro al pari entriamo.

[*Qui faranno vista di non poter entrare, e poi tutti in un tempo entreranno.*]

Scena Quarta
[Eugenio, Bernetta]

EUGENIO Non vidi giamai umor più stravagante di colui, se non erro, che aveva nome Orimberto, per quanto m'è stato detto: "Vita mia, cor mio!" Li diedi ben io un ricordo, con cinque avvertimenti a mano aperta, che se l'arricorderà.

BERNETTA Signora sì, lasciate far a me, or ora glielo porto. Oh che bel mazzetto! Oh che bei fiori! Oh che soavi odori! Tutto ora anderà in dono alla signora Lidia. In effetto, chi dona il cuore ogn'altra cosa è poco. Chi è questo bel soldatino? Un essercito di questi, i turchi subbito si renderebbero.

EUGENIO Costei mi guarda, qual che ruffiana che va a caccia, come la volpe a pollastri.

BERNETTA   Fa, la, la, la, son nata alla Ripetta,
              E Roma tutta m'ha detto Bernetta.

EUGENIO Bell'umore, canta, passeggia con isprezzatura, e in passando mi dà delle acute guardate.

BERNETTA Eh, eh, eh.

EUGENIO Orsù, costei è pazza.

BERNETTA Signor giovine mio, potta di Bao, com'è il vostro nome? Maramao? (Quest'è la signora Lidia, voglio far la balorda.)

EUGENIO Son Maramao. E voi dove avete la squacquara?

ORIMBERTO I'm coming too.

GRANELLO Without another word, let's go in together.

[*Here we see that the players can't get through the door, and then all at once they go through it together.*]

Scene Four
[Eugenio, Bernetta]

EUGENIO I never saw anyone act as bizarrely as that fellow, whose name, if I'm not mistaken, was "Orimberto" and who kept saying to me "my life, my love!" I gave him quite a souvenir so that he won't forget me: five pieces of advice delivered with the flat of my hand.

BERNETTA Yes, my lady, leave it to me; I'll take it to her right away. What a lovely bunch of flowers! How beautiful they are! What a sweet scent! Now all these will go as a gift to Mistress Lidia. But when you give your heart away, no other present can really compare. Who's this handsome little soldier? Against an army of fellows like him, the Turks would surrender right away.[lxxxviii]

EUGENIO That woman is staring at me as if she were a madame on the prowl or a fox going after chickens.

BERNETTA   Tra, la, la, la: I was born at Ripetta
                And all of Rome called me Bernetta.[lxxxix]

EUGENIO In a good mood, while singing and strolling nonchalantly, she passes by and throws me some sharp glances.

BERNETTA Well, well, well…

EUGENIO She's gone out of her mind.

BERNETTA My good young sir, by the cunt of St. Hussy, what's your name? Wait, I'll tell you: it's Pussy. (This is Lidia, or my name is "Stupid.")

EUGENIO That's me alright: Pussy. And where do you have it all warm

BERNETTA Su la camicia.

EUGENIO Oh brutta poltrona! Questo a me, questo a un cavaliere?

BERNETTA Siete cavaliero eh, il credo; ma ho udito a dire che 'l vostro cavallo non ha coda. Ah ghiotterella, che volete far in quest'abito? Volete soffocar la natura della femmina, chè d'andar sborrosa, o senza calzoni. State pur tanto bene; e perché far questo, che strana risoluzione avete presa? Attendete, che voglio chiamar la signora padrona.

EUGENIO Oh, che imbroglio!

BERNETTA O di casa? Signora Florinda signora Florinda, il signor Lidio, il signor Lidio!

EUGENIO Eugenio, Eugenio, non Lidio.

BERNETTA Sì, sì, quel signor Eugenio ch'ha tanto nei calzoni, com'ho io sotto la veste.

EUGENIO E qualche cosa di più.

BERNETTA Questo lo vedrà poi la mia padrona.

EUGENIO Di grazia, purché sia meritevole di tener del resto, mi contento.

BERNETTA Signora padrona uscite.

Scena Quinta
[Florinda, Eugenio, Bernetta]

FLORINDA Che vuoi, che vuoi, che tu mi chiami, con sì gran fretta?

EUGENIO Quest'è una bella signora.

and soft?[xc]

BERNETTA Let me lift this shirt.

EUGENIO You nasty good-for-nothing! How dare you do that to me—to a trooper like me!

BERNETTA Right, right, I believe you, you're really a trooper: but I've heard it said that your mount hasn't got a tail. You greedy little thing, what are you trying to do, dressed up like that? Do you want to smother woman's true nature, which is to go about flowing forth freely, or at least not in pants? You're so well off in life: why are you doing this? What strange fancy has taken hold of you? Wait here, for I want to call my mistress.

EUGENIO What kind of swindle is this?

BERNETTA Is anyone home? Mistress Florinda, Mistress Florinda! Master Lidio, Master Lidio is here!

EUGENIO It's Eugenio, Eugenio: I'm not Lidio.

BERNETTA Yes, yes, the same Eugenio who's got as much in his trousers as I have under this skirt.

EUGENIO And something more besides.

BERNETTA That will be for my mistress to decide.

EUGENIO Please, I'll be content if she's worthy to keep the change.

BERNETTA Come on out, mistress.

Scene Five
[Florinda, Eugenio, Bernetta]

FLORINDA What do you want, what do you want? Why are you calling for me with such great haste?

EUGENIO This is a lovely lady.

BERNETTA Signora Florinda, mi credo che la signora Lidia, per tema della corte, per aver, come Vostra Signoria sa, accusato il signor Silvio a torto, voglia fuggire; s'è perciò vestita in abito d'uomo, e fingendo non mi conoscere, dice ch'ha nome Eugenio; però quando m'ha sentito dir di chiamar la mia padrona, s'è fermata. Eccola in quel canto.

FLORINDA Lascia far a me. O 'l mio caro soldatino, o 'l mio vago amoretto armato, così eh? Convertir la faretra in ispada, la benda in sciarpa? Solo una cosa ha dello sproporcionato alla voce d'Amore, poiché Amor è spogliato e voi siete vestito. Entriamo adunque in casa che, dispogliato che sarete, vi porrò in letto, e io novella Psiche mi corcherò presso il mio novello Amore.

EUGENIO È ben un furfante chi non ci viene. Signora son Lidia femmina, Eugenio maschio, Amor vestito, spogliato, tutto quello che vuole, andiamo a letto, che 'l tempo caldo il ricerca.

FLORINDA Andiamo cor mio, andiamo.

BERNETTA Oh che signora Lidia cattiva! Ma quanto mi dispiace che Florinda rimarrà poi con le mani piene di mosche, come sarà nel letto. Promette, è vero, quell'abito d'uomo, che troverà Florinda cercando un baloardo; spogliata poi di quell'abito darà della mano in una piatta forma. Entro anch'io.

Scena Sesta
[Governatore, Sufronio, Silvio, Lidia, Melina, Peruccio, quattro labardieri]

GOVERNATORE Grandissima forza ha 'l piccolo fanciullo Amore; ma perché non si conosce errore dove regna Amore, per questo non volli men io esser così rigoroso com'averei potuto. Sarà bene però, signora Lidia, che il signor Silvio con licenza del suo signor padre, e per mie preghiere, si disponga a pigliar così cara signora per consorte. Che dite signor Sufronio?

SUFRONIO Quanto vuol Vostra Signoria Illustrissima altrottanto voglio anch'io.

BERNETTA Mistress Florinda, I think Lidia wants to flee because she fears the court; as Your Ladyship knows, she wrongly accused Silvio. So she's gotten dressed up as a man and, pretending not to recognize me, says that her name is Eugenio. When she heard me say that I was going to call my mistress, however, she stayed. See, she's over there.

FLORINDA Leave this to me. Oh my darling little soldier, oh my pretty little armed Cupid, so that's it, eh? You want to turn the quiver into the sword, or a blindfold into a neck-scarf ? There's only one thing that doesn't quite fit with the figure of Cupid: for Cupid is undressed, and you've still got your clothes on. Let's go into the house and, once you're undressed, I'll put you to bed, and then I'll be the new Psyche lying next to my new Cupid.

EUGENIO Only a knave could refuse her offer. My lady, I'm the woman named Lidia, the man called Eugenio; I'm Cupid, dressed or undressed; I'll be anything you like, but let's go to bed, as the heat of the day commands.

FLORINDA Let's go, my love, let's go.

BERNETTA Oh, but that Lidia is bad! How sorry I am that Florinda will end up with nothing for it, and in bed it'll be the same story. It's true enough, those men's clothes seem to promise that Florinda will find herself with a well-built bastion; but once those clothes are off, she'll instead lay her hands on only a little platform. I'm going inside too.

Scene Six
[Governor, Sufronio, Silvio, Lidia, Melina, Peruccio, four halberdiers]

GOVERNOR The little boy-child, Cupid, is extremely powerful, but because there are no errors wherever he reigns, I do not wish to be as rigorous in this case as I might have been. It would be well, Lidia, if, with his father's permission, and in accordance with my prayers, Silvio were to be disposed to take such a dear lady as his lawfully wedded wife. What say you, Sufronio?

SUFRONIO Whatever Your Excellency desires is my desire as well.

GOVERNATORE E voi, signor Silvio, che ne sentite?

SILVIO Benché l'animo mio fosse disposto ad altro ch'al pigliar moglie, nondimeno per sue preghiere, per la volontà del padre, e perché assai merita la signora Lidia, io mi contento.

GOVERNATORE Tocca solo a voi signora Lidia a compiacersi di questo, il che sarà facile, amando Vostra Signoria al vivo così fatto gentiluomo.

LIDIA Non nego signore di non aver amato il signor Silvio quanto amar si possa altro amante; ma accadono cose in un momento che non sono bastanti a capire in senso umano. Non ha molto ch'io, della signora Florinda invaghita, disprezzo l'amor di tutti gli uomini per provar quello d'una donna sola; la quale quanto amava sé stessa entro uno specchio, tanto s'è posta ad amar me, entro lo specchio del mio volto mirando tutto quel bello che già la faceva in se stessa contenta; e perciò abbiamo giurato ambe due di voler consevar il fior virginale col non saper d'uomini, con amarci ad ognor di vivo cuore.

GOVERNATORE Strana cosa invero ode Latanzio; e certo questa cosa è degna più tosto di silenzio che di racconto. E come dovranno due così belle signore viver digiune d'amanti e di consorti, e quel ch'è peggio, d'esser prive di dar in copia bellissimi e nobilissimi figli al mondo, da' quali si vegga e l'armi e le lettere fatte maggiormente gloriose? Ah, fugga da Vostra Signoria così, e mi perdoni, indegno pensiero.

LIDIA Signore così giurai, e così d'osservar prometto.

MELINA Signor Governator, credi a Melina da Bulogna, vedi che com' la mia fanesina ha dit una cosa l'è cusì vedi; uh poverina l'ha pur patì tant per quel signor Silvi de carton.

PERUCCIO E Peruccio ne fa fede signor Governatore, che tante volte sono andato a letto senza cena per la disperazione amorosa che questo signor Silvio poneva nel cuore alla mia povera signora Lidia. Oh, quanti cancheri gli ho tirato! Ma non si sono appiccati, che ne sarebbe tutto, tutto pieno; ve lo dico, perdonatemi.

GOVERNOR And you, Silvio, how do you feel about this?

SILVIO Although my thoughts were turned to other things than marriage, nevertheless—thanks to your prayers, my father's wishes, and the fact that Lidia is deserving indeed—I accept.

GOVERNOR Now it's up to you to agree to this, Lidia, which should be easy, since Your Ladyship loves so strongly this selfsame gentleman.

LIDIA I don't deny, sir, that I have loved Silvio as well as one might love one's lover. But in a single moment things can happen that can't be understood in human terms. It wasn't long ago that I, in love with Florinda, despised the love of all men, in order to experience that of a woman alone. She came to love me as much as she loved herself in the mirror; and in the mirror of my face she could gaze at all the beauty that used to make her happy in herself. And thus the two of us swore to preserve our virginal flower by not knowing men and loving each other with all our hearts.

GOVERNOR What strange things do I hear?[xci] Certainly this is better passed over in silence than told aloud. And how should such lovely ladies live without lovers and consorts and, what is worse, be deprived of bringing into the world an abundance of most handsome and noble sons, who would bring greater glory both to arms and letters? Pardon me for saying so, but may Your Ladyship banish such an unworthy thought.

LIDIA Sir, thus did I give my word, and thus do I intend to keep it.

MELINA Lord Governor, listen to Melina from Bologna. You see, if my little girl has said one thing, then that's the way it is, you see! Poor thing, she's suffered so much for that worthless fellow Silvio.

PERUCCIO And I, Peruccio, can testify that I've gone to bed many times without supper because of the lover's despair this fellow Silvio has put into the heart of my poor mistress Lidia. How many times I've wished the pox upon him! If my wishes didn't stick, it's a good thing, because he'd be totally full of it by now. There, I've said it: forgive me.

MELINA E mi ghe ho pur augurà tante code sel, e tanti tarvò.

GOVERNATORE Stavi fresco signor Silvio.

SILVIO Pacienza signor.

Scena Settima
[Bernetta, Governatore, Lidia, Silvio, Sufronio, Melina, Peruccio, Florinda]

BERNETTA Piano, cari signori, che Florinda è con il signor Eugenio.

GOVERNATORE Quest'altra è un grazioso umore; dice: "Piano di grazia, poiché Florinda è col signor Eugenio," e poi se n'entra.

LIDIA "Eugenio è con Florinda!" "Piano, cari signori?"

BERNETTA Ma sì, che indiscrizione è questa? Vi dico che facciate piano che Florinda è col signor Eugenio.

LIDIA Sì questo torto a me! Signor Governatore voglio far le mie vendette.

GOVERNATORE Piano, piano; noi vediamo quelle d'Amore in Vostra Signoria perché così rigida voleva esser al signor Silvio.

LIDIA Signor, abbisi pacienza il signor Silvio, che non mai sarò sua; Florinda m'ha ingannata.

BERNETTA Il vostro viso ha ingannata lei, semplicetta. Io so come l'è; ma perché Florinda è ormai vestita, e vuol dar lodi ad Amore, e chiederli publico perdono, lascerò la cura a lei. Eccola appunto.

FLORINDA Grande è la possanza d'Amore.

LIDIA Ah Florinda, così eh?

MELINA And I've wished him ill many times as well.

GOVERNOR You were certainly in trouble there, Silvio.

SILVIO What can I say, my lord?

Scene Seven
[Bernetta, Governor, Lidia, Silvio, Sufronio, Melina, Peruccio, Florinda]

BERNETTA Not so loud, good people: Florinda is in there with Eugenio.

GOVERNOR She's got a fine sense of humor, telling us "please, not so loud, because Florinda is with Eugenio," and then she walks right in there.

LIDIA "Eugenio is with Florinda?" "Not so loud, good people?"

BERNETTA Yes, there's nothing wrong with saying it: I'm asking all of you to keep it down because Florinda is with Eugenio.

LIDIA How dare she do this to me! My Lord Governor, I want to take my revenge.

GOVERNOR Not so fast, not so fast. We see here Cupid's revenge on Your Ladyship because you wanted to be so severe with Silvio.

LIDIA Silvio will have to accept that I'll never be his, my lord; but Florinda has deceived me.

BERNETTA You little dolt, it was your face that deceived her. I know how things really stand: but because Florinda is now dressed, and wants to praise Cupid while publicly asking his pardon, I'll leave it up to her to tell you. And here she is.

FLORINDA Great is the power of Love.

LIDIA Ah Florinda, so that's it, eh?

FLORINDA Ah, Lidia mia, uditemi.

LIDIA Che mia, non sia mai vero! Così tosto rompermi la fede!

FLORINDA Lidia mia, dir vi voglio, poiché ora più che mai, mia siete.

LIDIA Fui vostra mentre m'osservaste fede; or che l'avete rotta, anch'io la rompo e frango.

FLORINDA Uditemi signori, e s'io ho torto non solo Lidia ch'è il mio bene con la lingua m'ingiuri, ma con la mano mi castighi.

LIDIA No, no, signora io non voglio sentirvi; avete adulterate le santissime leggi dell'amicizia, avete franta la fede datami di conservar il fiore virginale, e avete annullato lo stretto obligo di non conoscer uomo. Non voglio udirvi, signora ciascuno mi scusi, io me n'entro.

GOVERNATORE Donna risoluta niun ceppo l'affrena. Dica adunque la signora Florinda, che con grandissima attenzione ascoltiamo.

FLORINDA Signori, credo che per cento lingue sia noto per la città di Firenze, com'io odiava tutti gli uomini per amar me sola. In questo tempo ch'entro un vetro la fragilità di questo mio bene godeva, ecco Amore vuol, se in un vetro errai, in un vetro faccia l'ammenda; così mentr'oggi colà dentro mi vagheggio e trastullo, scorgo un languido viso, che sì mesto mi sembrava ch'io, tutta intenta a consolarlo, miro d'intorno occhiuta da qual alto entro il basso dello specchio quella imagine veniva; tanto feci con le preghiere, e con inganni, ch'al fine vidi ch'era la giovinetta Lidia, che, usanza di Firenze, aveva in capo un finissimo cappellino con penne. La stessa, dalle finestre scende alla strada, e qui palesatasi amante, io biasimo Amore, ed ella così faconda il loda che di lei mi sento prigioniera amante; e per un certo dolcissimo rilassamento nelle sue braccia io le svenni. Ritornata in me stessa, è fatta così del mio mal pietosa che mi giura di non più conoscer uomo per amarmi. Così, con laccio di fede avvinte in promissione strettissima, giurammo di conservarsi verginelle.

Oh potenza d'Amore! In questo tempo, veggo un giovanetto chiamato Eugenio, fratello simile di Lidia. Io la credo la stessa Lidia, che per tema della querela data ingiusta a Silvio, voglia incognita allontanarsi da Fiorenza, e con parole brevi, e con atti risoluti

FLORINDA Ah my dear Lidia, listen to me.

LIDIA What do you mean, "my dear Lidia?" It was never true! You were so quick to break faith with me!

FLORINDA "My dear Lidia" is what I want to say to you, for now—more than ever—you're mine.

LIDIA I was yours while you were faithful to me; and now that you're not, I too will break faith with you and crush it to pieces.

FLORINDA Listen to me, one and all, and if I'm in the wrong may Lidia—whom I love—not only insult me with her tongue but chastise me with her own hand.

LIDIA No, no, madam, I don't want to listen to you. You've violated the most holy laws of friendship, you've broken the vow you made to me to preserve your maidenhead, and you've not respected our strict obligation not to know men. I don't want to listen to you, my lady. Now will you all please excuse me; I'm going back into my house.

GOVERNOR There are no fetters that can hold back a resolute woman. Speak, then, Florinda: we're all ears.

FLORINDA Good people, I think throughout the city of Florence it's known by one and all that I used to hate men and love only myself. I used to delight in the fragility of that love of mine within the glass; until one day Cupid decided to make amends in a glass for the error that I had made in a glass. Thus while I was looking lovingly at myself and praising myself in it, I saw appear next to mine a languid face that seemed so sad to me that I, all intent upon consoling it, looked around me high and low to discover whence that image in the mirror came. So keen was I that, with many prayers and tricks, at last I found the young Mistress Lidia, who, following the Florentine fashion, was wearing a very elegant little hat with feathers. She came down from the window to the street, and when she told me of her troubles in love, I condemned Cupid. She instead praised him so skillfully that I felt myself become her loving prisoner, and with a certain sweetest slackening of my senses I swooned into her arms. When I came to myself, she was so moved by my plight that she swore to me never to know

l'abbraccio, il conduco in casa, fo retirar le serve, mi chiudo in una camera, e per vestirmi anch'io de' panni per ischerzare, e per far che quelle spoglie ella deponesse, di mia mano lo spoglio, ed egli entrato nel letto, alor che mi vede spogliata dice: "O Florinda mia cara, vorrei dirvi un gran caso, e poi vestir vi potrete." Così con allegrezza saglio il letto e vicino lui mi corco, il bacio dolce e dicoli: "Che vuoi anima mia? Favella, ecco la tua Florinda." alor Eugenio, stringendomi disse: "Sappiate mia signora, come io non son donna come voi, ma sono, se giamai l'udiste nominare, un ermafrodito, cioè sono più uomo che donna."

In questo così fatto dire, non so io signor. Vago d'udir e di saper com'ogni donna suole, tanto fece e tanto disse, che dalle sue braccia non mi tolsi, che sua sposa rimasi, scoprendomi con l'opera che tutt'uomo egli era. Eccovi adunque detto come Amor i superbi castighi.

MELINA Quest'è la mazor cosa che mai sippa stada sentida da Borgonou a Saragoza.

GOVERNATORE Certamente qui si vede uno sforzo grandissimo di castigo amoroso. Signora Florinda, non bisognava nascer così bella se Vostra Signoria non voleva che Amor si sdegnasse contra lei, non volendo sentir parte di quel fuoco che tutto il mondo sente. Novella Psiche ancor voi oggi sarete, che sdegnando fastosa di sua beltà, di non amore amante alfin rimase, e amante del bellissimo Amore; però s'è così bello il signor Eugenio com'è la signora Lidia, si potrà sicuramente dir che di nuovo si sia rinovato in terra in questo punto il caso della stessa Psiche e dello stesso Amore. Ma ecco s'io non erro il vostro sposo. Oh com'è vago!

men and to love me only. Bound together tightly by our vows of love, thus we swore to one another to remain maidens.

Oh power of Love! Not long after, I saw a young man named Eugenio, who is Lidia's twin. I thought that she was Lidia herself,[xcii] who, because of the unjust accusations she'd made against Silvio, wanted to leave Florence in disguise. With brief words and resolute deeds I embraced him, led him into my house,[xciii] had the servants withdraw, and shut us up in a room. There I planned to dress up in some funny clothes of my own and to get her out of those spoils of conquest.[xciv] So I undressed him and took him to bed. When he saw me undressed, he said: "O my darling Florinda, I must tell you about an extraordinary circumstance, and then you may get dressed again." So I happily climbed onto the bed and lay down by him, kissing him sweetly and saying: "What do you want, my love? Go on, tell me, your Florinda is right here." Then Eugenio, holding me tightly to him, said: "Know, then, madam, that I am not a woman like you, but am (if you've ever heard the term before) an hermaphrodite, that is to say, I am more man than woman."[xcv]

Well, I wouldn't have known if he hadn't said so. I naturally wanted to know more, just as any woman would, and he did and said so much more that I never did leave his arms. I became his wife,[xcvi] and in doing so I discovered that he was all man. Thus, from what I've told you, you can see how Cupid punishes the proud.

MELINA This is the most incredible thing that has ever been heard in the whole world.

GOVERNOR We can certainly see here a truly great effort to chastise you in love. Florinda, you shouldn't have been born so beautiful if Your Ladyship didn't want Cupid to be angry with you when refusing to feel any part of that fire the whole world feels. You're still a new Psyche even today: she displayed her beauty but disdained love; yet she went from not loving to becoming a lover in the end; a lover of that most beautiful god of Love himself. If Eugenio is as beautiful as Lidia, we can safely say that once more the story of Psyche and Cupid has been repeated here on earth among us. But, if I'm not mistaken, here's your husband. My, how handsome he is!

Scena Ottava
[Eugenio e tutti quelli della scena settima]

EUGENIO Signora consorte, e dove soletto mi lasciaste? Quanta nobil gente a questi sposi fanno ampia corona?

GOVERNATORE Signor Eugenio, io parlerò per molti. Siamo a parte di questo caso amoroso e improviso; ed è ben tale, e così pellegrino, ch'io voglio farne di mia mano un poco d'abbozzo per farlo poi recitare alla nostra Accademia, e intitolarlo *Amor nello specchio*. Godetevi felici, che 'l cielo vi sia favorevole di lunga vita e di figliuoli assai; poiché sì come molte torri fanno bella una città, molte navi un porto, molta cavalleria un campo, così molti figliuoli fanno bella una famiglia. Rimane solo che la povera signora Lidia si chiami contenta.

EUGENIO Signori io sono ancora mezo spogliato, però con loro licenza me n'entro.

BERNETTA E io vengo a vestirvi, non già a dispogliarvi, poiché in questo dispogliamento la mia padrona è rimasta colta da quell'ermafrodito che sta in parte nascosta.

SUFRONIO Eh, eh, eh, che ghiottoncella. [*Tutti ridranno.*] Ma che suon di tamburo, che gente esce fuor di quella casa?

Scena Nona
[Mago, Lelio, Guerindo, Orimberto, Granello, Coradella, e tutti gli altri della scena ottava]

[*Qui tutti quelli che saranno in scena si tireranno dietro la prospettiva, e gli altri passeggeranno il palco con bella distanza; Granello suonerà il tamburo, Coradella volteggerà un'insegna, o bene o ridicolosamente, facendo delle cascate nel girarsela sotto e sopra; però la bandiera sarà una fatta a capriccio di coloro che reciteranno.*]

MAGO Signore questi erano amanti, o mio signor Governatore, e or sono soldati.

Scene Eight
[all the characters in the previous scene, plus Eugenio]

EUGENIO My wife, where did you leave me so all alone? How many noble people are here to celebrate the bride and groom!

GOVERNOR Eugenio, I'll deign to speak for everyone here. Although not a part of this sudden love story, it's so strange and unusual that I want to write a brief sketch of these events and have it put on stage by our own Academy. I'll call it *Love in the Mirror*. Be happy and enjoy one another: may heaven grant you long life and many children. As many towers make a city lovely, many ships make a port, and much cavalry makes a field of battle, so do many children make a family beautiful. All that's left now is for poor Lidia to find her happiness.

EUGENIO Sirs, I'm still half undressed, and by your leave I'll go back inside.

BERNETTA I'll come along to dress you, and not to further undress you, since in removing those clothes my mistress was taken by that half-hidden hermaphrodite.[xcvii]

SUFRONIO Ha, ha, ha, what a little glutton you are! [*All laugh.*] But what are these drumbeats and who are these people coming out of that house?

Scene Nine
[all the characters in the previous scene,
plus the Wizard, Lelio, Guerindo, Orimberto, Granello, and
Coradella]

[*Here all the onstage actors will withdraw behind the backdrop, while the others will walk onto the stage keeping a good deal of distance from each other. Granello will be beating a drum; Coradella will be waving a standard either well or comically, and falling down while passing it above or beneath his body. Coradella's flag will be improvised by the actors.*]

WIZARD My lord Governor, these men who were once lovers are now soldiers.

GUERINDO O Arfasat eccellente, già dato segno avete del vostro gran valore a questa città, non solo nel liberar da spiriti il più bel palazzo che 'n Fiorenza fosse, quanto in aver fatto trovare al Serenissimo Gran Duca quel tesoro che dal Re Totila fu lasciato sepolto in queste parti; e or non contento avete fatto divenir questi gentiluomini amanti, bellicosi guerrieri?

MAGO Certo sì signore, e fra poco partir mi dovrò da questi confini, per ridurmi nell'Anglia, dove di quelle vastissime parti il Rege con lettere mi chiama.

GOVERNATORE Perderà molto l'Italia, quadagnerà in buon dato l'Inghilterra.

GRANELLO O signor Governatore, se parlate solamente col mago, Vostra Signoria non lascerà parlare al tamburino, né all'alfier Coradella. Che vi par di questo tu pu tu, pu tu; e di quest'altro il volteggiare e 'l cadere?

GOVERNATORE Sono cose maravigliosissime.

CORADELLA Il diavolo fa far di queste resoluzioni, vedete.

GUERINDO Illustrissimo signor Governatore, era vergogna s'al nome di Guerindo, che son quell'io, fossi ad ognora stato alla città con le mani a cintola; mi sono accorto del mio errore, e però fuggendo Amore, seguo Marte.

LELIO E io, mio signore, Lelio sono, che ben la riconosco e le m'inchino umile, che per aver nel mar di Venere scorso grandissima borrasca, nel porto di Bellona mi son reticato, e in quello appendo le tabelle di voto solenne di non più entrar in simil acque.

ORIMBERTO Io poi signore non vi so dir altro, se non che, se mai più m'innamoro, mi possa affogare come fece quel filosofo il primo picciolo grano d'uva passa ch'io mi pongo in bocca; e bench'io non abbia sargentino, sciarpa, cappello con pennoni, e terzaruoli al fianco stralucenti, nondimeno mi fa tanto cuore in veder loro così ben disposti, ch'io mi risolvo di star alla città a mangiar le succiole ad onor loro, e bever buona verdea vicino il mio caldano. [*Qui tutti ridono.*]

GUERINDO O excellent Arfasat, you've already shown this city your great worth. Not only have you exorcized the spirits who were haunting the most magnificent palace in Florence, but you've led his Most Serene Highness, the Grand Duke, to discover the treasure that King Totila long ago left buried here.[xcviii] As if that weren't enough, you've now turned these gentlemen from lovers into combative warriors?

WIZARD Indeed I have, sir. Soon, however, I must leave here and travel to Anglia, as letters from the king of that immense land have called me there.[xcix]

GOVERNOR Italy's great loss will be England's gain.

GRANELLO My lord Governor, if you only talk with the Wizard, Your Excellency will let speak neither the drummer nor the standard-bearer Coradella. What do you think about this *rat-a-tat, rat-a-tat-tat* of mine, or his twirling and dipping the flag?

GOVERNOR These are most wondrous things indeed.

CORADELLA You see, the devil makes us take such decisions.

GUERINDO Your most illustrious Lord Governor, it would be shameful if Guerindo—for that's my name—were always hanging around the city with his hands in his pockets. I recognize the error of my ways, and renounce Cupid in favor of Mars.

LELIO And I, my lord, am Lelio, who know you well and humbly bow before you. I encountered a terrible storm on the sea of Venus; but having reached the port of Bellona, goddess of war, I've published there my solemn vows never to sail upon such waters again.[c]

ORIMBERTO I, my lord, instead don't know what to add, except that if I should ever fall in love again, may I choke to death (as that philosopher did[ci]) on the first little raisin that I eat. Although I haven't got a halberd, neck-scarf, feathered cap, or any long shiny arquebuses[cii] at my side, it nonetheless warms my heart to see these men so willing to serve, so much so that I've decided to stay in the city and, in their honor, eat boiled chestnuts, drink good white wine, and stay close to my brazier. [*Here everyone laughs.*]

CORADELLA Eh, eh, eh! Il signor Orimberto ha detto benissimo. Ma ecco la signora Lidia con bocca ridente.

Scena Decima
[Lidia, Bernetta, con tutti quelli che recitano]

LIDIA Signori non solo ho udite dalla mia porta socchiusa le resuluzioni del signor Lelio e signor Guerindo, ma la cagione lecitissima per la quale la signora Florinda è divenuta di nemica d'Amore amante. Ma dov'è Eugenio, mio capitano fratello, il quale, fuggito dal padre, oggi esser mi dovrà secondo padre?

BERNETTA Lo dirò io. Questa cattivuccia della mia padrona, sanguisuca amorosa, voleva, alor ch'era nel letto, succhiarli tutto il sangue; or non avendo potuto gliel'ha tutto commosso e avviato come si vede alor che si avene poppando a 'n capezzolo d'una donna, che benché tu non poppi, nondimeno il latte stilla; ver'è che cessato il primo, gli vien ora tanto sangue dal naso ch'è una bellezza; però è sopra il catino, né può venire.

GOVERNATORE Anderem noi a visitar lui, che è ben dovere mirar le maraviglie angeliche di natura sparse in questi duo bellissimi volti, e della signora Lidia, e del signor Eugenio.

GRANELLO Farete bene signori, entrate tutti.

MAGO Anch'io la seguito.

LELIO E così il signor Guerindo e io facciamo.

GOVERNATORE Signora Lidia.

LIDIA Mio signore.

GOVERNATORE Con patto che 'l signor Silvio sia suo consorte.

LIDIA Sia destino il suo potere.

SILVIO Oh fortunato Silvio! Anch'io me n'entro.

CORADELLA Ha, ha, ha! You said it alright, Master Orimberto. But here's Lidia with a smile on her face.

Scene Ten
[Lidia, Bernetta, and all the actors]

LIDIA Good people, because my front door was ajar I not only heard what Lelio and Guerindo have decided to do, but also the very legitimate reason for which Florinda became Cupid's lover rather than his enemy. Where is my captain and my brother, Eugenio, who once fled from our father but now should be a second father to me?

BERNETTA I'll tell you. My naughty and wicked mistress is a bloodsucking lover, and she wanted to suck out all of his blood once he was in bed with her. Although she wasn't able to do so, she stirred and fired up his blood so greatly that it was like what happens when you suck at a woman's nipple; even though you're not her infant, milk comes out anyway. In this case, although she finally let him be, now his nose is bleeding so profusely that it's a sight to behold. He's holding his head over a basin, and can't join us.

GOVERNOR We'll go to visit him, for we ought to gaze upon the angelic marvels of nature to be found in these two beautiful faces belonging to Lidia and Eugenio.

GRANELLO It would be good for one and all to do so: let's go in.

WIZARD I'll follow you.

LELIO Master Guerindo and I are coming too.

GOVERNOR Mistress Lidia.

LIDIA My lord.

GOVERNOR Only if you agree to take Silvio as your husband.

LIDIA I must yield to your power.

SILVIO O fortunate Silvio! I'm coming too.

MELINA Credi pur, che Melina gnanca liè la no vol star chi, mo' no alla fé bona.

PERUCCIO E Peruccio ti seguita.

CORADELLA Fratello, dove si mangia rinunzio l'alfiero e mi fo cuoco. Addio, qui getto l'insegna.

GRANELLO Signori io son qui solo, e per questo mi chiamo Granello, avendo così del tondo a star da me soletto. Ma come solo, se tanta gente rimiro? Oh, lasciatemi un poco suonar questo tamburo, e dar una passeggiatina, e poi vi dirò il resto. Signori, lasciatemi sputare un poco; lasciatemi dar un'altra ricercata, e poi segguiterò signori, o venga el canchero alla sputaruola, un'altra brevissima suonatina.
   Or comincio.

> Signor vi si fa intendere,
> che ve n' andiate a cena;
> che ben si può comprendere,
> ch'altro non vien in scena;
> rimasi io qui soletto,
> per dirvi: "Buona notte, andate a letto."

FINE

MELINA [*to Peruccio*] You can believe that not even Melina wants to remain here, not now: farewell!

PERUCCIO And Peruccio's following you.

CORADELLA Brother, if we've found a place where we can eat something I'm abandoning this standard to become a cook instead. Farewell, this is where I throw down the flag.

GRANELLO Ladies and gentlemen, I'm here all alone. That's why my name is Granello: like a grain of sand or wheat, I'm so round that I can stay within myself and all by myself. But what am I saying—"all alone"—when I see so many people? Oh, let me play this drum for a bit and take a little stroll, and then I'll tell you the rest. Ladies and gentleman, now let me spit a bit; let me look around again, and then I'll go on, ladies and gentlemen—oh the hell with the spittoon—with another very short piece of music. Here I go:

> Good people, don't think I don't know
> That dinner's where you want to go;
> So it's easy enough to grasp
> That this is our play's last gasp;
> And all that's left to be said
> Is "Good night, now go to bed."

THE END

Ordine per recitar Amor nello specchio *con gran facilità*

ATTO PRIMO

Scena Prima e Seconda
Nulla.

Scena Terza
Florinda avrà un picciolo specchio in seno o nella manica.

Scena Quarta, Quinta, Sesta, Settima
Nulla.

Scena Ottava
Quattro labarde per quattro labardieri, o vestiti da tedeschi o vero in ogn'altro modo.

Scena Nona
Nulla.

ATTO SECONDO

Scena Prima
Lo stesso specchio per Florinda.

Scena Seconda
Un libro, una verga, una ghirlanda, una candela per il Mago.

Scena Terza
Un libro, una verga, una ghirlanda, una candela.

Scena Quarta, Quinta, Sesta, Settima
Nulla.

ATTO TERZO

Scena Prima
Nulla.

Performance Instructions for Staging Love in the Mirror with Great Ease

ACT I

Scenes One and Two
Nothing.

Scene Three
Florinda will have a little mirror either hanging around her neck or in hand.

Scenes Four through Seven
Nothing.

Scene Eight
Four halberds for the four halberdiers, who will be dressed like lansquenets or something similar.

Scene Nine
Nothing.

ACT II

Scene One
The same mirror for Florinda.

Scene Two
A book, a staff, a wreath, and a candle for the Wizard.

Scene Three
A book, a staff, a wreath, and a candle.

Scenes Four through Seven
Nothing.

ACT III

Scene One
Nothing.

Scena Seconda
Un libro per il Mago e un anello grosso per dar ad Orimberto.

Scena Terza
Nulla.

Scena Quarta
Due baston di carta pecora, uno per Florinda, l'altro per Bernetta.

Scena Quinta
Un tulpante grande, grosso e ridicoloso; una vestaccia alla turchessa di tela bianca a nere lune, un libraccio, una verga.

Scena Sesta
Libro, verga, ghirlanda, candela per Lelio e per Granello.

Scena Settima
Una cassa, coperta d'un tappeto bello, la qual averà accomodato un capo d'essa come un finestrino per aprire e serrare, in modo che colui ch'è dentro possa per quella parte uscire.

E alor che questa cassa si dovrà portar in palco per far la burla, si dovrà far veder tutta fuora d'una cantonata, eccetto quel capo finestrato, che dovrà rimaner dentro; uscita poi che sarà Florinda, doppo essere stata veduta, ed entratoci lo spirito, porteranno tutta la cassa in scena; avvertendo che la Florinda per uscire più spedita da quel finestrino, potrà fingersi in sottanino, senza faldiglie e sopravesti, o vero in camicia; parimente lo spirito entrando averà un ingegno da gittar fuoco, e nel tempo che s'aprirà la cassa getterà una volta una gran fiamma, e salterà fuori con un bastone di carta pecora bastonando tutti, in quello.

Da tutte la strade del teatro si getteranno fiamme contra Lelio, contra Granello, e facendosi terremoto continuo co' piedi, nel gittar le fiamme, facendosi ancor de' fischi, finirà la burla.

Scena Ottava
Libro, ghirlanda, verga, candela per Guerindo e per Coradella.

Scene Two
A book for the Wizard and a big ring to give to Orimberto.

Scene Three
Nothing.

Scene Four
Two cudgels made of stiff parchment, one for Florinda and one for Bernetta.

Scene Five
An oversized, ridiculous-looking turban; a Turkish-style robe made of white canvas with black moons on it, a thick book, and a staff.

Scene Six
A book, a staff, a wreath, and a candle for Lelio and Granello.

Scene Seven
A chest covered with a fine carpet. At one end of the chest there will be a small trap door that can be opened or closed, so that whoever is in the chest can get out.

When the chest is carried onstage for the trick, it should be placed just beyond a street corner, and entirely visible to the audience, except for that part containing the trap door, which should remain behind the set. Once Florinda, after having been seen on stage, is out of the chest, and once the spirit has taken her place in it, the chest will be moved completely out onto the stage. In order to get out of the chest more quickly, Florinda may not wear a farthingale or other heavy clothing, instead appearing in a soutane or shirt. Likewise the spirit who gets into the chest will have a flame-throwing device with him. When the chest is opened he will first spray a large tongue of flame, then jump out with a stiff parchment stick and beat everyone around him.

All the streets onstage will erupt with flames aimed at Lelio and Granello; as the flames appear, backstage the other actors will stomp on the floorboards with their feet without stopping, to make it sound like an earthquake; they will also whistle until the scene has come to an end.

Scene Eight
A book, a staff, a wreath, and a candle for Guerindo and Coradella.

Scena Nona
Un sacco con dentro la Morte, e altre fiamme per gittar dalle strade con lo stesso modo della Scena Ottava, con altri quattro vestiti da Morte per far che possano saltar fuora dalle quattro strade al loro tempo; e se più strade fossero, come tali sono i teatri alcuna volta, si farà ancora che sieno più Morti.

Scena Decima
Tulpante per Orimberto, veste a lune, libro, verga, candela.
    Una cassa dorata o inorpellata con vetri, in modo che sembrino gioie; dovrà la stessa aver nel fondo tanta finestra, per la quale possano uscir degli spiriti.
    Il palco nel mezo averà altrettanta finestra, sopra la quale si porrà la cassa, sì che per di sotto il palco uscendo gli spiriti, paiano uscir dalla stessa cassa.

E qui pur dal disotto si getterà fuor di quella istessa cassa fiamme infinite, accogliendo sovente fra le stesse fiamme quelli ch'usciranno, per far la cosa più ridicolosa. Così con lo stesso modo del gittar fuoco dalle parti delle strade e di far terremoto gettando dalle parti delle strade fiamme addosso a quelli che dovranno entrare, finirà la burla, avvertendo ch'ad ognor si getteranno fiamme dalla cassa, e nel disotto del palco si farà rumor di tamburo, di fischi e di catene.

ATTO QUARTO

Scena Prima, Seconda, Terza, Quarta, Quinta, Sesta, Settima
Nulla.

ATTO QUINTO

Scena Prima
Duo fastelli d'erba, quali dovranno esser al collo uno di Granello, l'altro di Coradella.

Scena Seconda e Terza
Nulla.

Scene Nine
A sack with Death in it, and more flames to appear in the streets as in Scene Eight. Four other actors dressed as Death who, at the right time, jump out onto the stage from the four streets. If there should be more streets, as is the case in some theaters, there should be even more actors dressed as Death.

Scene Ten
A turban for Orimberto, plus the robe with the moons on it, the book, the staff and the candle.

    A gilded chest with colored glass that looks like jewels. This chest must have a trap door on its underside to allow the spirits to pass through.

    There will be another trap door in the middle of the stage, over which the chest will be placed, so that when the spirits come out from under the stage they will seem to be coming out of the chest instead.

From underneath the stage a vast number of flames will come shooting out of that same chest, often at the same time as the spirits are emerging from it, in order to heighten the comic effect. In the same way, there will be flames coming from the four streets, and an earthquake will be simulated by shooting flames from the four streets onto the actors who have to enter through them. Thus the scene will come to an end: and as long as the flames shoot out of the chest, from underneath the stage there should be heard the sound of a drum, whistles and chains.

ACT IV

Scenes One through Seven
Nothing.

ACT V

Scene One
Two bundles of herbs: one of these should be around Granello's neck, and the other around Coradella's neck.

Scenes Two and Three
Nothing.

Scena Quarta
Un bel mazzetto di fiori per Bernetta.

Scena Quinta, Sesta, Settima, Ottava
Nulla.

Scena Nona
Un tamburo per Granello, insegna per Coradella, non troppo grande, due sargentini, due sciarpe, due terzaruoli per Lelio e per Guerindo.

FINE

Scene Four
A big bunch of flowers for Bernetta.

Scenes Five through Eight
Nothing.

Scene Nine
A drum for Granello, a standard (not too big) for Coradella, two halberds, two neck-scarves, and two arquebuses for Lelio and Guerino.

THE END

Notes

i. The Rue Clopin, on the Left Bank (in what is now the Fifth arrondissement), was in a university neighborhood known for its printers in the early modern period. Although the street itself no longer exists, the little-known Passage Clopin still follows its former route, now passing through the building complex of the ex-École Polytechnique bounded by the Rue Monge, the Rue Descartes, the Rue Clovis and the Rue des Écoles. The Italian text makes reference to the "College du Petit-Navarre," which was part of the venerable College of Navarre, founded in 1304 and suppressed during the French Revolution.

ii. François de Bassompierre (1579–1646) was one of France's most important and wealthiest nobles under Henry IV and Louis XIII. He was a notorious rake as well as a renowned soldier, and his *Journal de ma vie* confirms that he took part in the theatrical festivities at Carnival in Paris in 1622.

iii. In Greek mythology the handsome youth Narcissus was courted by many lovers of both sexes, but in his pride he spurned them all. He was punished by Nemesis: Narcissus, when stopping to drink at a spring, saw his own reflection in it and fell in love with it. Unable ever to embrace this beautiful image, however, the youth pined away, and eventually died at the edge of the spring. See Ovid, *Metamorphoses*, III.339–510.

iv. In his writings on the theater, Andreini argued that comedy was an imitation of the true that could teach the members of the public which errors to avoid in life, thus making it a highly moral art form. He noted, not long after the publication of *Love in the Mirror*, that "although in comedies we often see lascivious acts and profane actions, they are not put there in order to teach us [how to perform] them, but in order to show us the way in which we may avoid them" (G. B. Andreini, *Lelio bandito: tragicommedia boschereccia* [Venice: G. B. Combi, 1624], 12).

v. I have been unable to identify this reference to Plato.

vi. *Speculum vitae humanae* translates into English as "the mirror of human life."

vii. Thalia is the Greek Muse of Comedy, as well as the name of one of the three Graces of Greek mythology. The personification of prudence was traditionally represented with a mirror in hand by early modern iconographers such as Ripa.

viii. Numerous devices exploiting optical effects created by multiple mirrors circulated in Europe in the early seventeenth century. See Laurent Mannoni, *The Great Art of Light and Shadow: Archaeology of the Cinema*, ed. and trans. Richard Crangle (Exeter: University of Exeter Press, 2000 [1995]), 6–19. Salvatore Maira's film version of *Love in the Mirror* (1999), although anachronistic in its approach, also examines some of these.

ix. See the introduction to this volume concerning the importance of Mars and Venus in the play.

x. For unknown reasons there are two (somewhat different) lists of *dramatis personae* contained in the 1622 *editio princeps*. I follow here the first modern editors of the play (1997) who combine the two lists, emend them to eliminate mistakes and inconsistencies, and group the characters just as Andreini did in 1622. The main characters are grouped in terms of either kinship (father/son, etc.) or household (master/servant), while the others are associated loosely in terms of either magic or law. Eugenio, the Judge, Melina, and Peruccio are not mentioned in either list of *dramatis personae* in the 1622 edition.

xi. See Pliny, *Natural History*, XVI.24, on the antagonism between the ash tree and the serpent. Pliny (*Natural History*, XXIII.80) explains that the berries of the laurel are an antidote to snake venom, as well as a natural snake repellent. Although not mentioned in Pliny, it is worth noting that the laurel tree was sacred to Apollo, slayer of the Python.

xii. Hart's tongue, a fern with many common names (hind's tongue, buttonhole etc.), is the *Lingua cervina* of the medieval apothecaries. Its name refers to the shape of its fronds.

xiii. See Giambattista Della Porta, *Magiae naturalis* (Naples: Orazio Salviano, rev. ed. 1589 [1558]); *Natural Magic* (London: Thomas Young and Samuel Speed, 1658), I.7: "There is likewise a wonderful enmity between Cane and Fern. So that one destroys the other. Hence it is that a Fern root pounded, does loose and shake out the Darts from a wounded body, that were shot or cast out of Canes. And if you would not have Cane grow in a place, do but plow up the ground with a little Fern upon the Plough-shear, and Cane will never grow there."

xiv. Hermes (Mercury) was originally a phallic god in ancient Greece. His name comes from the Greek word *herma*, referring to a square or rectangular pillar of stone, terracotta, or bronze; a bust of Hermes' head was set on top, and male genitals adorned the base. These unusual objects were used to bring good luck or fertility. Guerindo seems to be referring here not only to the phallic symbolism of the *herma*, but also to Hermes's association with the clever, cunning, and even deceitful use of words, exemplified in the Homeric "Hymn to Hermes" (in which the infant Hermes tries to smooth-talk his way out of a predicament). It is Hermes who gives the lyre—and hence the faculty of poetry—to Apollo.

xv. Although a wired collar called a "whisk," which stuck out horizontally, was fashionable in the 1620s, Coradella here appears to refer to a collar with multiple points of cloth hanging down from it, which was popular with merchants at the time (Venice was one of the chief centers of commerce in northern Italy in this period, particularly for luxury goods).

xvi. The lotus flower, which played such a great role in ancient Egyptian culture, rises up from the mud at the bottom of ponds and streams. Florinda is likely playing with the word here in order to squeeze an erotic meaning from it, by suggesting not only the muddy origins of the plant but also the fact of its "rising" (like the aroused male sexual organ).

xvii. The Roman god Cupid is usually equated with the Greek god Eros. Cupid is also known as "Amor" (Love) in the Latin tradition, which represents him as a playful little boy, devoid of Eros's dignity. Throughout *Love in the Mirror* Andreini plays with the double meaning of the term, which at times may refer to the god or to love itself, and there are any number of passages in which its sense remains ambiguous.

xviii. Literally her words are: *Florinda thus loves herself so deeply / That in a mirror she, in love, dies; / That in a beautiful glass she has set all of her heart.*

xix. See the "Dedication," footnote iii.

xx. Diana was a chaste Latin goddess, usually identified with the Greek virgin goddess Artemis. The latter was a huntress who kept the company of other virgins, yet was also the goddess of childbirth. Artemis was sometimes known as Phoebe and associated with the moon. Venus, on the other hand, originated as a Roman goddess of the fertility of gardens but was identified with the Greek goddess of love, Aphrodite. Eros was Aphrodite's son, as were—among others—Priapus (a phallic god) and Hermaphroditus, whose father was Hermes. In some cults, such as Sparta's, she served as both goddess of love and goddess of war, and was often worshiped together with Ares (Mars), the god of war. The planet Venus is both the morning star and the evening star.

xxi. The Pleaides were the seven daughters of Atlas and Pleïone, all but one whom had affairs with the gods. One version of their myth recounts that Zeus transformed them into stars and set them in the heavens in order to save them from the lust of the giant Orion: in the form of a constellation, the latter now pursues the Pleaides eternally across the night sky. Another version, to which Florinda may also be alluding, maintains that they died of grief at the death of their sisters, the Hyades, and were changed by Zeus into stars.

xxii. Literally, Florinda says, repeating the word "glass" four times: *Not because I live as a lover/ In a shining glass, / And my love is made of glass, / Does Cupid turn glass into diamond; / But sweet are the pains / Of which I speak as I go rejoicing; / And, always happy, I cry aloud: / Whoever is Love's phoenix burns in a glass.* More ancient than Greek myth, the phoenix was a legendary and often sacred firebird, which reproduced by bursting into flames and arising from the ashes as a new phoenix. Frequently associated with the sun, the bird's autonomous power of regeneration made it virtually immortal and invincible.

xxiii. Literally, Testuggine says: "Since you always take your ziziphus berries [i.e. testicles] with you to the whorehouse, you're going to be in trouble." He thus puns on the resemblance between the surname "Zizolieri" and the "zizole" or ziziphus berries. In English the closest equivalent would perhaps be "the family jewels."

xxiv. Originating in Egypt, the Sphinx was a monster with a human head and the body of a lion: usually its gender was female. In Greek mythology the Sphinx appears most memorably in an early episode in the story of Oedipus in Thebes. The Sphinx, who plagued the city, destroyed all those who could not answer her famous riddle about the three ages of man. Oedipus came to Thebes, answered the riddle successfully, and either the Sphinx killed herself or he slew her in combat. In exchange for this service, the Thebans made him their king.

xxv. The text literally reads: "Then my name isn't Sufronio Giuggiolieri," thus continuing the untranslatable punning between "zizole" and "giuggiole," which are both Italian names for ziziphus berries, here extended to the surnames "Zizolieri" and "Giuggiolieri."

xxvi. Samson is described in the Old Testament (Judges 13–16) as both a judge in Israel and a man possessing supernatural strength. He loved Delilah, who was bribed by the Philistines to discover the secret of Samson's strength, which lay in his unshorn hair. She then betrayed her lover to them, and they blinded and enslaved him. Eventually, however, his hair grew back and, when brought out of prison to amuse the crowd in a large public building where the Philistine chiefs were assembled, he pulled down the pillars to which he had been chained, burying both himself and many hundreds of his enemies beneath the rubble.

xxvii. Pan is a rural Arcadian (Greek) god of fertility, half-human and half-goat in appearance. The son of Hermes, who was also from Arcadia, Pan was usually represented as an eroticized figure, in keeping with his goatlike being.

xxviii. A very similar pun is employed by Shakespeare in *The Merry Wives of Windsor*, IV.1:
EVANS. What is your genitive case plural, William?
WILLIAM. Genitive case?
EVANS. Ay.
WILLIAM. Genitive: horum, harum, horum.
QUICKLY. Vengeance of Jenny's case; fie on her! Never
  name her, child, if she be a whore.
EVANS. For shame, oman.
QUICKLY. You do ill to teach the child such words. He
  teaches him to hick and to hack, which they'll do fast
  enough of themselves; and to call "horum;" fie upon you!

xxix. *Achores* is in fact a French medical term (of Greek origin) that indicates a fungal infection of the scalp, i.e. ringworm.

xxx. Timon was a citizen of ancient Athens who was a legendary misanthrope. According to the historian Plutarch, Timon lived during the era of the Peloponnesian War (431–404 BCE). Shakespeare's *Timon of Athens* is concerned with this same Athenian man-hater.

xxxi. Granello refers to a Venetian sailing vessel known as the "marciliana," which first appeared in the Middle Ages. Usually rather small, it could, however, also be built as a large transport ship of considerable tonnage. Hundreds of these seagoing vessels were in use in the eastern Mediterranean as late as the eighteenth century.

xxxii. Granello plays on two meanings of the Italian word "l'estremità," which may mean "the tip or point of a shoe" as well as "the end of a rope."

xxxiii. In one of the two lists of *dramatis personae* included in the 1622 edition of *Love in the Mirror*, the Governor is identified as "Latanzio." It seems possible that here the Judge is referring to the Governor's name, rather than to Lucius Caelius Firmianus Lactantius (250–320 CE circa), early Christian theologian and apologist who attempted to defend the Church against the worst of the Roman persecutions.

xxxiv. The she-bear was widely believed to lick her newborn cubs (born toothless, blind and bald) into the shape of a bear. The origins of this belief, although unknown, are undoubtedly of great antiquity and can be found already in early Greek civilization and mythology.

xxxv. In the Greek myth, Hippomenes won the fleet-footed Atalanta's hand thanks to the ruse of the three golden apples, which were provided to him by Aphrodite.

xxxvi. Cleopatra VII Thea Philopator (69–30 BCE) was the last pharaoh of ancient Egypt and the last ruler of its Hellenistic era. Her notorious liaisons with Julius Caesar and, later, Mark Antony made her name synonymous with sexual license from the Middle Ages on. Cleopatra was a favorite subject of Baroque writers and artists, from Shakespeare (*Anthony and Cleopatra*) to Artemisia Gentileschi.

xxxvii. The legendary Lucretia was a Roman noblewoman violated by Sextus Tarquinius, the son of the last king of Rome prior to the foundation of the Republic. Instead of hiding her shame, Lucretia denounced her rapist to her family before killing herself to preserve her honor. When her lifeless body was displayed to the people of Rome, they rose in revolt and, led by Lucius Junius Brutus, overthrew the monarchy. Lucretia was a favorite subject of early modern art and literature, including Shakespeare's long poem, *The Rape of Lucrece* (1594).

xxxviii. The birthplace of Aphrodite or Venus (as she was known in Latin), the goddess of love, was usually attributed either to Cyprus or to the island of Cythera, located between the Peloponnesus and Crete. Aphrodite's mortal and divine loves were legion, although she was married to Hephaestus (associated with the Roman god Vulcan). Hephaestus once caught Aphrodite in bed with her lover Ares, also known as Mars, the god of war: using chains to bind them fast, the cuckolded husband brought all the other Olympian gods together to mock the pair.

xxxix. In Greek mythology, Endymion was an exceptionally beautiful young nobleman with whom the goddess of the moon, Selene, fell in love. Later ages tended to conflate Selene with the chaste Artemis. As the conversation continues, it is clear that Lelio considers the moon goddess and Artemis to be one and the same, as does Florinda.

xl. In Greco-Roman mythology Artemis/Diana was the goddess of the hunt as well as the personification of chastity. Forest groves of oaks were considered sacred to her. Roman poets sometimes called her "Cynthia," in honor of the hill of Cynthus on the island of Delos, which was believed to be her birthplace. Here the crescent moon that was one of her symbols when she was conflated with the moon goddess is, Florinda suggests, like the horns worn by a cuckolded lover.

xli. In one version of the Greek myth, the handsome Adonis was killed by the tusks of a wild boar, sent by Artemis in retaliation for Aphrodite (who loved Adonis) having caused the death of a favorite of the huntress goddess.

xlii. Andreini's beloved mother, Isabella Canali Andreini, died in childbirth in 1604 while traveling in France.

xliii. Proteus was a minor sea god in Greek mythology, capable of rapidly transforming himself into many different shapes. See Homer's *Odyssey* IV.363–570 for the tale of Proteus and Menelaüs.

xliv. Echo was a nymph and attendant of the goddess Hera, wife of Zeus. Her chatter distracted the queen of the gods while her husband was seducing other nymphs. When this ruse was discovered, Hera punished Echo by condemning her forever only to repeat the words of others. The nymph later fell in love with Narcissus, who coldly rejected her; she wasted entirely away with love-sickness, until there was nothing left of her but her voice, which could be heard in caves and on mountainsides.

xlv. The theory of the humors, already present in the Hippocratic writings dating from the late fifth century BCE on, was central to the great Greek physician Galen's (129–c. 210 CE) explanatory system of health and illness, which was still dominant in the early seventeenth century in Europe. This theory endorsed blood-letting and other manipulations of bodily fluids.

xlvi. Here the Wizard identifies himself, in the text of the 1622 edition (p. 46), as "Stefasat." However, this name never is used again in the play, and the list of *dramatis personae* identifies him as "Arfasat" instead.

xlvii. I have been unable to locate the source of this citation, also found in other, unrelated texts of the same period.

xlviii. Psyche was a stunningly beautiful mortal woman who eventually became Cupid's wife and was herself made immortal. The tale of Cupid and Psyche is known only from Apuleius's *The Golden Ass* IV.28–VI.26.

xlix. Both Egeria and Arethusa were nymphs transformed into fountains by Diana; Egeria was said to have melted into tears while mourning the death of her husband Numa (Ovid, *Metamorphoses* XV.479–546).

l. Literally, Bernetta says: "this time it was helpful to me to be born on Frying-Pan Square, where all the good seeds get fried." She implies, however, that in the part of town where she was born, gentlemen of distinction have been impregnating the local lower-class women; she will later indicate that her birthplace is in fact a university neighborhood known for its prostitutes (the Ripetta district).

li. Aristotle is "the Philosopher," and Florinda perhaps refers to either the *Nicomachean Ethics* (Book 4), where Aristotle examines the necessary role of anger in human behavior, or the *Rhetoric* (II.2).

lii. In Greek mythology, Æolus ruled the winds. In one account of this wind god, Æolus gave his name to the Aeolian Islands near Sicily. In another, which Homer includes in the *Odyssey* (Book X), Æolus lived on the floating island of Aeolia, and was visited there by Odysseus and his crew.

liii. The Pactolus river was celebrated in antiquity, according to Pliny, for the medicinal and curative properties of its waters. According to myth, King Minos washed himself in the river, turning its sands into gold. The Achelous river was instead associated with a legendary cornucopia—a symbol of fertility, abundance, and prosperity.

liv. In battle, Achilles gave King Telephus a thigh wound that refused to heal. In one version of the myth, Telephus then consulted an oracle, who told him that "only what wounded you shall heal you." Achilles's comrade, Odysseus, reasoned that if Achilles' spear had inflicted the wound, that same spear must be able to heal it. Rust from the spearhead was scraped off onto the wound, and Telephus was finally healed.

lv. This citation seems to blend "Amor, per lo tuo calle a morte vassi" from Giovanni Della Casa, *Rime* (4.1) and "ché per la strada presa a morte vassi" from Torquato Tasso, *Gerusalemme liberata* (XX.110), confirming the hypothesis that Andreini sometimes cites literary and philosophical works from memory in *Love in the Mirror*.

lvi. I have been unable to locate the source of this citation.

lvii. Sufronio calls Orimberto a "beccaccione," which is another way of calling him a cuckold, an insult still favored by contemporary Italians.

lviii. The hippomanes, according to the O.E.D., is "a small black fleshy substance said to occur on the forehead of a new-born foal," reputed by the ancients to be an aphrosidiac.

lix. Pietro d'Abano (1257–1315) was a renowned doctor, university professor, and philosopher who taught in Paris and Padua. Expert in astrology, he was eventually accused of heresy and atheism, and died in prison. Cecco d'Ascoli (c. 1269–1327) was a doctor, university professor and poet who was also a famous astrologer. Zoroaster, the Middle Eastern prophet, was, by the beginning of the Seicento, widely considered by Europeans to have been a great magician and sage. See original on facing page (124).

lx. *Grimoires* are books of magical knowledge and demonology, such as the anonymous and popular seventeenth-century *Lemegeton Clavicula Salomonis* or *Lesser Key of Solomon*, to which Andreini may be referring here (it is known to have circulated in French in manuscript form in the 1600s, although the exact date of composition is not certain). One section of the work, the *Ars Almadel*, tells how to make the almadel, which is a wax tablet with protective symbols drawn on it, by employing the proper colors, materials, and rituals.

lxi. The name "Sibyl" comes from the ancient Greek word *sibylla*, meaning prophetess. There were many Sibyls in the ancient world, most famously at Cumae, but the tradition had died out long before the Wizard's day.

lxii. The 1622 text reads "Sufronio" instead of "Orimberto," but this is clearly a mistake.

lxiii. Ludovico Ariosto, *Orlando furioso*, Canto XXVII.1.1–2.

lxiv. Ariosto, *Orlando furioso*, Canto XXXV.27.6.

lxv. In antiquity every important fountain or well was consecrated, and sacrifices were offered to them, as well as to the deities that presided over them (see Ovid's *Fasti*, III.300). The ancient Greeks, when consulting the oracle of Amphiaraüs, threw money into the well sacred to the hero, and the Romans threw money into springs, wells, and rivers, often for the purpose of divination. The later tradition of the wishing well, into which money was thrown in exchange for the fulfillment of a wish, arose from this practice. Orimberto appears to have been skimming the Florentine fountains for coins, perhaps a comment by Andreini on the traditionally tight-fisted nature of the city's inhabitants. The term "rame" (copper) may be used for "coins" in general. Here, however, it also has the comic effect of indicating the very slight value of the coins (because those made of copper were the least valuable of all) that the foolish and avaricious Orimberto has been stuffing into his pockets.

lxvi. *Domine ad quid* appears to be generic or parodic here, rather than a citation of a specific text.

lxvii. The Hecatonchires were three monstrous giant offspring of Gaia and Uranus, or the earth and sky, in the prehistory of Greek mythology. Briareus the Vigorous and Gyges the Big-Limbed, like their sibling Cottus, each possessed a hundred hands and fifty heads. They were known in the Latin literary tradition as the *Centimani* or "hundred-handed ones."

lxviii. A legendary creature with a lion's body and, usually, an eagle's wings. The griffon, although bizarre-looking, is usually associated with noble or religious themes in medieval and early modern culture. Here it instead has the aspect of a fabulous monster, like the Ogre.

lxix. Granello resorts to Latin here: "*quam primum*" would appear to be parodic.

lxx. Literally: *O kind voice, / O welcome words, / O sound as fine / As a sunbeam; / What the Wizard wants / We will do, / Amidst these bright lights / Of stars on high, / We'll take her out, / We'll take her out.*

lxxi. Literally: *Oh great lord of the dark and fearful kingdom, / With your two-pronged scepter, / At these words of mine / Put aside your disdain, / Make me happy in love, I'm suffering, / Arfasat's only sign to Guerindo is / He promises him Florinda as his woman, / You who obey circles and exorcisms, / Send me the sun by way of dark clouds.*

lxxii. In a typically Baroque conceit, Orimberto puts together two capital F's (one of them backward) to form a figure resembling a gallows.

lxxiii. A legendary and rare winged creature that was the offspring of a griffon and a mare. Orimberto refers to the tale of Astolfo and the Hippogriff in Ariosto's *Orlando furioso*: the knight Astolfo mounts this mythical steed in order to travel to the moon to recover Orlando's lost wits (Canto XXXIV).

lxxiv. Here Orimberto lists a series of demons whose names may have been invented by Andreini. I have not translated them, but they can be found in the facing Italian text.

lxxv. For the ancient Greeks, Persephone (known as Proserpina to the Romans) was the queen of the underworld and the wife of its lord, Hades (known as Pluto to the Romans).

lxxvi. In modern Italian the term "zazzera"—used to describe long and somewhat scruffy locks of hair, especially those of men—tends to have a pejorative meaning. In the early 1620s, however, men's hair (among the elites) was worn collar-length and carefully brushed back from the forehead. The most fashion-conscious men wore a lovelock, i.e. a single long strand of hair hanging down over one shoulder.

lxxvii. The rose is the soundhole under the strings of the instrument. Bernetta puns on "cicalare," which means "to chat" but whose root is the noun "cicala" (cicada), an insect that rubs its legs together in order to emit sound. "Frictrix" or "fregatrice," both of which indicate the action of rubbing together, were terms for "lesbian" in the seventeenth century.

lxxviii. Bernetta is describing here a modern stringed instrument such as a violin, rather than an ancient lyre.

lxxix. Many local Jewish cuisines in early modern Europe used the goose exactly as their Christian counterparts employed the pig: nothing was left unused, from the rendered fat to the neck and feet.

lxxx. The meaning of this sentence is unclear; but men's shirts, in this period, often featured long cuffs covering the hand as far as the fingertips.

lxxxi. "Libreria" may also mean "bookstore": either way, Eugenio makes his point.

lxxxii. In Renaissance erudite comedy, the pedant—trained in letters and philosophy—was often represented as a sodomite and pedophile. See, for instance, Aretino's *The Stablemaster* (*Il Marescalco*), first published in 1533.

lxxxiii. Aurora was the Roman name for the goddess of the dawn, who was known as Eos in Greek mythology. She was the sister of Selene (the moon goddess) and of Helius (the sun god).

lxxxiv. The Furies, known in Greek mythology as the Erinyes, were ferocious avenging female spirits. They punished those who had offended blood kin, setting wrong to right by exacting terrible retribution from the guilty. The Graces were female personifications of beauty and grace, often shown in ancient art as scantily clothed (or nude) dancers. Curiously, in some parts of ancient Greece the Graces were closely associated in cult with the Erinyes.

lxxxv. See the "Dedication," footnote four.

lxxxvi. Melina is the one character in the play who, true to the Arte tradition, speaks mainly in dialect. In this case, however, although her speech is suggestive of the dialect of the central Veneto region (Padua-Vicenza-Polesine), there are many inconsistencies indicating that these words are to be attributed largely to Andreini's inexhaustible inventiveness with

language. The playwright bases Melina's imaginary dialect on the Latinized and Tuscanized literary *koiné* of the eastern Po valley—where a veritable Babel of dialects coexisted in close proximity—that had already been in circulation for several centuries. It is worth recalling here that Andreini's mother was born in Padua.

lxxxvii. The 1622 text reads "Governor," but the Governor is not in this scene.

lxxxviii. The expansionist Ottoman Empire was in conflict with Christian Europe, especially the Venetian Republic and the Spanish Empire, during the early years of the seventeenth century. Bernetta's words have a double meaning here, because many Europeans—thanks in part to early modern Orientalism—believed the Turks to be not only sexually licentious, but sodomitic.

lxxxix. The Ripetta neighborhood in Rome, along the eastern bank of the Tiber, was in transition in the late sixteenth and early seventeenth centuries. There was a great deal of port traffic, although the famous Porto di Ripetta had yet to be built; but what Bernetta refers to here is the fact that the area was widely known to be the residence of many Roman prostitutes. See Tod A. Marder, "The Porto di Ripetta in Rome," *The Journal of the Society of Architectural Historians* 39, no. 1 (1980): 33.

xc. Bernetta and Eugenio exchange a series of untranslatable but sexually charged double meanings here. "La squacquara" is, literally, "diarrhea."

xci. Literally, "what a strange thing does Lactantius hear." Possibly the Governor's name is Lactantius ("Latanzio"), as stated in the first of the two lists of *dramatis personae* published in the 1622 edition, as well as suggested in act 1.

xcii. Florinda deliberately refers to Eugenio as a "she" ("la") here, for reasons that will become clearer shortly.

xciii. Florinda now calls Eugenio "him."

xciv. Florinda now switches back to seeing Eugenio as a "she."

xcv. See the introduction in this volume concerning hermaphrodites in Italy and France between the Cinquecento and Seicento.

xcvi. The question of early modern marriage and its rituals is very complex, linked as it is to specific religious cults and local social practices. Even if we assume the couple to be Catholic, and thus bound by the Tridentine rule (1563) that a Catholic marriage must be presided over by a priest, the play seems to suggest that the far older tradition, in which marriage is formed without the intervention of state or church, simply by spoken mutual consent of the couple and the consummation of their union, still has validity here.

xcvii. Literally, "that hermaphrodite who remains in a hidden part."

xcviii. Totila (whose real name was Baduila) was king of the Ostrogoths in Italy from 541 until his death in 552 CE. His reign was marked by near-constant military campaigns against the Byzantines for control of the peninsula. He partly destroyed Florence in 552, when he took the city and killed many of its inhabitants.

xcix. Anglia is the medieval and neo-Latin name for England.

c. Bellona was an ancient Roman war goddess, who appeared armed with spear and torch. She accompanied Mars into battle and may be identified as his sister, wife, or daughter. See Ovid, *Metamorphoses* V.155.

ci. I have been unable to identify this ancient philosopher.

cii. The arquebus ("terzarolo") was a large-caliber firearm with a very long barrel, in use until the sixteenth century in Europe. It was already obsolete by 1622.

Bibliography

Primary Sources

A.   Giovan Battista Andreini

The following are works by Andreini referred to in the present volume. They are listed here by date of publication. For a complete bibliography, see Carandini 2003 (below).

Andreini, Giovan Battista. *Il pianto d'Apollo. Rime funebri in morte d'Isabella Andreini comica Gelosa.* (with *Lo sfortunato poeta. Rime piacevoli con una essagerazione [sic] in prosa*). Milan: Girolamo Bordoni e Pietro Martire Locarni, 1606.

La Maddalena. Venice: Somasco, 1610. Rpt. Florence, Eredi Marescotti, 1612.

Lo schiavetto, commedia. Milan: Pandolfo Malatesta, 1612. Rpt. Venice: Giovan Battista Ciotti, 1620, and Venice: n.p., 1621.

La Maddalena, sacra rappresentatione [sic]. Mantua: Aurelio e Ludovico Osanna, 1617. Rpt. Milan: Malatesta, 1620.

La campanazza, commedia. Paris: Nicolas Della Vigna, 1621. Rpt. 1622; Venice: Angelo Salvadori, 1623 and 1627; Milan: Pandolfo Malatesta, 1627 and 1674.

La Ferinda, commedia. Paris: Nicolas Della Vigna, 1622.

Amor nello specchio, commedia. Paris: Nicolas Della Vigna, 1622. Modern edition. Rome: Bulzoni, 1997.

La sultana, commedia. Paris: Nicolas Della Vigna, 1622.

Li duo Leli simili, commedia. Paris: Nicolas Della Vigna, 1622.

La centaura, suggetto diviso in commedia, pastorale e tragedia. Paris: Nicolas Della Vigna, 1622. Rpt. Venice: Imberti, 1625; Venice: Sanzonio, 1633. Modern edition Genoa: Il Melangolo, 2004.

Le due commedie in commedia, suggetto stravagantissimo. Venice: Imberti, 1623. Rpt. 1625 and 1632. Modern edition in Ferrone, 1985–1986, 2: 17–105.

Lelio bandito, tragicomedia boschereccia. Milan: Giovan Battista Bidelli, 1620. Rpt. Venice: G. B. Combi, 1624.

Comici martiri e penitenti. Paris: Nicolao Callemont, 1624.

Il convitato di pietra. Unpublished ms., 1651, Rome, Archivio Cardelli.

Il nuovo risarcito 'Convitato di Pietra.' Unpublished ms., 1651, BNCF, *Magl.*, VII, 16. Modern edition Rome: Bulzoni, 2003.

La Maddalena lasciva e penitente. Milan: Giovan Battista e Giulio Cesare Malatesta, 1652. Modern edition Bari: Palomar, 2006.

B.　Other Primary Sources

Ariosto, Ludovico. *Orlando furioso.* Milan: Garzanti, 1990 [1532].

Basile, Giambattista. *Lo cunto de li cunti.* Ed. Michele Rak. Milan: Garzanti, 1998 [1634–36]. Translated into English as *The Tale of Tales, or Entertainment for Little Ones.* Trans. Nancy Canepa. Detroit: Wayne State University Press, 2007.

Boileau, Nicolas. *Satires, Épîtres, Art poétique.* Ed. Jean-Pierre Collinet. Paris: Gallimard, 1985 [1660–1668].

Corneille, Pierre. *L'Illusion comique.* Ed. Jean Serroy. Paris: Gallimard, 2000 [1639].

Della Porta, Giambattista. *Magiae naturalis.* Naples: Orazio Salviano, rev. ed. 1589 [1558]. Translated as *Natural Magic.* London: Thomas Young and Samuel Speed, 1658.

Genealogía, origen y noticias de los comediantes de España. Ed. N. D. Shergold and J. E. Varey. London: Tamesis Books, 1985.

Guazzo, Stefano. *La civil conversazione.* Ed. Amedeo Quondam. 2 vols. Modena: Mucchi, 1993 [1574].

Kircher, Athanasius. *Ars magna lucis et umbrae n X. libros digesta. Quibus admirandae lucis & umbrae in mundo, atque adeò universa natura, vires effectusque uti nova, ita varia novorum reconditiorumque speciminum exhibitione, ad varios mortalium usus, panduntur.* Amsterdam: J. Jansson, 1671.

Shakespeare, William. *The Norton Shakespeare.* Ed. Stephen Greenblatt, et al. New York and London: W. W. Norton & Co., 1997.

Tesauro, Emanuele. *Il cannocchiale aristotelico.* Savigliano: Editrice Artistica Piemontese, 2000 [1670].

Secondary Sources

Andreadis, Harriette. *Sappho in Early Modern England : Female Same-Sex Literary Erotics, 1550–1714.* Chicago: University of Chicago Press, 2001.

Andrews, Richard. *Scripts and Scenarios: The Performance of Comedy in Renaissance Italy.* Cambridge: Cambridge University Press, 1993.

Comici dell'arte: corrispondenze. Ed. Claudia Burattelli, Domenica Landolfi, and Anna Zinanni. 2 vols. Florence: Casa Editrice Le Lettere, 1993.

Carandini, Silvia and Luciano Mariti. *Don Giovanni o l'estrema avventura del teatro: 'Il nuovo risarcito Convitato di Pietra' di Giovan Battista Andreini.* Rome: Bulzoni, 2003.

Cohen, Elizabeth S. "Evolving the History of Women in Early Modern Italy: Subordination and Agency." *Spain in Italy: Politics, Society and Religion 1500–1700.* Ed. Thomas J. Dandelet and John A. Marino. Leiden and Boston: Brill, 2007. 325–54.

Spain in Italy: Politics, Society and Religion 1500–1700. Ed. Thomas J. Dandelet and John A. Marino. Leiden and Boston: Brill, 2007.

Evangelista, Annamaria. "Le compagnie dei comici dell'arte nel teatrino di Baldracca a Firenze: notizie dagli epistolari (1576–1653)." *Quaderni di teatro* 24 (1984): 50–72.

_____. "Il teatro dei comici dell'arte a Firenze." *Biblioteca teatrale* 23–24 (1979), 70–86.

Commedie dei comici dell'arte. Ed. Laura Falavolti. Turin: UTET, 1982.

Ferrone, Siro. *Arlecchino: vita e avventure di Tristano Martinelli attore.* Bari: Laterza, 2006.

_____. *Attori mercanti corsari: la commedia dell'arte in Europa tra Cinque e Seicento.* Turin: Einaudi, 1993.

_____, ed. *Commedie dell'arte.* 2 vols. Milan: Mursia, 1985–86.

_____. "Il teatro." *Storia della letteratura italiana.* Ed. Enrico Malato. Rome: Salerno, 1997. 5: 1057–1110.

Fiaschini, Fabrizio. *L'"incessabil agitazione": Giovan Battista Andreini tra professione teatrale, cultura letteraria e religione.* Pisa: Giardini, 2007.

Athanasius Kircher: the Last Man Who Knew Everything. Ed. Paula Findlen. New York, Routledge, 2004.

Finucci, Valeria. "Isabella Andreini." *Routledge Encyclopedia of Italian Literature.* 2 vols. New York: Routledge, 2006. 1: 38–41.

Italia 1650: comparazioni e bilanci. Ed. Giuseppe Galasso and Aurelio Musi. Naples: CUEN, 2002.

García Arranz, José Julio. *Ornitología emblemática: las aves en la literatura simbólica ilustrada en Europa durante los siglos XVI y XVII.* Cáceres: Universidad de Extremadura, 1996.

Henke, Robert. *Performance and Literature in the Commedia dell'Arte.* New York: Cambridge University Press, 2002.

Katritzky, M. A. *The Art of Commedia: a Study in the Commedia dell' Arte 1560–1620, with Special Reference to the Visual Records.* Amsterdam and New York: Rodopi, 2006.

_____. "Reading the Actress in Commedia Imagery." *Women Players in England, 1500–1660: Beyond the All-Male Stage.* Ed. Pamela A. Brown and Peter Parolin. Burlington, VT: Ashgate, 2005. 109–43.

Long, Kathleen. *Hermaphrodites in Renaissance Europe.* Burlington, VT: Ashgate, 2006.

MacNeil, Anne. *Music and Women of the Commedia dell'Arte in the Late Sixteenth Century.* Oxford and New York: Oxford University Press, 2003.

Maira, Salvatore [films]. *Riflessi in un cielo scuro* (1991). *Donne in un giorno di festa* (1993). *Amor nello specchio* (1999), 104 minutes, with Anna Galiena, Peter Stormare and Simona Cavallari. Story, screenplay and direction by Salvatore Maira. A Factory and G. M. F. production, in collaboration with RAI Radiotelevisione Italiana.

_____. Introduction. *Amor nello specchio.* By G. B. Andreini. Ed. Maira and Anna Michela Borracci. Rome: Bulzoni, 1997. 9–34.

Malanima, Paolo. "A Declining Economy: Central and Northern Italy." *Spain in Italy: Politics, Society and Religion 1500–1700.* Ed. Thomas J. Dandelet and John A. Marino. Leiden and Boston: Brill, 2007. 383–403.

Mannoni, Laurent. *The Great Art of Light and Shadow: Archaeology of the Cinema.* Ed. and trans. Richard Crangle. Exeter: University of Exeter Press, 2000 [1995].

_____, Donata Pesenti Campagnoni, and David Robinson. *Light and Movement: Incunabula of the Motion Picture 1420–1896/Luce e movimento: incunaboli dell'immagine animata 1420–1896/ Lumière et mouvement: incunables de l'image animée 1420– 1896.* Gemona, Italy: Le Giornate del Cinema Muto, 1995.

Maravall, José Antonio. *Culture of the Baroque: Analysis of a Historical Structure.* Trans. Terry Cochrane. Minneapolis: University of Minnesota Press, 1986 [1975].

Marder, Tod A. "The Porto di Ripetta in Rome." *The Journal of the Society of Architectural Historians* 39, no. 1 (1980): 28–56.

Marin, Louis. "Neither the True Sex nor the False." *Cross-Readings.* Trans. Jane Marie Todd. Atlantic Highlands, NJ: Humanities Press, 1998 [1992]. 228–34.

The Oxford Short History of Italy, Vol. 4. Early Modern Italy 1550–1796. Ed. John A. Marino. Oxford and New York: Oxford University Press, 2002.

Mazzuchelli, Giammaria. *Gli scrittori d'Italia; cioè, Notizie storiche, e critiche intorno alle vite, e agli scritti dei letterati italiani.* Vol. 1. Brescia: Giambatista Bossini, 1753.

Minor, Vernon Hyde. *The Death of the Baroque and the Rhetoric of Good Taste.* Cambridge: Cambridge University Press, 2006.

Muto, Giovanni. "Dopo 'l'estate di San Martino' dell'economia italiana," *Italia 1650: comparazioni e bilanci.* Ed. Giuseppe Galasso and Aurelio Musi. Naples: CUEN, 2002. 71–86.

Nicholson, Eric. "Romance as Role Model: Early Female Performances of *Orlando furioso* and *Gerusalemme liberata.*" *Renaissance Transactions: Ariosto and Tasso.* Ed. Valeria Finucci. Durham, NC: Duke University Press, 1999. 246–69.

Powell, John S. *Music and Theatre in France, 1600–1680.* Oxford and New York: Oxford University Press, 1998.

Rebaudengo, Maurizio. *Giovan Battista Andreini tra poetica e drammaturgia.* Turin: Rosenberg & Sellier, 1994.

Rosand, Ellen. *Opera in Seventeenth-Century Venice: The Creation of a Genre.* Berkeley: University of California Press, 1991.

Snyder, Jon R. *L'estetica del Barocco.* Bologna: Il Mulino, 2005.

_____. "*Mare magnum*: the Arts in the Early Modern Age." *The Oxford Short History of Italy, Vol. 4. Early Modern Italy 1550–1796.* Ed. John A. Marino. Oxford and New York: Oxford University Press, 2002. 143–165.

_____. "Publish (f)or Paris? G. B. Andreini in France." *Renaissance Drama* 36–37 (2010): 351–375.

Storia della letteratura italiana. Ed. Enrico Malato. Vol. 5. Rome: Salerno, 1997.

Taviani, Ferdinando. "Bella d'Asia: Torquato Tasso, gli attori e l'immortalità." *Paragone/ letteratura* 35 (1984), 3–76.

_____. *La commedia dell'arte e la società barocca: la fascinazione del teatro.* Rome: Bulzoni, 1991 [1969].

Tessari, Roberto. "Il mercato delle maschere." *Storia del teatro moderno e contemporaneo, 1: la nascita del teatro moderno Cinquecento-Seicento.* Ed. Roberto Alonge and Guido Davico Bonino. Turin: Einaudi, 2000. 119–91.

Tylus, Jane. "Women at the Windows: Commedia dell'Arte and Theatrical Practice in Early Modern Italy." *Theater Journal* 49 (1997): 323–42.

Vermeir, Koen. "The Magic of the Magic Lantern (1660–1700): On Analogical Demonstration and the Visualization of the Invisible." *British Journal of the History of Science* 38, no. 2 (2005): 127–59.

Vescovo, Piermario. "Narciso, Psiche e Marte 'mestruato': una lettura di *Amor nello specchio* di Giovan Battista Andreini." *Lettere italiane* 56, no. 1 (2004): 50–80.

_____. "Virginia Ramponi e Virginia Rotari nello specchio di Giovan Battista Andreini." *Donne e teatro.* Ed. Daria Perocco. Venice: Ca'Foscari/Comitato per le pari opportunità, 2004.

Viganò, Aldo, ed. "Il gioco e i suoi 'generi': conversazione con Luca Ronconi." *La centaura.* By G. B. Andreini. Genoa: Il Melangolo, 2004. 213–19.

Weinberg, Bernard. *A History of Literary Criticism in the Italian Renaissance.* 2 vols. Chicago: University of Chicago Press, 1961.

Zampelli, Michael. "Trent Revisited." *Journal of Religion and Theater* 1, no. 1 (2002): 120–33.

Index

Appendix: Arfasat

An anonymous reader of the manuscript of this book has provided me with the following explanation of G. B. Andreini's choice of the name of the magus or Wizard in *Love in the Mirror*. I include it in this appendix because it not only enhances our reading of the play, but throws further light on the extraordinarily dense texture of the Baroque literary culture of citation, allusion, and appropriation, with which Andreini the writer was on intimate terms.

The name 'Arfasat' "is clearly an Italianization of Arphaxad (Genesis 11:11, Vulgate). As the first-born of Noah's son Shem, this biblical personage may have been chosen by Andreini as a foil to Noah's other son Ham, widely seen since at least the twelfth century as identical to Zoroaster, the inventor of magic (e.g. in Peter Comestor and Vincent of Beauvais). While the historical Zoroaster may be the referent here (see note lix, p. 228), this is open to question, as the identification of Ham was still current in early modern occult texts. Thus, as a "white" or "natural" magician, Arphaxad/Arfasat would have been a logical namesake to counter the "black" magic of Ham/Zoroaster, either by Andreini's own choice, or, more likely, through reminiscence of an actual occult text such as *The Treatise of Shem* (see Owen Davies, *Grimoires*, Oxford and New York: Oxford University Press, 2009, pp. 7–8)."